Academic Women

SRHE and Open University Press Imprint
General Editor: Heather Eggins

Current titles include:

Mike Abramson *et al.* (eds): *Further and Higher Education Partnerships*
Catherine Bargh, Peter Scott and David Smith: *Governing Universities*
Ronald Barnett: *Improving Higher Education*
Ronald Barnett: *Limits of Competence*
Ronald Barnett: *The Idea of Higher Education*
Tony Becher (ed.): *Governments and Professional Education*
Hazel Bines and David Watson: *Developing Professional Education*
John Bird: *Black Students and Higher Education*
Jean Bocock and David Watson (eds): *Managing the Curriculum*
David Boud *et al.* (eds): *Using Experience for Learning*
Angela Brew (ed.): *Directions in Staff Development*
Ann Brooks: *Academic Women*
Frank Coffield and Bill Williamson (eds): *Repositioning Higher Education*
Rob Cuthbert: *Working in Higher Education*
Roger Ellis (ed.): *Quality Assurance for University Teaching*
Maureen Farish *et al.*: *Equal Opportunities in Colleges and Universities*
Shirley Fisher: *Stress in Academic Life*
Sinclair Goodlad: *The Quest for Quality*
Diana Green (ed.): *What is Quality in Higher Education?*
Susanne Haselgrove (ed.): *The Student Experience*
Robin Middlehurst: *Leading Academics*
Henry Miller: *The Management of Change in Universities*
Jennifer Nias (ed.): *The Human Nature of Learning: Selections from the Work of
   M.L.J. Abercrombie*
Keith Noble: *Changing Doctoral Degrees*
Gillian Pascall and Roger Cox: *Women Returning to Higher Education*
Graham Peeke: *Mission and Change*
Moira Peelo: *Helping Students with Study Problems*
John Pratt: *The Polytechnic Experiment*
Tom Schuller (ed.): *The Changing University?*
Peter Scott: *The Meanings of Mass Higher Education*
Michael Shattock: *The UGC and the Management of British Universities*
Harold Silver and Pamela Silver: *Students*
John Smyth (ed.): *Academic Work*
Geoffrey Squires: *First Degree*
Kim Thomas: *Gender and Subject in Higher Education*
David Warner and Elaine Crosthwaite (eds): *Human Resource Management in
   Higher and Further Education*
David Warner and Charles Leonard: *The Income Generation Handbook*
David Warner and David Palfreyman (eds): *Higher Education Management*
Graham Webb: *Understanding Staff Development*
Sue Wheeler and Jan Birtle: *A Handbook for Personal Tutors*
Thomas G. Whiston and Roger L. Geiger (eds): *Research and Higher Education*
John Wyatt: *Commitment to Higher Education*

Academic Women

Ann Brooks

Society for Research into Higher Education
Open University Press

Published by SRHE and
Open University Press
Celtic Court
22 Ballmoor
Buckingham
MK18 1XW

and 1900 Frost Road, Suite 101
Bristol, PA 19007, USA

First published 1997

A catalogue record of this book is available from the British Library

ISBN   0335 19599 7 (pb)   0335 19600 4 (hb)

Library of Congress Cataloging-in-Publication Data

Brooks, Ann, 1952–
    Academic women / Ann Brooks.
        p.   cm.
    Includes bibliographical references (p.   ) and index.
    ISBN 0–335–19600–4 (hardcover).   — ISBN 0–335–19599–7 (pbk.)
    1. Women college teachers—Great Britain—Cross-cultural studies.
    2. Women college teachers—New Zealand—Cross-cultural studies.
    3. Sex discrimination in higher education—Great Britain—Cross-
cultural studies. 4. Sex discrimination in higher education—New
Zealand—Cross-cultural studies.   I. Title.
    LB2332.3.B76   1997
    378.1'2'082—dc21   96–47866
                                                                                  CIP

Typeset by Graphicraft Typesetters Limited, Hong Kong
Printed in Great Britain by St Edmundsbury Press Ltd, Bury St Edmunds, Suffolk

Contents

Acknowledgements vi
List of Tables and Figures vii
Foreword x

Introduction 1

1 Jobs for the Boys: Academic Women in the UK, 1900–1990 8

2 Women's Experience of the UK Academy 32

3 Academic Women in Aotearoa/New Zealand, 1970–1990 62

4 Academic Women's Experience of the Academy in
  Aotearoa/New Zealand 85

5 Gender, Power and the Academy: Patterns of Discrimination
  and Disadvantage for Academic Women in the UK and
  Aotearoa/New Zealand 119

Conclusion 128
Appendix 1: Researching the Academic Community –
  Methodological Issues 133
Appendix 2: Questionnaire – Researching the Experience
  of Women Academics in Higher Education 141
Appendix 3: Massey University – Academic Salaries 144
Notes 145
Bibliography 152
Index 167
The Society for Research into Higher Education 175

Acknowledgements

I would like to acknowledge a number of people who supported this project. I would particularly like to thank Professor Ann Oakley for her incisive academic critique, her wit and her ongoing encouragement. I would also like to extend my thanks to the academic women in the UK and New Zealand, without whose contribution this book would not have been possible. I am grateful to Dr Kay Morris-Matthews and Dr Alison Jones for their comments and their feminist scholarship. John Skelton at the Open University Press was a keen advocate of the project from the outset. The production of the manuscript would not have been possible without the commitment of two people: Stephanie Brennan's editorial skills proved invaluable; and a very special thanks to Heather Hodgetts for her patience, expert assistance, advice and support.

List of Tables and Figures

Tables

1.1 Numbers, ranks and types of universities of women
academics, UK, 1912–13   10

1.2 Numbers and rank of academic women in Great Britain,
1951   12

1.3 Women academics at the University of London and in
Great Britain, 1912–51   13

1.4 Number of universities with at least one woman academic
in a subject within the subject group, UK, 1912–51   14

1.5 Women academics in selected subjects, UK, 1912–51   15

1.6 Numbers, distribution and representation of women and
men academics in subject groups in selected years, UK   18

1.7 Percentage of women in various UK academic groups, 1990   19

1.8 Percentage of women full-time academic staff in Great
Britain wholly funded for selected cost centres and
percentage of women students in the same cost centres,
1987–88   20

1.9 Academic staff (teaching/research) by grade and gender
at university in England and Wales as at 31 December 1991   21

1.10 Academic staff (research) by grade and gender at university
in England and Wales as at 31 December 1991   22

1.11 Total academic staff by grade and gender at university in
England and Wales as at 31 December 1991   22

1.12 Total academic staff by grade and gender at the Universities
of Oxford and Cambridge as at 31 December 1991   23

1.13 Total academic staff by grade and gender at the University
of London as at 31 December 1991   23

1.14 Total academic staff by grade, gender and method of
employment at universities in England and Wales as at
31 December 1991   25

1.15 Academic staff at professorial rank by gender and method
of employment (full-time) at universities in England and
Wales, 1981–91   26
1.16 Academic staff at reader/senior lecturer grade by gender
and method of employment (full-time) at universities in
England and Wales, 1981–91   26
1.17 Academic staff at lecturer and related grade by gender
and method of employment (full-time) at universities
in England and Wales, 1981–91   26
1.18 Academic staff at lecturer and related grade by gender
and method of employment (part-time) at universities
in England and Wales, 1981–91   27
1.19 Total academic staff by grade and gender at selected
cost centres at universities in England and Wales as at
31 December 1991   28
1.20 Total academic staff by gender in main subject departments
at universities in England and Wales as at 31 December
1981   30
1.21 Total academic staff by gender at selected cost centres at
universities in England and Wales as at 31 December 1991   30
3.1 Women enrolled in New Zealand universities, 1890–1990   67
3.2 Courses taken by all internal university students
(including degree, diploma and certificate courses)
showing percentage of females for each course,
New Zealand, 1987   68
3.3 Courses taken by internal university students showing
percentage of females at each level, New Zealand, 1977
and 1987   68
3.4 Academic staff by gender and method of employment
at universities in New Zealand, 1980   69
3.5 Academic staff by gender and method of employment
at universities in New Zealand, 1991   69
3.6 Academic staff at professorial rank by gender and method
of employment (full-time) at universities in New Zealand,
1980–91   70
3.7 Academic staff at associate professor/reader/senior lecturer
(and lecturer-in-charge) grade by gender and method of
employment (full-time) at universities in New Zealand,
1980–91   70
3.8 Academic staff at associate professor/reader/senior lecturer
(and lecturer-in-charge) grade by gender and method of
employment (part-time) at universities in New Zealand,
1980–91   71
3.9 Academic staff at lecturer grade by gender and method of
employment (full-time) at universities in New Zealand,
1980–91   71

3.10 Academic staff at lecturer grade by gender and method of
employment (part-time) at universities in New Zealand,
1980–91   71
3.11 Academic staff at assistant (junior) lecturer grade by gender
and method of employment (full-time) at universities in
New Zealand, 1980–91   72
3.12 Gender differences in marital status, New Zealand   74
3.13 Gender differences in caregiver status, New Zealand   74
3.14 Females as percentage of total university staff by academic
rank, New Zealand, 1970–83   75
3.15 Academic status at time of first appointment to a university
position, New Zealand   76
3.16 Academic status of women at first appointment to a
university position, New Zealand   76
3.17 Highest qualifications gained by academic staff, New Zealand 77
3.18 Gender differences in highest degree obtained, New Zealand 77
3.19 Relationship between highest qualification held and status
of first appointment, New Zealand   78
3.20 Relationship between university of employment and
percentage of tenured staff, New Zealand   79
3.21 Number of publications (academic women and men),
New Zealand   80
3.22 Academic papers presented in last three years, New Zealand 81
3.23 Positions of authority held within the university by academic
staff, New Zealand   82
3.24 Positions of authority that have been or are held,
New Zealand   82

Figures

1.1 University entrance in Great Britain, 1938–47   9
1.2 University entrance in the UK, 1948–89   19
3.1 Women enrolled in New Zealand universities, 1890–1900   67

Foreword

Arguments for and against sex equality have a repetitive history in western culture. Periods of political organization to advance women's rights which lead to some improvement in these tend to be followed by long moments of resentment and retrenchment. The voice that dominates these is one which contends several reactionary positions: that women have acquired as much equality as their social and biological position merits; that too much equality is economically inefficient, not least because it serves to demotivate men, whose shoulders must, after all, continue to bear the whole weighty structure of patriarchy.

These last years before the millennium are marked by a profound back-lash against the 'second wave' feminism of the late 1960s and 1970s, and thus by a rehearsal of many old arguments against the need for further advances in women's position. Given this context, there is an urgent need for us to know just what is going on: where did women get to as a consequence of the political struggles of the 1970s? What effect have equal opportunities policies and practices really had? In this book, Ann Brooks sets out to answer this question with respect to women's activity in higher education. She shows that there was a period of real advance but that the pinnacle reached was a small one: in the UK in 1991 women made up under a quarter of the total university sector. Moreover, there was a strong relationship between gender and hierarchy: fewer than one in twenty professors were women, but almost one in three of the eponymous category 'other'. Women academics work predominantly in low status, low paid, temporary, part-time jobs. Within 'other', the largest contingent is short-term contract researchers whose working conditions ensure that they remain, to all intents and purposes, outside the academy.

These are some of the 'facts' which contradict the rhetoric so aptly stated in that by-line of many job advertisements these days: 'Working *towards* equal opportunities'. The statistics state the outcomes; so what about the processes? How and why does this massive discrimination happen? By inter-viewing academic women about their experiences, Dr Brooks is able to document the structural basis of power, patronage and prejudice which underlies the statistics, and which must be seen as constituting a serious indictment of a system formally committed to values of openness, justice and equality.

The picture painted in this valuable and timely book relives the strains within the academy that creep consistently into media headlines: 'Britain backward on sex bias' (*Times Higher Education Supplement*, 10.5.91); 'Women "undermined" by male values in higher education' (*The Independent*, 16.4.90); 'Men's room at the top' (*The Guardian*, 12.5.93). Recent surveys by the Association of University Teachers are particularly damning as regards the situation in the UK (Bryson and Tulle-Winton, 1994; Court, 1994), and especially with respect to the exploitation of women as contract researchers, and the greater burden of routine teaching and administrative duties carried by women academics at all levels. Universities, in other words, are like families: women do most of the work, but men get most of the credit.

An important strand in Dr Brooks' analysis is a comparison between the UK and New Zealand, a country with an overlapping, but also different, tradition. While the experiences of academic women in the two countries were broadly similar, it is interesting to note that women in New Zealand were more likely to frame their accounts in the language of 'sexism' and 'patriarchy'. Since the situation of women in the UK is demonstrably not better, British women either have a lower political consciousness or are more polite (or both). The fundamental point here is that cross-cultural comparisons are necessary to undermine the logic of fatalism: it does *not* have to be the way it is, because it *can* be done differently. As Dr Brooks so ably shows, a policy of affirmative action is capable of reaching parts unstimulated by a less robust commitment to equality. In the same way, we can see from analyses of the position of women in different societies that different policies do have different effects, but that what is required is a shift within the dominant value-system to reconceptualize citizenship in women-friendly terms (Stockman et al., 1995). A second critical conclusion to be derived from international comparisons is that equal opportunities legislation really does work – though sometimes in unexpected ways (Dex and Sewell, 1995).

Education is important of, and for, itself, but also because it is highly related to a whole range of social and health outcomes. What women academics are able to do is important to them as individuals; but also to female students in the academy, whose own notions of identity and autonomy are partly framed in response to this. The implications of this process extend beyond higher education, of course, and are another reason why Dr Brooks' study should be read and valued by a wide audience.

This was not an easy study to carry out. The experience of studying a process one is part of is not unusual for social science researchers, but the particular problems of tackling higher education as a case study for a doctoral degree on the topic of sex equality are not to be underestimated. There is a hidden history to Dr Brooks' thesis that may be told one day.

Meanwhile, I hope that her efforts will be amply rewarded, and that the story she tells in this book is both heard and acted on, so that the tide of the recent reaction against women's interests begins to turn. What we need, as Dr Brooks' analysis makes clear, is a new attention to the problems of women in higher education which goes beyond the vision of white middle-class feminism to embrace a much more heterogenous range of 'feminisms' with the strength to contend the historical equation between masculinity and the academy.

Professor Ann Oakley
Director, Social Science Research Unit
University of London, Institute of Education

References

Bryson, C. and Tulle-Winton, E. (1994) *Survey of Contract Research Staff in UK Universities*. London, Association of University Teachers.

Court, S. (1994) *Long Hours, Little Thanks: A Survey of the Use of Time by Full-time Academic and Related Staff in the Traditional UK Universities*. London, Association of University Teachers.

Dex, S. and Sewell, R. (1995) Equal opportunities policies and women's labour market status in industrialised countries. In J. Humphries and J. Rubery (eds) *The Economics of Equal Opportunities*. Manchester, Equal Opportunities Commission.

Stockman, N., Bonney, N. and Xuewen, S. (1995) *Women's Work in East and West*. London, UCL Press.

Introduction

Evidence from the UK and elsewhere points to the fact that institutions of higher education are masculinist institutions, with limited and rigid career patterns for academic women. Such evidence indicates a clear contradiction between the model of the academic community characterized by equality and academic fairness, which academic institutions purport to have, and the reality of academic life within these institutions. As Ramazanoglu argues, 'characteristically they are run according to hierarchical systems of organization which are not consistent with the democratic and liberal ethic adopted by these institutions' (Ramazanoglu, 1987: 61). It is the intention of the research outlined in this book to investigate the gap between this model of equality and academic fairness and the sexist reality of the academy. In this context this research will consider the apparent contradiction between the liberal ideology and egalitarian aims of the academy, and the reality of competitive academic careers in male-dominated hierarchies which leads to endemic sexism and racism in defence of male privilege. Ramazanoglu (1987) notes that there are general structural mechanisms in higher education 'which reproduce a patriarchal order which constructs academic women as actual or potential threats to this order, and which act to subordinate female academics' (ibid.). This book investigates the relationship between gender, power and the academy.

Despite some awareness in the UK of the apparent contradictions in higher education institutions, there appears to have been a reluctance to investigate the area, in the same way that has occurred in countries such as Australia (see Allen, 1990; Blackmore and Kenway, 1988; Byrne, 1987; DEET, 1993; Kenway, 1990; NTEU, 1995; Yates, 1990) and the United States (see Aisenberg and Harrington, 1988; Bognanno, 1987; Freeman, 1977; Simeone, 1987; Smith, 1991; Weiler, 1988). *The Report of the Hansard Society Commission on Women at the Top* (1990) states that 'it is likely that the persistence of outdated attitudes about women's roles and career aspirations constitutes the main barrier stopping women from reaching the top in academic life' (Hansard Society, 1990: 66). The Hansard Society Commission Report

continues, that for the UK there is 'little empirical evidence about the processes at work which bar women's progress . . . academics have only just begun
to research themselves' (Hansard Society, 1990: 67). The lack of research
which has resulted in so little information on the barriers academic women
face in higher education has been compounded by the fact that such work
as has been done fails to take account of differences between academic
women at different levels in the academic hierarchy and between subject
areas. In addition, little comparative research has been undertaken on the
position of academic women in different countries. This text attempts to
address some of these issues.

The primary focus of the book is an investigation of the position of
academic women in the academy in two cultural contexts, the UK and New
Zealand. While the issue of access and recruitment of students, specifically
female students, to higher education is not a primary focus, the issues
raised relating to the culture of the academy and, specifically, the role of
women academics in this context, clearly have implications for both recruitment and retention of women students. There is no formal division of
labour along gender lines among academics in the academy in areas such
as research, teaching and administration. It is maintained that, based on
this 'ungendered' division of labour, lip service is paid to equality in the
academy, which is then undermined in numerous and effective ways. It is
the operation and processes of power at work in academic institutions which
form one of the key areas of interest in this text, as well as how academic
women are located within these processes.

A feminist framework of analysis

Data, evidence and debates around the position of academic women are
presented within a feminist framework of analysis. The contribution of feminist theoretical debates to research on academic women, and to women's
educational experience more generally, has been considerable. It is important, at this point to understand the significance of the contribution more
generally, and to consider the particular relevance of contemporary feminist debates to this research.

Arnot (1992a) provides an outline of the relationship between feminism,
social policy and social justice in the context of understanding feminism's
critique of 'social democratic educational policy' (Arnot, 1992a: 42). She
maintains that the coincidence of two social movements in the 1960s, the
movement towards social democratic reforms and the women's movement
produced, on the one hand, major contradictions and, on the other, 'a new
agenda for women' (ibid.: 43). Arnot contends that the research which
emerged on women's education in the early 1970s highlighted an increasing
disillusionment with 'the social democratic principles underlying education
and social policy' (ibid.: 42). This was particularly evident in understanding
issues of social equality and equal opportunity where the version being used

'emphasised equality of access rather than equality of outcome' (ibid.: 43). As Arnot notes it was these social democratic principles and not just those of 'the women's movement which informed feminist educational theory and practice' (ibid.). This emphasis was still apparent even in the 1980s. However, as Arnot (1992a: 46) claims 'feminist critiques of social democracy bit deeper and deeper, challenging the liberal philosophy at the heart of educational policy and the specific sets of relations constructed within the liberal democratic state and its institutional arrangements'.

This was seen by feminist theorists and researchers not as an expression of the democratic politics of consensus, but as the result of the operation and exercise of male power. The challenge posed by the feminist critique eroded many of the 'illusions of the social democratic project' (Arnot, 1992a: 59). Arnot goes on to claim that many of the fundamental beliefs intrinsic to social democratic principles such as equality of opportunity and universalism were challenged by feminist theory and research.

At the same time as feminist theoretical debates and research were challenging social democratic principles, feminism was subjecting itself to a similar scrutiny. Two converging trends have been clearly identified by Arnot (1993a) as the defining ones for feminist educational theory and research in the 1980s and 1990s. Feminism's scrutiny of its own basic tenets have encouraged:

> leading educational feminists to respond to new currents of thinking, particularly in the light of the development of, for example, black feminist scholarship and postmodernist feminism . . . Secondly economic recession and the emergence of free market philosophies in a range of countries had generated a crisis in education and a new pattern of educational reform.
>
> (Arnot, 1993a: 2)

Arnot and Weiler's *Feminism and Social Justice* (1993) brings together these converging trends, addressing the need to understand and frame educational research within contemporary feminist theoretical and methodological debates. The goals of the research undertaken in this book share these aims. One of the key developments to have emerged in feminist educational research and in feminist theorizing more generally is identified by Arnot:

> there is an increasing awareness of the limits and constraints of a common academic agenda. The commonalities of women's experiences of schooling [and higher education] across different societies are now being actively questioned and the ways in which white feminist thought has channelled and colonized indigenous national concerns and have sustained particular power relations between women (especially between white and black women) are clearly on the agenda.
>
> (Arnot, 1993a: 2)

These influences have been reflected in the work of feminist educational theorists in the US, Canada, Australia and New Zealand and have in many ways shifted the feminist analytic framework. As Arnot (ibid.) comments: 'Feminist theorizing is clearly both the condition for a recognition of our unity across national boundaries but also the condition for recognizing our diversity between nations and within nations.' These developments within feminist thinking have produced a more reflexive feminism. This is recognized by Acker (1994: 135) when she argues that: 'Feminist work can become more sensitive to diversity when it crosses national borders, for women's position within higher education responds to particular social, cultural and economic forces . . . Feminism itself takes different forms in different countries (Gelb, 1989; Eisenstein, 1991).'

Both the ongoing debates within feminist theoretical analysis and the specificities related to the analysis of the academy and the position of academic women within these contexts have informed this research. Thus the framework selected for research within this book draws on these influences and attempts to understand the position of academic women within specific historical, political and cultural contexts as they apply in different national settings. Central in these debates has been the shift in analytic thinking within feminist theorizing from discourses around 'equality' to those of 'difference'. As Acker observes:

> In recent years feminist writers have furiously debated how difference among women can be accorded the respect and analytical importance they deserve without destroying the integrity of the concept of 'women' upon which much of feminism as a political practice rests (Hirsch and Keller 1990).
>
> (Acker, 1994: 134)

This remains a contentious and difficult area of debate within feminism and is one which will be seen to emerge within the debates and evidence framing this analysis of academic women. The priority within this research has been a concern to provide an analysis of academic women. However, the influence of the debates outlined can be seen in the chapters of this book in their attention to the construction of 'difference' around gender, race and ethnicity, age, nationality and a range of other factors and in the recognition of the complex interrelationship of these modes in understanding the position of women in the academy.

Within this book the relationship between gender, power and the academy is investigated through an analysis of the 'discourses' of the academy. The analysis of organizational and institutional power is facilitated through the concepts of discourse and power within a feminist poststructuralist analysis. Feminist poststructuralism, as developed in the work of feminist theorists, has impacted significantly on theoretical and methodological developments in the area of gender and education. Feminist poststructuralism is important in terms of the development of a more reflexive feminist analysis. It highlights feminism's attempt to incorporate 'difference', within feminism's traditional frame of reference. It is for these reasons that it is drawn on. Feminist poststructuralism's relevance to the debates outlined in this book needs to be clarified at this point.

As will be indicated in this book, feminist theory has undergone a period of considerable change and a more critical feminism is developing. This critical feminism is cautious of concepts such as 'patriarchy', women's 'oppression', experience and even 'gender' as used in traditional feminist analysis. These concepts are considered too broad in their understanding of the operation of power, as well as avoiding the diversity and complexity of how power impacts on different groups of women. This more critical feminism does not reject earlier feminist analyses but identifies their limitations and cultural biases. Feminist poststructuralism is not another branch of feminist theory, it is rather more a critical strategy for understanding which draws on a range of concepts and analytical models, including the concept of discourse.

In addition, feminist poststructuralism, because it is interested in multiplicity and diversity facilitates new ways of understanding the diverse and contradictory way women experience power. Women's experience of the discourses of the academy is not a 'unitary' experience and is intersected by factors such as race, ethnicity, class, age and nationality. In the process of understanding the diversity of social power relations that academic women experience, a broader based understanding of both resistance and contestation can be accommodated. The term 'discourse'[1], as used within feminist post-structuralist analysis, facilitates an understanding of the different responses of academic women to the discourses of power in the academy in both challenging, resisting and, in some cases, accepting the sexism of the academy. The application of the concept of discourse within a feminist poststructuralist framework facilitates an analysis of power[2] within organizational and institutional structures and practices. The implications for the operation of masculinist and patriarchal discourses within the academy are investigated within this framework.

Evidence will be considered that universities are masculinist institutions. Ramazanoglu (1987), in an article entitled 'Sex and violence in Academic life or you can keep a good woman down', argues that general structural mechanisms in higher education reproduce a patriarchal order. Academic women are seen as actual or potential threats to this order and academic institutions and male academics act to subordinate female academics. Further, she argues that the mechanisms used to subordinate academic women need to be understood as forms of violence. Ramazanoglu links violence with social control in academic life and maintains that:

> The exercise and experience of violence in academic life is part of the general need for men to control women and the general dependence of women on men ... A violent academic situation is not so much an experience of fisticuffs and flying chairs as one of diminishing other

human beings with the use of sarcasm, raised voices, jokes, veiled insults
or the patronising put down.

(Ramazanoglu, 1987: 61)

A wide range of empirical[3] data is drawn on to develop an analysis of the
position of academic women; and methodological issues in my research are
explored in Appendix 1. In analysing empirical data drawn from women in
the academy in two cultural contexts, the UK and New Zealand, the concept of discourse is used to investigate diversity and 'difference' in the experiences of academic women. Analysis of the data is framed within an analytical
focus around 'identity', subjectivity and 'difference' framing the position of
academic women within the discourses of the academy. Chapter 1 examines
patterns of exclusion, segregation and differentiation for academic women
in the academy for the period 1900–90. In particular, patterns of differentiation for academic women are investigated through an analysis of statistical
data from universities in the UK for the period 1970–90. Chapter 2 examines the experiences of academic women at universities and polytechnics in
the UK.

Analysis of the position of academic women within the academy in New
Zealand is assessed through an investigation of patterns of discrimination
and differentiation for academic women in the New Zealand academy. A
limited investigation is provided of literature in the form of academic reports
from universities in New Zealand, together with a statistical profile of the
New Zealand academy, for the period 1970–90. Chapter 3 investigates
feminist research and background reports on the status of academic women
in the academy in New Zealand. Feminist poststructuralist implications for
research are considered within a broader analysis of their implications for
the growth of an indigenous feminist research methodology in a New Zealand
context. The position of academic women in New Zealand is considered in
the context of the particular discourses operating in the academy in New
Zealand. A comprehensive analysis of the educational history and sociology
of the New Zealand academy is beyond the scope of this book. However,
the New Zealand academy is considered through an analysis of feminist
critiques of the academy, through a review of the literature in the form
of academic reports on the position and status of academic women within
the academy and through a limited statistical profile of the New Zealand
academy.

Chapter 4 explores academic women's experience of the academy in
Aotearoa[4]/New Zealand based on data drawn from interviews with academic
women. While this book does not attempt to make direct comparisons between the position and experience of academic women in different cultural
contexts, Chapter 5 explores patterns of discrimination and disadvantage
for academic women in the UK and New Zealand. An assessment is made
of the relative significance of the various factors which define the position
of women in the academy. It highlights the similarities and differences in
patterns that flow from considering the position of academic women in the

UK and NZ and suggests mechanisms for changing the institutional climate of higher education.

Conclusion

The literature produced on the position of academic women in Britain is very limited, and reflects a tendency within both feminist and educational research in the UK to consider academic women as members of a largely white, middle-class, elite group and as such not a priority in terms of research. Acker (1994: 147) notes that: 'Britain appears to lag behind other, similar countries in its commitment to improving the status of women in general and women academics in particular.' She goes on to point out that the reasons for this might be sought in its particular historical and political traditions. It has been maintained (Gelb, 1989) that by comparison with the USA and Sweden, feminist groups in the UK are more 'radical, ideological and decentralized. There has been no extensive feminist infiltration into bureaucracies' (ibid.) as has been the case of the 'femocrats' in Australia (see Eisenstein, 1991; Franzway et al., 1989; Yates, 1990, 1993; Yeatman, 1988, 1990). As with Australian developments Acker (1994: 147) notes that: 'Canadian universities also benefit from a higher level of feminist activism than British ones, reflecting the greater prominence of the women's movement generally, and there is evidence that such efforts have been influential' (Drakich et al., 1991). Acker also maintains that while feminist theory gives broad reasons for understanding inequalities of gender, it is 'focused studies in specific countries and educational systems which are necessary to fill in the details' (ibid.). It is the intention of this book to address both of these issues.

1

Jobs for the Boys: Academic Women in the UK, 1900–1990

Historical position of academic women in the academy

> From the eighth to the eleventh centuries, women lectured in law (and served as judges) in Cordoba, Granada and Seville . . . Throughout the late Middle Ages, women studied and graduated from Italian universities . . . Other women studied and taught in Bologna and other Italian universities and in Spanish, German and Dutch universities . . . These were exceptional women and their circumstances may have been unusually favourable . . . In Britain women were excluded from all universities until they were admitted to all scientific courses at the University of Durham, College of Science in Newcastle in 1981.
>
> (Rendel, 1980: 142)

This first chapter reviews the literature and background data outlining the historical position of women academics in the academy in the UK. First, an attempt is made to define the position of academic women in relation to the academy for the period 1900 to 1970 in terms of access to academic institutions, appointments and subject areas. The second part of the chapter charts the more recent trends between 1970 and 1990.

Charting the position of academic women in higher education, Margherita Rendel argues that at the end of the nineteenth century in England, the relevance of higher education to the professions and occupations other than the church had become apparent. The partial removal of exclusionary practices in institutions such as education and in workplaces for women was part of a shift in the form of patriarchy in the twentieth century from private to public.[1] Changes in the form of patriarchy were reinforced by changes in legislation, opening up the possibilities for women's employment. 'First wave feminism'[2] was influential in changing aspects of patriarchy and this was

Figure 1.1 University entrance in Great Britain, 1938–47

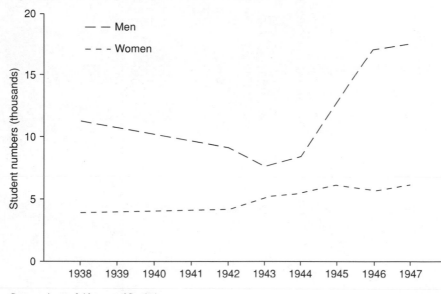

Source: *Annual Abstract of Statistics*

clearly evident in the area of higher education. Despite the significant gains of first wave feminists in relation to women's access to universities in Britain, significant closure remained in terms of access to academic institutions, subject areas and to academic appointments. Both areas of academic life, that is, access by students and the appointment of women to academic posts, have been shown to be highly contested. Sutherland (1985) notes that in the latter part of the nineteenth century there was a reluctant opening up of universities to women students which proved controversial and fiercely fought in the case of medicine. In Britain, during the 1920s, attitudes towards female students were initially enthusiastic, but this interest declined between the wars.

Blackburn and Jarman (1993: 197), in their analysis of changing patterns of access to and growth of university education between 1938–90, show that in 1938 'less than 2 per cent of the relevant age group were entering universities, and among women it was less than 0.5 per cent'. They note that the picture is complicated by patterns during and immediately after the war, the pattern of women's access to universities shows a small but steady increase (see Figure 1.1). However, they comment that: 'The increase in women students by no means matched the decline in the number of men, nor did it enable the number of female students to catch up with the number of men, but in 1943 it narrowed the gap to an extent that has not been repeated since' (Blackburn and Jarman, 1993: 198). The Annual Abstract of Statistics shows that in the immediate postwar years, men outnumbered women by three to one and as Blackburn and Jarman note, it was 1948

Table 1.1 Numbers, ranks and types of universities of women academics, UK, 1912–13

University	Professors	Readers, senior lecturers, etc.	Percentage of women holding senior posts	Lecturer	Asst. lecturer	Other	Total women	Total staff	Percentage of women staff
All Universities	4	5	5.9		152		161	3135	5.1
Excluding Oxbridge	4	5	5.9		152		161	2791	5.8
Oxbridge	*Note*: No women held university posts at Oxford or Cambridge								
London	2	5	13.2		46		53	696	7.6
Old Civic					60		60	1190	5.0
University Colleges: Exeter, Reading, Nottingham, Southampton	1		4.3		22		23	193	11.9
Wales	1		7.1		13		14	156	9.0
Scotland					11		11	556	2.0

Source: Commonwealth Universities Yearbook, 1914. (Cited in Rendel, 1980: 146)

before Cambridge University 'admitted women as full voting members of the University' (McWilliams-Tulberg, 1975) (ibid.).

While historical data highlighting access to a university education for women as students are documented in the literature, the position of women academics is more difficult to assess historically. This is partially, as Rendel argues, because of the lack of available statistical data. Writing in 1980 Rendel states, 'I am aware of little or no work on the obtaining by women of academic posts and of their progress in them' (Rendel, 1980: 144). Rendel indicates that statistics from the University Grants Committee provide information on students from 1919 onwards and statistics on academic staff run from 1923 by grade and university, but the data do not indicate gender or subject area.

Several writers, including Deem (1981) and David (1989), have linked the general position of women in education with state policy and ideology. As Deem argues, changes in educational policy have been closely linked to the needs of the economy rather than issues of equity. Educational policies have reflected prevailing ideologies regarding women's role in society. Deem maintains that such ideologies serve the dual purpose of masking patriarchal relations of male dominance and capitalist social relations. Deem argues that, as a result, women have not understood the structural causes of their oppression. This has implications for the subjective experience of individual women and how the sphere of education is seen and experienced by women. As Ramazanoglu comments: 'Women still differ politically over whether the struggle is against men or against a more institutionalised conception of patriarchy' (Ramazanoglu, 1987: 73).

Patterns of exclusion for academic women in the academy: charting the trends, 1900–1970

> In Britain a woman was first appointed to an academic post in 1893 and to a chair in 1894. The proportion of women academics now is virtually the same as in the 1920s and the proportion holding senior posts virtually the same as in the 1930s . . . individual women have learnt it is not enough to be better than men . . . they are not perceived as scholars.
>
> (Rendel, 1980: 143)

The work of Margherita Rendel (1980, 1984) is one of the few systematic analyses charting patterns of access and exclusion to the academy for academic women in the period 1900–80 in the UK.[3]

Drawing on statistical data from the *Commonwealth Universities Yearbook*, Rendel charts the position of women academics for the period 1912 to 1951. She shows that, while the percentage of female staff has more than doubled for this period, in some universities it seems to have deteriorated (see Tables 1.1 and 1.2). Rendel shows that for all universities in Great Britain the percentage of women staff increased from 5.1 per cent in 1912–13

Table 1.2 Numbers and rank of academic women in Great Britain, 1951

University	Professors	Readers	Senior lecturer	Percentage of women holding senior posts	Lecturer	Asst. lecturer	Other	Total women	Total staff	Percentage of women staff
All Universities	23	54	73	11.4	719	305	145	1320	10861	12.2
Excluding Oxbridge	20	47	73	11.5	637	296	143	1216	9541	12.7
Oxbridge	3	7	*	9.6	82	9	3	104	1320	7.9
London	14	38	35	21.9	201	73	35	397	2422	16.4
Old Civic	3	8	19	7.1	221	92	81	424	3685	11.5
University Colleges: Exeter, Reading, N'ttm, Southampton and Young Civics			2	1.4	105	22	15	144	816	17.6
Wales	2		12	20.6	35	12	7	68	641	10.6
Scotland	1	1	5	3.8	75	97	4	183	1977	9.3

Note: * No rank of senior lecturer at these universities.
Source: Commonwealth Universities Yearbook, 1914. (Cited in Rendel, 1980: 149)

Table 1.3 Women academics at the University of London and in Great Britain, 1912–51

Year	London		All universities		Percentage of women at London	
	Senior women	All women	Senior women	All women	Senior women	All women
1912	7	53	9	161	77.8	32.9
1921	20	83	27	390	74.1	21.3
1930	43	150	56	514	76.8	29.2
1951	87	397	150	1320	58.0	30.1

Source: *Commonwealth Universities Yearbooks*, 1914, 1922, 1931, 1952. (Cited in Rendel, 1980: 150)

to 12.2 per cent in 1951. At the 'old civic' universities (e.g. Manchester and Birmingham) the percentage of women staff rose from 5 per cent in 1912–13 to 11.5 per cent in 1951. In all periods, the proportion of women holding university posts at Oxford and Cambridge was far below the national average, whereas it was above the national average at the 'young civic universities' (Exeter, Reading, Nottingham and Southampton). Rendel argues that the explanation for the absence of women at Oxford and Cambridge lies in the long refusal of the two universities to admit women to full membership. In fact, women academics were not admitted to Oxford until the 1930s and Cambridge until the late 1940s, and even then only gradually and in very limited numbers. It is not clear why women did so well at the young civic universities. Rendel argues that these posts would have been less attractive to candidates for university posts likely to succeed elsewhere.

London University tended to have slightly more women academics than the national average. This position was clearly helped by the presence of women's colleges. Further, at London the proportion of women academics holding senior posts was consistently above the national average for women (see Table 1.3). Rendel (1980) considers the number of women academics in senior positions in women's colleges and mixed colleges at the University of London. She states that, in comparing women's colleges and mixed colleges, the proportion of women academics holding posts was the same, at 29 per cent. However, in terms of more senior posts, women academics held 19 per cent of senior positions in the women's colleges, compared with 2 per cent in the mixed colleges. Thus, in the case of the University of London, women's colleges were important in providing senior posts for academic women. In drawing conclusions on the number of women academics holding positions at universities in the UK, Rendel argues that by the 1950s the proportion of women academics overall had risen and in some cases had doubled.

Table 1.4 Number of universities with at least one woman academic in a subject within the subject group, UK, 1912–51

Subject group	1912		1921		1930		1950	
	No. of universities with women	No. of universities with subject	No. of universities with women	No. of universities with subject	No. of universities with women	No. of universities with subject	No. of universities with women	No. of universities with subject
Education	14	22	16	23	16	23	23	26
Medicine	4	16	12	17	15	17	16	16
Engineering, vocational, etc.	1	18	4	20	4	20	7	20
Agriculture	1	14	3	14	3	13	12	13
Science	13	22	21	24	22	25	26	28
Social administration, etc.	5	22	13	23	16	23	24	27
Humanities	15	22	22	23	23	24	25	27
Total of universities	19	22	23	24	24	25	28	29

Note: Owing to the way in which the *Commonwealth Universities Yearbook* is compiled, London is counted as one university throughout, Dundee is counted as part of St Andrews throughout; Newcastle is counted as a separate university throughout. When they are listed, St David's Lampeter, the Welsh School of Medicine and the Royal Technical College, Glasgow, are included as separate institutions.
Source: *Commonwealth Universities Yearbooks*, 1914, 1922, 1931, 1952. (Cited in Rendel, 1980: 153)

Table 1.5 Women academics in selected subjects, UK, 1912–51

Subject	Number of women		Number of universities with at east one woman in the subject			
	1912	*1930*	*1912*	*1921*	*1930*	*1951*
Biology		6		3	4	2
Botany						
(inc. agric. botany)	14	31	8	14	15	18
Physiology/anatomy	4	15	3	8	10	11
Zoology						
(inc. natural history)	7	21	6	10	13	16
Maths	6	19	3	7	8	20
Chemistry						
(inc. tech. chemistry)	5	23	3	13	10	17
Physics	1	4	1	9	2	8
English	16	37	10	18	16	19
French	10	48	4	7	17	25
German	4	17	3	10	11	17
History	9	27	6	13	14	22
Philosophy	3	9	1	5	6	8

Source: *Commonwealth Universities Yearbooks*, 1914, 1922, 1931, 1952. (Cited in Rendel, 1980: 154)

Patterns of exclusion and segregation for academic women in relation to subject areas, 1900–1950

Some of the most significant struggles of first wave feminism were to secure access to education in the nineteenth century and early twentieth centuries, thereby gaining access to middle-class occupations and professions. Women were, as a result, successful in breaking into a wide range of subject areas in the academy.

Rendel (1980) charts the appointment of women to senior posts in different subject areas in the early decades of the century. She shows that women academics held senior posts in a wide range of subjects. In 1913 the four chairs held by academic women were in botany, education and two in English. By 1922, women held chairs in languages, history and in medical subjects, and by 1930, in zoology and the social sciences. Rendel notes that, at the reader/senior lecturer level, the range of subject areas where women were represented was extensive, including the sciences and social sciences. However, even by 1951, women academics did not hold senior posts in engineering, mathematics and dentistry. The number of women academics in different subject departments from the period 1912–51 is highlighted in Tables 1.4 and 1.5.

One of the emergent subject areas in the first half of the century was the 'social sciences', comprising business and management studies, economics, geography, accountancy, government and public administration. Social science originally developed in European universities. The social sciences in British universities were 'late developers', and were more tied to a professional or applied area of academic life. David (1989) notes that it is surprising, given the subject matter of the social sciences, that no specific consideration was given to either the gender composition of the students who chose to enter higher education or to the representation of academic staff in gender terms. As David indicates: 'The academic careers that initially developed from the social sciences flowed from this and were very much in the general academic mould – new specialised careers, essentially for men although the exclusion of women was not by design' (David, 1989: 205). By the 1950s, women were represented within most subject groups in nearly all universities.

Patterns of access, exclusion and segregation, 1960–1970

The social democratic ideology of the 1950s and 1960s provided an ideological framework supporting women's role in higher education. As Deem (1981) maintains, once again educational policy reflected economic considerations and needs and a somewhat altered ideological position on the role of women in relation to higher education. The growth of white-collar and professional occupations required the recruitment of female labour. So state ideologies reflected a dual role (work and family) model for women, and encouraged women into education and training. State ideology was also reflected in social welfare service provisions to enable women to participate more fully in the labour market, albeit in segregated sectors. As a result, the 1960s saw an upsurge in women students' entry to universities. Deem notes that in 1965 the percentage of female undergraduates in the UK as a whole was 27.7 per cent; ten years later it has risen to 36.2 per cent, and in 1980–81 it had reached 39.8 per cent; a quota system had, more or less, openly been applied to keep female entrants at 10–25 per cent of the total admitted.

Changes in educational policy and ideology resulted in the expansion of higher education in Britain in the 1960s. Blackburn and Jarman (1993: 200) note that the 'number of entrants rose from 40,875 in 1963 to 61,201 five years later, a rise of 50 per cent'. There was a concomitant expansion of academic posts in the late 1960s and 1970s. In terms of the position of women academics at universities during the 1970s, the number of women academics employed full-time in universities between 1972 and 1979 increased, along with an increase in the number of academics generally resulting from the expansion of higher education. However, Rendel notes that there were big differences in gender distribution in terms of grades and subject areas in which the increases occurred. The distribution was one of vertical and horizontal segregation. Horizontal segregation exists when men and women are working in different types of occupation. Vertical occupational segregation exists when there is greater differentiation in the level at which women and men are found within the same occupation. In the case of vertical segregation, men are generally working in higher grade occupations and women in lower grade occupations, or vice versa. In her earlier work, drawing on the period 1912 to the mid-1970s, Rendel (1980) (see Table 1.6)[4] suggested that the significance of horizontal segregation was diminishing as women obtained posts in a wider range of subjects, but that vertical segregation remained unchanged. However, Rendel's (1984) analysis of the Universities Statistical Record (USR) data for the years 1972–79 suggests that both horizontal and vertical segregation were increasing.

Charting the trends in the UK academy, 1970–1990

As the first part of this chapter has shown, the period from 1900 to 1970 indicated some change for academic women and they were seen to have made some progress towards achieving parity with academic men. However, while the period 1900–70 showed some increased access for academic women, both the numbers and representation of academic women at different levels and in different subject areas remained small by comparison with academic men.

During the period 1970–90, there was almost continuous growth in the number of both men and women entrants to universities. As Blackburn and Jarman (1993: 198) comment: 'The growth has been based on the creation of new universities, the conversion of existing colleges to universities, and expansion of intakes through the system. By 1989 there were four times as many entrants as in 1948' (see Figure 1.2); in 1996, around half of entrants to higher education are women.

Blackburn and Jarman note that from 1970 to 1989, while there was a rise of 49 per cent among full-time university students, the number of part-time students increased 145 per cent. Blackburn and Jarman point out that the increase was mainly in the polytechnics and colleges, although there was a significant growth in numbers at the Open University and 'a more modest increase in other universities (Halsey, 1992a)' (ibid.).

The number of full-time women lecturers in universities has also increased, but as can be seen from statistics cited by Halsey (1990) (Table 1.7), the proportion of women among the total number of professors, readers and senior lecturers remains very low.

Figures also show that the recruitment of large numbers of women undergraduate and postgraduate students into certain subject areas is not reflected in the numbers of academic women appointed to those areas. In addition, figures for 1987–88 from selected cost centres (Table 1.8), compared with

Table 1.6 Numbers, distribution and representation of women and men academics in subject groups in selected years, UK

Subject groups	Distribution								Representation			
	1912 Women		1930 Women		1966		1975		1966 Women		1975 Women	
	N	%	N	%	% Women	% Men	% Women	% Men	N	%	N	%
Education	44	27.3	81	15.9	8.1	4.3	6.7	4.4	236	19.9	295	17.6
Medicine	9	5.6	48	9.4	20.1	15.6	23.6	16.8	585	13.7	1035	16.2
Engineering, vocational	1	0.6	10	2.0	1.6	12.5	3.9	14.7	47	1.4	171	3.1
Agriculture	2	1.2	5	1.0	3.5	4.1	2.7	2.7	102	9.0	118	11.6
Science	38	23.6	133	26.1	21.6	32.4	17.4	28.0	627	7.1	764	7.2
Social administration	9	5.6	39	7.7	17.6	13.9	21.3	7.1	511	13.4	933	14.3
Humanities, languages	58	36.0	193	37.9	27.4	17.2	24.3	16.3	797	16.9	1065	17.1
Total %		99.9		100	99.9	100	99.9	100				
N	161		509		2905	27404	4381	38067	2905	10.6	4381	11.5
Education	44	27.3	81	15.9	8.1	4.3	6.7	4.4	236	19.9	295	17.6
Sciences	50	31.0	196	8.5	46.8	64.6	47.6	62.2	1361	7.7	2088	8.8
Humanities, etc.	67	41.6	232	45.6	45.0	31.1	45.6	33.4	1308	15.3	1998	16.7

Source: *Commonwealth Universities Yearbooks*, 1914 and 1931; *Statistics of Education*, Universities, 1966 and 1975. (Cited in Rendel, 1980: 152)

Figure 1.2 University entrance in the UK, 1948–89

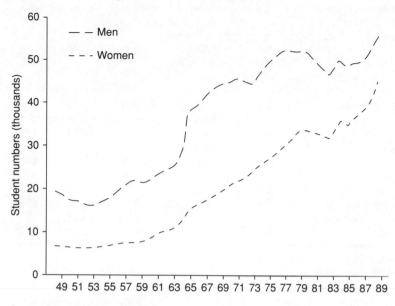

Source: *Annual Abstract of Statistics*

Table 1.7 Percentage of women in various UK academic groups, 1990

Designation	University %	Polytechnic %
Professors, heads of department	3.0	6.7
Readers, senior lecturers, principal lecturers	9.1	18.7
Lecturers	19.5	22.9
Research workers	25.4	28.6

Source: Halsey (1990).

the corresponding percentages of women students, suggest that in cost centres where women are in preponderance, for example psychology and social studies, women staff are not more likely to be in senior positions. Thus the appointment and promotion of women academics to senior positions has not kept pace with the recruitment of women students.

Fulton (1993: 111) assesses patterns of university access along the lines of age, gender, full-time and part-time enrolment. He considers figures for the period 1981–91 and notes that in 1981, 57 per cent of full-time first degree entrants were men but by 1991 the situation had changed considerably, with women outnumbering men in the oldest age group and almost reaching parity in the under 21 age group. For part-time students, women from older

Table 1.8 Percentage of women full-time academic staff in Great Britain wholly funded for selected cost centres and percentage of women students in the same cost centres, 1987–88

Cost centre	Prof	Reader and senior lecturer	Lecturer	Pg	Ug
1 Clinical medicine	2.7	12.1	19.1	47.8	45.5
7 Nursing	71.4	80.0	79.5	48.0	96.3
9 Biochemistry	4.6	4.1	11.5	39.4	47.5
10 Psychology	3.3	6.8	20.7	60.5	71.7
15 Physics	0.5	0.2	4.4	11.5	16.1
17 Mathematics	0.9	2.4	7.7	19.7	30.8
21 Civil engineering	1.3	1.2	2.8	6.4	8.5
31 Other social studies	3.4	8.9	20.0	56.1*	45.6*
34 Language based studies	5.6	15.3	27.4	56.1	70.5
37 Education	8.0	12.5	23.4	57.3	76.7

Note: * = Estimated.
Source: *Universities' Statistical Record.*

age groups dominate the higher education figures. Fulton concludes that: 'The 1990s have truly been the decade of the woman student' (ibid.).

However Acker (1994), drawing on figures from the Universities Funding Council, shows that subject divisions have persisted along gendered lines in the 1990s:

> For UK domiciled full-time undergraduates, male students outnumbered female students in engineering and technology (in the ratio of 6 : 1), mathematical sciences, and architecture and related studies (approximately in the ratio 3 : 1) and, in physical sciences (approximately in the ratio 2 : 1). In contrast, female students outnumbered male students in education (in the ratio 4 : 1) and in studies allied to medicine, languages and related studies and, librarianship and information sciences (approximately in the ratio 2 : 1) (Universities Funding Council, 1993: 8).
>
> (Acker, 1994: 154)

The period from 1980–92 has thus witnessed considerable expansion in student numbers in higher education. The pace has been further accelerated in the 1990s by the expansion of the university sector, including the development of new universities, increases in the number of overseas students and the increase in part-time higher education.

Against this backdrop, I will go on to chart and assess the representation of academic women in the academy across and within different grade boundaries and subject areas. The analysis covers aggregates of universities in England and Wales; aggregates to include England and Wales, Oxford and Cambridge and London University.

Information on specific universities cannot be presented here because

Table 1.9 Academic staff (teaching/research) by grade and gender at university in England and Wales as at 31 December 1991

Grade	Men	%	Women	%	Total
Professor	4353	95.3	216	4.7	4569
Reader/senior lecturer	7675	89.7	880	10.3	8555
Lecturer	12759	76.9	3839	23.1	16598
Other	186	40.3	276	59.7	462
Total	24973	82.7	5211	17.3	30184

Source: *Universities Statistical Record* (1992)[5].

of the requirement of confidentiality made by a number of universities. Statistical data from the Universities Statistical Record (USR) were available from 1972 (not 1970) and the last convenient date that seemed appropriate to use was 31 December 1991, so in effect the period of time considered was 1972–92. The USR were asked to provide tabulated data on the following areas:

(a) The number of women and men academic staff in the following grade of post[6] as at 31 December 1991: professor; reader/senior lecturer; lecturer and the equivalent research grades.
(b) The number of women and men academics in different grade of post, employed on a full-time and part-time basis between the years 1980–91.
(c) The number of women and men academics employed in different grade of post in the following selected cost centres for the period 1980–91:
   1. Clinical medicine
   7. Nursing
   9. Biochemistry
   10. Psychology
   15. Physics
   17. Mathematics
   21. Civil engineering
   31. Other social studies
   34. Language based studies
   37. Education

The number of academic women, 1981–1991

Statistics on the distribution of those academic staff who combine both teaching and research (by grade and gender in universities in England and Wales as at 31 December 1991; Table 1.9) show that the proportion of professorships held by women academics was 4.7 per cent; the proportion of reader/senior lectureships held by women academics was 10.3 per

Table 1.10   Academic staff (research) by grade and gender at university in England and Wales as at 31 December 1991

Grade	Men	%	Women	%	Total
Professor	113	87.6	16	12.4	129
Reader/senior lecturer	419	76.6	128	23.4	547
Lecturer	7725	68.6	3529	31.4	11254
Other	2927	57.7	2145	42.3	5072
Total	11184	65.8	5818	34.2	17002

Source: *Universities Statistical Record*, 1992.

Table 1.11   Total academic staff by grade and gender at university in England and Wales as at 31 December 1991

Grade	Men	%	Women	%	Total
Professor	4466	95.0	232	4.9	4698
Reader/senior lecturer	8094	88.0	1008	11.0	9102
Lecturer	20484	73.5	7368	26.4	27852
Other	3113	56.2	2421	43.7	5534
Total	36157	76.6	11029	23.3	47186

Source: *Universities Statistical Record*, 1992.

cent; and the proportion of lectureships held by women academics was 23.1 per cent.

For research posts only (see Table 1.10), there was a higher proportion of women academics in each grade. This higher proportion of research posts, as opposed to teaching and research posts, held by women academics is related to the fact that much research is contract based research and, by definition, short-term and frequently part-time. It is perhaps not surprising that this area is characterized by a preponderance of women contract researchers.

The nature of contract based research work generally means that funding for such posts comes from bodies outside the university such as research councils. As Acker (1994: 136) notes for contract researchers: 'Their job security only extends for the duration of their contract, which might be as short as 6 months. For some, a succession of contracts constitute a career. Contract researchers are often excluded from other academic employee benefits such as maternity leave and are not always well integrated into academic life.'

Figures for the *total* academic staff are shown in Table 1.11.

The following section considers figures for academic women in different grades for two aggregates of universities, Oxford and Cambridge and London

Table 1.12 Total academic staff by grade and gender at the Universities of Oxford and Cambridge as at 31 December 1991

Grade	Men	%	Women	%	Total
Professor	349	95.6	16	4.3	365
Reader/senior lecturer	332	91.9	29	8.0	361
Lecturer	2966	76.6	903	23.3	3869
Other	135	46.0	158	53.0	293
Total	3782	77.3	1106	22.6	4888

Note: (i) Oxford does not employ the senior lecturer status and has a slightly extended lecturer scale, (ii) a number of academic posts at the University of Oxford are not on national scales.
Source: *Universities Statistical Record*, 1992.

Table 1.13 Total academic staff by grade and gender at the University of London as at 31 December 1991

Grade	Men	%	Women	%	Total
Professor	1096	92.1	93	7.8	1189
Reader/senior lecturer	1897	80.1	471	19.8	2368
Lecturer	3879	66.5	1952	33.4	5831
Other	835	52.4	756	47.5	1591
Total	7707	70.1	3272	29.8	10979

Source: *Universities Statistical Record*, 1992.

University. Figures for the Universities of Oxford and Cambridge (Table 1.12) show that the proportion of posts held by women academics at the Universities of Oxford and Cambridge was slightly lower than the national average, confirming the findings of Rendel (1980). The proportion of academic posts held by women academics at universities in England and Wales in 1991 was 23.3 per cent compared to 22.6 per cent at the Universities of Oxford and Cambridge.

The proportion of posts held by women academics at the University of London (see Table 1.13) is slightly larger than the national average, again confirming the findings of Rendel (1980). The proportion of academic posts held by women academics at universities in England and Wales in 1991 was 23.3 per cent compared to 29.8 per cent at the University of London.

With regard to the overall low porportion of women academics in the UK, Acker asserts that:

The impact of the imbalance on British academic life is extreme, especially when it is combined with tendencies towards hierarchy and elitism still found within many of the universities. Professors in British universities are people who head departments, represent the university to government, serve on working parties, act as external examiners, make hiring and promotion decisions. In many universities, the numbers of women professors can literally be counted on the fingers of one hand, while the men number in the hundreds.

(Acker, 1994: 137)

Acker goes on to note that when she left a British university post in December 1990, only two women at that university held the post of professor, although by the time of her writing (1993/94) the number had increased to six.

As we have seen from Tables 1.9, 1.10 and 1.11, the proportion of academic women in *senior* positions remains small by comparison with academic men. Further, as has been indicated a disproportionately large number of academic women are found at the lower end of the appointment scale. These findings confirm those of earlier research (Rendel, 1984) which shows the segregation of academic women into the lowest grades and as a result shows that women were disadvantaged in terms of promotion opportunities by comparison with academic men. The initial low level of appointment of academic women results in more limited access to senior positions because academic women may, as a result, lack the experience to be considered for promotion to senior positions.

The concentration of women academics at lower levels of the academic hierarchy is compounded by the fact that they are disproportionately found in untenured and part-time positions. This pattern is repeated in other countries including: Canada (see Drakich et al., 1991; Statistics Canada, 1992); Australia (see Allen, 1990; Bacchi, 1993; DEET 1993; NTEU, 1995); and New Zealand (see Massey University, 1989; MoEdNZ, 1992, 1993; Morris-Matthews, 1993; Vasil, 1992, 1993). However, patterns of access to more senior positions do vary, as is shown by Acker in her comparison between women academics in universities in the UK and in Canada. She notes that:

Women make up 18.8 per cent of Canadian academics, a figure similar to the British one (Statistics Canada, 1992). There is also a tendency for women to be disproportionately located in contractually limited appointments and part-time positions (Drakich et al., 1991). But once in the 'tenure track' women's chances of advancing to middle levels are greater than those of their counterparts in Britain. A third of women and 35 per cent of men hold the middle rank of associate professor. The difference comes at the full professor rank, which is held by 13 per cent of women and 40 per cent of the men (Statistics Canada, 1992).

(Acker, 1994: 147)

The disproportionate number of academic women in part-time positions is confirmed by Table 1.14. It is particularly striking that in the category of 'other', including lecturer grade and other related posts, the proportion of full-time appointments at this level held by women academics was 27.3 per

Table 1.14 Total academic staff by grade, gender and method of employment at universities in England and Wales as at 31 December 1991

Grade and gender of post	Method of employment				
	Full-time	%	Part-time	%	Total
Professor					
Men	4189	95.1	277	94.8	4466
Women	217	4.9	15	5.2	232
Total	4406	100	292	100	4698
Reader/senior lecturer					
Men	7534	89.7	560	79.9	8094
Women	867	10.3	141	20.1	1008
Total	8401	100	701	100	9102
Other					
Men	22489	72.7	1108	44.9	23597
Women	8429	27.3	1360	55.1	9789
Total	30918	100	2468	100	33386
Total	43725		3461		47186

Source: *Universities Statistical Record*, 1992.

cent and the proportion of part-time appointments held by women was 55.1 per cent.

It is revealing, in terms of trends, to backtrack ten years, and to compare the position in 1991 with that in 1981. The total proportion of posts (full-time and part-time) held by academic women in 1981 stood at 15.0 per cent (23.4 per cent in 1991). The total proportion of full-time posts held by academic women in 1981 was 14.0 per cent (22 per cent in 1991); the total proportion of part-time posts held by academic women in 1981 was 42.2 per cent (in 1991 it was virtually the same at 43.8 per cent).

In the ten years between 1981 and 1991, the proportion of women academics in all grades of post based on method of employment has increased. However, by not comparing absolute numbers of men and women at different grades between the period 1981 and 1991, significant changes in the numbers and method of employment of academic women employed are obscured. In considering the numerical increase (increase in absolute numbers) in both grade and method of employment for academic men and women, further trends become apparent. The number of full-time male professors has increased from a figure of 3689 in 1981 to a figure of 4189 in 1991, a percentage increase of 13.5 per cent. However, while the actual numbers of academic women holding chairs is much lower – 89 in 1981 and 217 in 1991 – the percentage increase in women professors is 143.8 per cent during that

Table 1.15 Academic staff at professorial rank by gender and method of
employment (full-time) at universities in England and Wales, 1981–91

Gender of post	Year		% increase
	1991	*1981*	
Men	4189	3689	13.5
Women	217	89	143.8
Total	4406	3778	16.6

Source: *Universities Statistical Record*, 1992.

Table 1.16 Academic staff at reader/senior lecturer grade by gender and
method of employment (full-time) at universities in England and Wales, 1981–91

Gender of post	Year		% increase
	1991	*1981*	
Men	7534	7134	5.6
Women	867	519	67.0
Total	8401	7653	9.8

Source: *Universities Statistical Record*, 1992.

Table 1.17 Academic staff at lecturer and related grade by gender and method
of employment (full-time) at universities in England and Wales, 1981–91

Gender of post	Year		% increase
	1991	*1981*	
Men	22489	21020	7.0
Women	8429	4555	85.0
Total	30918	25575	20.9

Source: *Universities Statistical Record*, 1992.

period (Table 1.15). Thus, while the total percentage increase in full-time
professors is 16.6 per cent, the rate of increase in female professorships far
outstrips that of male professors, despite the relatively small numbers of
women professors overall. (The same pattern is apparent in part-time posts
at this level.) A similar trend can be seen in the increase in the numbers
of academic men and women holding full-time reader/senior lectureships
(Table 1.16) and full-time lectureships (Table 1.17) for the period 1981–91.

Table 1.18 Academic staff at lecturer and related grade by gender and method of employment (part-time) at universities in England and Wales, 1981–91

Gender of post	Year		% increase
	1991	1981	
Men	1108	474	133.8
Women	1360	539	152.3
Total	2468	1013	143.6

Source: *Universities Statistical Record*, 1992.

The number of academic women holding part-time lecturer and related grade posts for 1981 and 1991 exceeds the number of academic men in the same position (Table 1.18). Thus, the only grade of post where academic women outnumber academic men is the very lowest grade – the part-time lecturer and related grade.

In summary, in the ten years between 1981 and 1991, the proportion of women academics in all grades of post based on method of employment has increased. However, in comparing absolute numbers of men and women at different grades, significant changes can be seen. Throughout the grades the percentage increase for women far outstrips that for men, and the rate of increase in both full-time and part-time positions held by women is far greater than that for men. There are real increases for women including an improvement in full-time and part-time positions.

This is despite the fact that throughout the grades the numbers of academic women remain small. The greater gains being made by academic women in full-time positions must also be set against the lower base point from which women started. At the most senior level, women at full-time professional level did better than men proportionately, although the actual numbers of women are very small. The only grade at which, in absolute numerical terms, women outnumber men is at the lowest rung of the scale, at the level of part-time lecturer and related grade. This confirms the findings of earlier research (Rendel, 1984) and in addition confirms the difficulties for academic women of gaining security of tenure or promotion. The appointment of academic women to the lowest positions on the scale and the implications for promotion opportunities for academic women are discussed at various points in this text. Acker (1994: 148) maintains that 'demographic trends and educational policies that expanded then contracted the system have led to an ageing academic profession with large numbers at the top of the "lecturer scale" (reached at about 40) competing for promotion. Because promotions to middle levels are typically internal ones, the system discourages geographical mobility'. Thus despite the overall figures and the real increases for academic women at professorial level, the numbers of academic women compared to academic men remain small. The nature of appointments for

Table 1.19 Total academic staff by grade and gender at selected cost centres at universities in England and Wales as at 31 December 1991

| Cost centres | Professor | | | Academic staff by grade and gender | | | | | | Total |
| | | | | Reader/senior | | | Other lecturer | | | |
	Men	Women	Total	Men	Women	Total	Men	Women	Total	
01 Clinical medicine	675	36	711	1352	351	1703	3139	2391		5530
07 Nursing	4	8	12	4	5	9	28	102		130
09 Biochemistry	68	7	75	145	5	150	525	295		820
10 Psychology	78	7	85	128	24	152	414	302		716
15 Physics	205	1	206	400	7	407	1424	162		1586
17 Mathematics	239	3	242	339	15	354	856	144		1000
21 Civil engineering	82	–	82	138	1	139	518	61		579
31 Other social studies	450	32	482	700	103	803	1590	830		2420
34 Language based studies	307	41	348	524	106	630	1270	953		2223
37 Education	92	19	111	263	54	317	757	571		1328
Total	2200	154	2354	3993	671	4664	10521	5811		16332

Source: Universities Statistical Record, 1992.

academic women still lack parity with academic men in terms of the grade and method of appointment.

The subject areas of academic women, 1981–1991

The next section of this chapter turns to selected subject areas for universities in England and Wales. The selection of cost centres follows Halsey's selection as outlined in his article 'Long open road to equality' (Halsey, 1990). Rendel's (1984) work on the distribution of women academics at universities in the notes that by the 1970s academic women were represented in most subject areas. However, she also notes that there were big differences in the representation of academic women and men in both grades and subject areas. She argues that patterns of vertical and horizontal segregation can be seen to be operating.[7]

Table 1.19 presents total numbers of academic staff by grade and gender in selected subject areas at universities in England and Wales as at 31 December 1991. As might be expected, traditionally male-dominated cost centres such as physics, maths and civil engineering show a huge discrepancy in terms of the number of academic staff by gender in every grade. In civil engineering, for instance, out of a total of 800 academic staff, women hold 62 posts with no women academics holding chairs, and 1 woman in the position of reader/senior lecturer. The proportion of women academics represented in civil engineering in 1991 is only 7.8 per cent.

Perhaps more surprising are cost centres where female students are in preponderance, but where the numbers of women academic staff remain small, particularly in senior positions. Psychology is a typical area where, out of a total of 953 academic staff, the proportion of posts held by academic women is 34.9 per cent. More starkly, women academics constitute 8.2 per cent of professorships, 15.7 per cent of readers/senior lecturers and 42.2 per cent of lecturer and related grades. Women academics are disproportionately located in the lowest grades. It is clear that the 'feminization' of the social sciences is having an impact on the appointment and promotion of women academics to senior positions. Subjects such as psychology, which attract a large number of women students, clearly show an increase in the number of academic women holding posts but their representation in senior positions remains limited and academic women are overwhelmingly represented at the lowest grades. Similarly, in the case of Cost Centre 31, 'other social studies', out of a total of 3705 academic staff, women academics comprise 26 per cent of academic staff, 6.6 per cent of professorships and 12.8 per cent of reader/senior lecturer grade. The same pattern can be seen in education and language based studies; women remain clustered in the lower grades and constitute a relatively small percentage of the total academic staff in these cost centres.

What were the trends for academic women in different subject areas in the ten years leading up to 1991? There are difficulties in making comparisons

Table 1.20 Total academic staff by gender in main subject departments at universities in England and Wales as at 31 December 1981

Subject departments	Academic staff by gender				
	Men	%	Women	%	Total
Clinical medicine	3621	76.0	1139	23.9	4760
Biochemistry	473	76.9	142	23.0	615
Psychology	497	75.4	162	24.5	659
Physics	2013	95.4	97	4.5	2110
Mathematics	2076	93.3	149	6.7	2225
Civil engineering	697	96.2	27	3.7	724
Language based studies	2540	76.3	788	23.6	3328
Education	1206	77.5	350	22.4	1556
Total	13123	82.1	2854	17.8	15977

Source: *Universities Statistical Record*, 1992.

Table 1.21 Total academic staff by gender at selected cost centres at universities in England and Wales as at 31 December 1991

Cost centres	Academic staff by gender				
	Men	%	Women	%	Total
01 Clinical medicine	5166	65.0	2788	35.0	7944
07 Nursing	36	23.8	115	76.1	151
09 Biochemistry	738	70.6	307	29.3	1045
10 Psychology	620	65.0	333	34.9	953
15 Physics	2029	92.2	170	7.7	2199
17 Mathematics	1434	89.8	162	10.1	1596
21 Civil engineering	738	92.2	62	7.7	800
31 Other social studies	2740	73.9	965	36.0	3705
34 Language based studies	2101	65.6	1100	34.3	3201
37 Education	1112	63.3	644	36.6	1756
Total	16714	71.5	6636	28.4	23350

Source: *Universities Statistical Record*, 1992.

between 1981 and 1991 because they are based on different classifications (i.e. subject departments and cost centres), but some comparison is possible. Tables 1.20 and 1.21 show total academic staff by gender at selected subject departments or cost centres at universities in England and Wales as at 31 December 1981 and 1991. So, for instance, the proportion of posts in civil engineering held by women academics increased from 3.7 per cent in 1981 to 7.7 per cent in 1991. Similarly, for physics, the proportion of posts held by academic women in 1981 was 4.5 per cent, while by 1991 it had increased to 7.7 per cent. The proportion of posts held by academic women in psychology for 1981 was 24.5 per cent, while in 1991 it was 34.9 per cent. The figures for education show a similar trend.

There has clearly been an increase in the numbers of women academics in some subject areas in the ten years between 1981 and 1991, although there are still traditional male-dominated subject areas, for example physics and civil engineering. Subjects such as psychology and education show an overall increase in the number of academic women at all levels. However, the number of academic women in senior positions and throughout the grades within these subject areas remains small. Evidence of the under-representation of women in different subject areas is complex. Women academics are clearly doing better in almost all areas but overall are still seriously under-represented.

Conclusion

By 31 December 1991, the proportion of posts held by academic women was 23.3 per cent. The proportion of academic posts held by academic women thus remains small compared to the proportion held by academic men. Similarly, the total proportion of senior posts held by women academics at universities in England and Wales was 9.0 per cent. Thus, the proportion of academic women in senior posts again remains small by comparison with academic men. In addition, a disproportionate number of academic women are found at the lower end of the appointment scale. The low level of appointment of academic women results in more limited access to senior positions because academic women, as a result, lack the experience for promotion to senior positions.

Between 1981 and 1991 there were very real increases for women, including an improvement in full-time and part-time positions. Nevertheless, the actual numbers of women involved remain small. The only grade at which, in absolute numerical terms, women outnumber men is at the lowest rung of the scale, at the level of part-time lecturer and related grades. Despite the real increases for academic women at professorial level, both the numbers and proportions of academic women compared to academic men remain small. In terms of the grade and method of employment, women academics still lack parity with academic men.

In terms of subject areas, the situation is both complex and uneven. While in some cost centres the increase for women has been dramatic and is much greater than the increase for academic men, other cost centres remain resolutely male dominated. Even where dramatic increases have occurred, caution should be taken in arguing that parity has been achieved in the position of academic men and women. Where increases have occurred, the number of academic women in senior positions and throughout the grades remains small. Women academics are clearly doing better than previously but are still seriously under-represented by comparison with academic men in the academy.

2

Women's Experience of
the UK Academy

The relationship between feminist knowledge and women's experience has been shown to be problematic as a result of recent debates within feminism. Ramazanoglu (1993) maintains that some feminists claim that a woman's subjective knowledge is 'true' because it directly articulates women's experience. However, she notes that this position is problematic: she highlights the difficulty of discussing women's experience in unitary terms and contends that 'we always have to interpret and conceptualise accounts of women's disparate experiences' (Ramazanoglu, 1993: 7). This chapter investigates the diverse experiences of academic women framed around issues of, 'subjectivity', 'identity' and 'difference'. It shows how academic women are differentially positioned within the academy, across a range of contradictory sites and locations.

The concepts of 'experience' and 'difference' within feminist research

The issue of women's experience within feminist theory and methodology has been shown to be problematic. It was stated earlier that the use of feminist poststructuralism challenges feminism's tendency to view women's experience as 'unitary' and undifferentiated. A feminist poststructuralist approach, establishes 'experience' as highly differentiated and contradictory. The responses of different academic women and their experiences of the academy will be related to such factors as ethnicity, race, nationality, marital status, age, parenthood, class and academic status (e.g. seniority, tenure, method of employment and promotion opportunities). Some academic women will accept, some challenge, some resist and some reject, the discourses of the academy and their position within in.

The issue of 'difference' has been the subject of considerable discussion within feminism. Barrett (1987) assesses the significance of the concept of 'difference', theorizing and contextualizing the concept within feminist theoretical debates of the 1980s. She maintains that 'the idea of difference within the category of woman is radically challenging to conventional feminist arguments. This is because it is attempting to deconstruct the very historical identity on which feminist politics has traditionally been based' (Barrett, 1987: 29).

Barrett goes on to explain two different meanings of the term 'difference'. The first 'drawing on the idea of difference between women and men (whether seen in timeless, essentialist terms or in a more socially constructed approach) and the other a more deconstructive model that emphasizes the difference(s) within the category of woman itself as well as within the specific social existences of women' (ibid.). Barrett outlines three particular uses of the idea of difference which are (i) a sense of difference effectively to register diversity of situation and experience between women; (ii) difference as an understanding of the positional rather than absolute character of meaning, and (iii) modern psychoanalytic accounts of sexual difference. The following analysis is concerned with the first two uses.

The first form of difference – 'Difference 1' – is difference as experiential diversity. Barrett outlines how a sense of 'difference' as the recognition of diverse social experience has become politically important. Both class and race are now seen as two major axes of difference. Barrett points out that the claims of nation, region and ethnicity as well as age, sexual orientation, disability and religion are also seen as important elements of 'experiential diversity'. While Barrett recognizes this level of diversity as important, she maintains that it can equally be argued against this view that a substantive focus on women can easily leave 'untouched the dominant theoretical and methodological paradigm of the various academic disciplines' (Barrett, 1987: 31).

Barrett develops this position further in showing that, more recently within feminism, 'pluralism has emerged as the least threatening solution to the dilemmas posed by the recognition of difference between women (as opposed to difference between women and men). Pluralism has in fact emerged as the lowest common denominator of feminism' (Barrett, 1987: 32). Barrett makes the important point that while pluralism may appear to solve problems within feminism it does not necessarily strengthen feminism in relation to the world in general. Barrett cites the work of the feminist poststructuralist post-colonialist theorist Gayatri Chakravorty Spivak (1983) in highlighting the implications of this form of feminist pluralism. Drawing on Spivak's work, she notes that pluralism is traditionally 'the method employed by the central authorities to neutralize opposition by seeming to accept it. The gesture of pluralism on the part of the marginal can only mean capitulation to the centre' (ibid.). Barrett maintains that the category of experience is in many ways a problematic one.

She states that some feminists associated with 'feminist standpoint epistemology', which she describes as 'a theory of knowledge based on the social positioning of women' (Barrett, 1987: 32), are problematizing some of the issues (see Harding, 1987a). Harding (1993) has further developed the debate around the relationship between feminist knowledge and women's experience. She argues that:

It is thinking from a contradictory position that generates feminist knowledge. So the logic of the standpoint directive to start thought from women's lives requires starting from multiple lives that are in many ways in conflict with one another and each of which has its own multiple and contradictory commitments.

(Harding, 1993: 153)

The second type of difference described by Barrett – 'Difference II' – is difference as positional meaning. Barrett links the development of this concept of 'difference' to the work of the French philosopher Jacques Derrida (1976, 1978). Derrida makes the now famous distinction between 'difference' and 'différance', where the notion of 'différance' is associated with a broad attempt 'to dismantle the claims of what is called "foundationalist thought": this refers to the supposed certainty with which a discourse proposes its view of the world' (Barrett, 1987: 32). Barrett develops this form of difference more broadly in terms of its relationship of feminism particularly as developed in the work of Michel Foucault and Jacques Lacan. Barrett proceeds to consider the question of whether these poststructuralist theoretical positions are compatible with feminism. Barrett notes that 'the politics generated from these perspectives tend towards the textual and the local' (Barrett, 1987: 34). She further notes in discussing the implications of Foucault's work that 'the "micro-politics" stemming from Foucault's work are, whilst obviously in harmony with feminism's convictions about the interrelatedness of personal and political life, scarcely likely to transform any major social institution overnight' (ibid.).

Barrett maintains that one of the major achievements of poststructuralism has been 'to criticise and deconstruct the "unified subject" whose appearance of universality disguised a constitution structured specifically around the subjectivity of the white bourgeois man' (ibid.). However, while noting the strengths of this position, Barrett argues that it is not clear that this model offers any model of change and she points out that one of the major weaknesses of poststructuralism is its failure to theorize 'agency', resistance and political challenge. Barrett's analysis of the concept of difference has opened up traditional feminist analysis to considerable scrutiny and has been valuable in the analysis of the experiences of academic women in this research.

Investigating 'difference' in the experiences of academic women

The following analysis investigates the concept of 'difference' in the experiences of academic women in the UK and assesses their contradictory experiences of university life. Details of the methodology are outlined in Appendix 1. Based on the returns of 108 questionnaires (54 per cent) sent to academic women at 20 'established' universities and 'new universities' (polytechnics) in the UK, the breakdown of academic women by grade is as follows:

Distribution of women academics by grade of post[1]

Teaching/research
Professor/HOD	22
Reader/senior lecturer	32
Lecturer	29
Assistant lecturer	1
Senior research fellow	1
Research fellow	3
Teaching fellow	1
[Principal lecturer in new universities ex polytechnics]	4

Research
Senior research associate	2
Research associate	3
Senior research officer	2
Research officer	3
Research assistant	2

Administrative
Senior administrative officer	1
Administrative officer	2

Academic women's perceptions and experiences were sought on a number of issues including: promotion opportunities; issues of productivity; workload/responsibility issues; discrimination; sexual harassment; mentorship; equal opportunities issues/policy and practice.

Women's experience and being a woman is not equivalent to being a feminist, experiencing the world from a feminist perspective. Nevertheless, it is hard to imagine that academic women could have remained untouched by the 'feminist experience'. However, assumptions about a shared language, understanding, even sympathy among women academics were challenged in a number of ways. As will be seen, the contradictory experiences of academic women, as shown in the analysis of the data, reveal a low level of awareness of many aspects of sexism and patriarchy in the academy. While it is the case that academic women, in many cases, do reveal a concern about patronage, prejudice, discrimination and discriminatory practices facing women in the academy, there appears to be a failure to link this in any systematic way to the operation of sexism or patriarchy in the academy.

The lack of a shared experience among academic women was reflected in the views of a senior lecturer in education who made the following comment about the issues raised: 'I have answered this questionnaire to the best of my ability, but with great reluctance. My own experience and self-perception are not in tune with the issues as normally presented ... My position as a woman academic has certainly been no worse than that of my male colleagues in the same age cohort.' These views were shared by a senior lecturer in educational studies who made the following comments: 'I felt that your questionnaire expected me to identify problems. I do not perceive myself as having problems in the area of equal opportunities because of my sex ... I work in a department in which women are unusually well represented (roughly 50 per cent of department academic staff are female) at all levels. My problem in this area is an unusual one, how to attract good quality male candidates onto the course!'. These views come from academic women in tenured senior academic positions, and whose subjectivity appears closely allied with male academics. However, a similar response came from a contract researcher whose lack of job security (fixed-term contract) and lack of awareness of feminist issues led her to accept, or at least accommodate, the masculinist discourses of the academy, as was shown in the following response: 'Many [questions] are loaded with feminist "buzz words" or are phrased in such a way that they will probably only be understood by feminists – many women have not studied and do not care about feminist issues' (research associate).

These responses, coming from women in different academic positions, highlight the difficulty of generalizing from women's experience and confirm the imperative already established within feminist theoretical debates, of understanding diversity and difference in the experiences of academic women. Other academic women in similar positions express very different subjective perceptions as can be seen in the following comments. A senior lecturer stated: 'I should be interested to know what comes of this [research]. I have been active in EO [equal opportunities] issues at this university for many years and was one of a group which agitated to have a Women's ... Committee set up and it wasn't easy.' A senior lecturer in law acknowledged the need for research in the area: 'Thank you for the invitation [to take part]. I wish you every success in the future. It is an area which can indeed benefit from investigation.' A lecturer in government was also very supportive: 'I wish you the very best of luck with your research, there is far too little info on this general area. I would be most interested in reading the results, not least because I would like to do something to change the situation, so if you produce some articles or papers I would be delighted if you would send me the references.' Further support came from a lecturer in human sciences and a professor of paediatrics: 'If you want someone who feels passionately about these issues for qualitative interviewing I'd be happy to help ...' (lecturer); 'Best of luck in your research' (professor in paediatrics). A senior lecturer in computing, reader in social policy and lecturer in educational studies all wanted to see the results: 'I would be grateful if you could send me the results of this survey once they are published' (senior lecturer in computing); 'Would like to see a summary of your results' (reader, social policy) and (lecturer in educational studies). A senior lecturer in statistics offered additional help: 'I hope your research goes OK and if you need any further help then please let me know'; as did a lecturer in humanities: 'I'm glad, *very* glad you're doing research in this area and would be very happy to offer more info. Good luck.' These comments reflect the views of a range of academic women at different levels of seniority and in different academic disciplines. All reflect an awareness of, and a resistance to, their location within the discourses of the academy. Their 'subjectivity', and their experience of their social and academic location is a contradictory one.

In the process of theorizing the relationship between experience and knowledge, Harding (1993) argues that there are two positions to be avoided:

> One is the conventional western tendency to start thought from 'the view from nowhere', to perform what Donna Haraway [1988] has called 'the God Trick' . . . This tendency which might be called transcendental or ahistorical foundationalism leads to parochialism because it can never recognise the possible greater legitimacy of views that claim to be historically situated but contradict the speakers. The other is the tendency in reaction to this ahistoricism, to insist that the spontaneous consciousness of individual experience provides a uniquely legitimating criterion for identifying preferable or less false beliefs.
>
> (Harding, 1993: 141)

In analysing the empirical data drawn from the perceptions and experiences of academic women in the UK and conscious of these two problematic tendencies, an attempt will be made to reflect diversity and difference around a range of 'social and academic locations' for academic women in universities in the UK. As Harding argues:

> It is a struggle to articulate the forbidden 'incoherent' experience that makes possible new politics and subsequent analyses. On the other hand . . . our actual experiences often lead to distorted perspectives and understandings because a male supremacist social order arranges our lives in ways that hide their real nature and causes.
>
> (Harding, 1993: 151)

The following analysis assesses the position of academic women over a range of discourses and practices within the academy. These include: the gendered nature of power in leadership positions; promotion; productivity; responsibility/workload; discrimination; sexual harassment; 'violence' in academic life; mentoring and equal opportunity policy and practice.

The gendered nature of power in leadership positions within the academy

The Report of the Hansard Society Commission on Women at the Top (1990) in its analysis of a range of organizational contexts notes that discrimination against women is still widespread. In addressing itself specifically to the situation in universities in the UK, the Report describes them as 'bastions of male power and privilege'. Harding notes that academic men in positions of power in the academy establish patterns of control in the maintenance of power:

> Men love appropriating, directing, judging and managing everything they can get their hands on – especially the white, western, heterosexual and economically over-privileged men with whom most feminist scholars and researchers most often find themselves interacting in various workplaces and social institutions.
>
> (Harding, 1993: 149)

The responses from academic women in different social and academic locations, to the issue of control by men in leadership positions in the academy presented the following responses. A succinct response from a professor of humanities encapsulated where control by male academics was most clearly felt: 'Appointments, promotions and membership of committees making both!' (professor of humanities). Additional comments from a range of women academics present a similar picture with regard to the underrepresentation of academic women in leadership positions and to their position within the academy more generally:

'Under-representation of women in permanent, promoted and highly paid posts' (professor).

'Promotion to chairs' (lecturer in women's studies).

'Informal but powerful "boys" network' (senior lecturer).

'Lack of role models' (lecturer).

'It seems to me that Cambridge is reluctant to have women in university posts except fairly conservative ones at the top' (professor ex-Cambridge).

'Patronage of chairs re promotion – male colleagues favoured' (teaching fellow).

'Access, funding, performance criteria and a general ethos that promotes the white male' (lecturer).

Promotion opportunities and 'tenure'[2]

The Report of the Hansard Society Commission on Women at the Top (1990) shows that significant obstacles exist within institutions in general and universities in particular which prevent women attaining positions of seniority. The Report identifies two obstacles in particular in academic life. The first is the generally poor promotion opportunities for women and the second is the lack of job security. The Report also notes that even where women had gained tenure they were promoted less frequently than men. In investigating the issues of promotion and job security for academic women in universities in the UK, it is important to assess the practices operating around the issue of promotion within the academy, and to understand the position of academic women within the promotion framework. Academic women define promotion differently depending on their position in the academic hierarchy. Subjective perceptions are an important factor in how promotion is viewed and experienced by different groups of women academics.

Academic women showed a high degree of unity on the question of whether they viewed their present post as a promotion on their last position; 75 per cent thought that their present post represented promotion. The reasons given include the following factors: academic status; job satisfaction; financial reward; a combination of these; or other factors. Thirty-six per cent of academic women said they would see promotion in terms of academic status; 16 per cent said job satisfaction; 16 per cent said financial reward; 34 per cent said a combination of the above; 5 per cent said there were 'other' factors.

In cases where there had been a move from a senior lecturer to reader, the respondent did not see this as a promotion, seeing it as a 'sideways move'. This was also a reason given in other cases. For example, a lecturer in archaeology who had moved from the Council of British Archaeology into a lectureship said that she did not see the move as one of promotion: 'Others seem to see entry into academia as de facto promotion which is interesting . . . Within the CBA I was quite a big fish. Here I'm important by virtue of status alone as much as by the impact of my work.' Similarly, a lecturer in education who had moved from a deputy head of science in a secondary school did not see herself as gaining promotion: 'Drop in salary, level of responsibility – but I guess the job has perceived higher status than that of a teacher.' A professor in the humanities gave the following response to her experience of being promoted to a chair: 'At last the men in my department began to accord me a grudging respect.'

Academic women were asked about the type of 'tenure' the post carried. Forty-seven per cent of respondents said their post continued until retirement, 24 per cent said their post had no specific term of contract; 16 per cent said their post carried a fixed-term contract, 2 per cent said their post was probationary, 11 per cent did not answer. The tenured and contractual nature of posts has implications for how promotion is perceived by academic women. With regard to contractually based posts 98 per cent of academic research is carried out on short-term contracts. In relation to tenured posts a move from an untenured to a tenured position is seen as promotion. Academic women in this sample clearly saw themselves as having access to promotion opportunities. In terms of tenure, 71 per cent of the respondents had job security. Factors such as the number of senior academic women in the sample who had job security and would have experienced either promotion or opportunities for promotion at points in their career, could partially explain the perceived experiences of academic women. Subjective perceptions around seniority and tenure are contributory factors in this model of diversity as far as issues of promotion are concerned.

Related to the question of 'promotion', are issues of career structure and appraisal. Fifty-four per cent of academic women thought that their post carried a recognized career structure, 30 per cent said it did not, 9 per cent said it was not applicable, 8 per cent did not answer. The perceptions of academic women were closely related to whether posts were contractual or permanent. The majority of the 30 per cent of academic women who felt that that post did not carry a career structure were contract research staff. A second category consisted of a fairly large number who were on fixed-term contracts. Some respondents said the question was 'not applicable' because they had 'reached the top' – they held chairs, either departmental or personal. Thus, academic women's position contributed to difference and diversity in the experience of academic women.

Further differences also arose in academic women's perceptions of whether they had been made aware and/or been given access to promotion opportunities. Sixty-three per cent said they had been made aware of promotion opportunities. One academic women commented: 'Yes, but not encouraged to apply.' Another answered: 'Only by seeking out information.' One 'junior' academic woman's experience had been positive: 'Yes, my HOD suggested I could pursue accelerated promotion since I was appointed fairly low on the scale due to age and experience' (lecturer).

Twenty-five per cent of academic women thought they had no access to promotion opportunities because of their academic position; research assistants and those on temporary contracts saw little possibility of career development. A senior research officer maintained: 'They [promotion opportunities] don't really exist for those on temporary contracts. The main thing is to make enough money to get the contract renewed.' An assistant lecturer stated: 'Promotion tends not to be an issue in a temporary post.' A research associate saw little opportunity for advancement: 'No, this is largely because there are no real opportunities for research staff. I don't want to become a lecturer.' At the other end of the scale, a senior academic woman also saw career opportunities blocked for different reasons: 'No, there weren't any [promotion opportunities] – I hold a personal chair' (professor of paediatrics).

Differences also emerged in academic women's responses as to whether they had ever been encouraged to apply for more senior posts in their present institution. Thirty-nine per cent said they had been encouraged to apply for more senior posts; 40 per cent said they had not been encouraged to apply for more senior posts; 11 per cent said it was not applicable; 10 per cent did not answer. Some academic women who were located in relatively senior positions responded positively, as the following response from a 'reader' in the social sciences, indicates: 'Yes, all the bloody time –

constantly nagged by senior men to go up.' A second 'positive' response came from another senior academic woman: 'Yes, my department has asked for me (without my asking)' (that she be proposed for a personal chair) (reader). A principal lecturer had also had a positive experience: 'Yes, my head of school has put my name forward for a professorship.' A professor in education had been encouraged to apply for promotion but had turned it down: 'Yes, I was leaned on to become Dean. I refused.'

In addition, another group of senior academic women also responded positively but more guardedly: 'Invited yes – encouraged no' (teaching fellow); 'Yes, but generally my feeling is women have to push themselves' (professor of English). A more diverse group of academic women (40 per cent) considered that they had not been encouraged to apply for more senior positions. This group included those at 'the top' of the academic hierarchy; new appointees; fixed-term contract appointments; and research assistants. Academic women's experiences were marked by their 'location' in the academic hierarchy and the 'tenured' or otherwise nature of their post.

A crucial mechanism in the process of promotion is the system of academic appraisal. This can be seen to have both positive elements (support) and negative elements (managing academic women's aspirations). While a large percentage (69 per cent) of academic women had experienced appraisal, the experience of an appraisal for different groups of academic women located at different levels of seniority showed considerable diversity. Academic women holding professorial posts were united in their support of the appraisal process and generally in their own experience of appraisal: 'Yes – I'm sure it hastened my promotion' (professor of English); 'Yes, agreement that I should put more effort into research and less into admin for the next few years' (professor in social sciences); 'Yes, to improve work organisation and to gain feedback on current perspective and performance' (professor – social policy); 'Yes . . . I could still find a proper review helpful in planning work and career' (professor in humanities).

Those academic women who held the position of reader/senior lecturer had experienced the appraisal process as strategically useful for both promotion and personal development more generally: 'Yes – decision by my HOD to go for a personal chair' (reader); 'Yes – more structured approach to personal development and skills updating' (senior lecturer); 'Yes. It helped me to see where to go and to outline a strategy' (senior lecturer); 'Yes. Largely to let other people in the department know what I'm doing' (reader in politics).

Academic women holding the position of lecturer were not as united as their more senior colleagues in either their response to, or experience of, the appraisal process. For some, the experience had been a positive one: 'Yes. Positive feedback and encouragement' (lecturer); 'Yes – useful as a chat. I would find it very useful if it was done by an outside female, in other words outside my school/institution' (lecturer); 'Yes – I have the good fortune of having an exceedingly conscientious director [of studies] who is very helpful with both short and long term goals' (lecturer). For others, the experience had been a more negative one: 'Yes. Not constructive, paying lip service to the staff review system' (lecturer); 'Yes. Purely form, no real effect' (lecturer human sciences); 'Yes – it was a bit of a waste of time' (lecturer).

A large group of academic women had no experience of the appraisal process or were regarded as sufficiently senior not to 'need' an appraisal. Those academic women who had not had an appraisal, frequently saw the advantages of such a process. In the former group were those involved in different areas of research or administration. In answer to a question on whether they had experienced an appraisal their views are reflected as follows:

'No. An appraisal scheme exists for academic staff and will be extended to research staff next year. It can be beneficial if carried out by the right person with the right motives and appropriate back up. Contract research tends to have a short term outlook so a chance to plan ahead would be welcomed. It would also help to identify training needs' (contract researcher).

'No [appraisal]. I feel I could benefit from a review. Researchers are invariably isolated and departments hardly acknowledge they exist, let alone know what skills they may have or jobs they may wish to do' (senior research officer).

'No [appraisal]. It might help direct my efforts in ways which would improve my prospects of a future post' (research associate).

'No [appraisal]. I believe I could benefit knowing what additional skills would be advantageous to acquire for my future' (research assistant).

'No [appraisal]. Depends on the purpose of the review. Any activity which encourages personal "taking stock", reflection and setting personal goals is likely to be helpful' (research fellow).

'No [appraisal]. Yes [could benefit]. Encouragement to seek realistic goals and to discuss problems on both sides constructively' (administrative officer).

In the latter group were academic women whose seniority seemed to 'remove' them from the appraisal process: 'No [appraisal]. Could clarify strengths and weaknesses – requirements for promotion' (professor social sciences).

The process of institutional appraisal, as viewed by the academy, is an aspect of managed career development for academic women and is directly linked with the process of promotion. The process of appraisal is frequently not seen as something that applies to those on short-term fixed-term contracts, or in administration. Appraisal, however, can be seen as part of a more general process of professional development, as some of the comments made by academic women imply.

There are clear divisions in terms of career structure, promotion opportunities, 'tenure', and even the opportunity to discuss professional development through an 'appraisal' for different groups of academic women. The career structure for lecturers through readers to professors provides the opportunity of promotion for those in permanent posts in theory if not in practice. Those in 'untenured' positions and in teaching and research fellowships are outside the normal 'promotion round'. Academic women found in research posts are generally appointed on a contractual basis because of the funding structure in which they work. They are not part of, and do not experience, a career structure and promotion opportunities similar to those of lecturers. These groups do not have access to the process of appraisal which could assist them in their professional development. Thus, academic women are differentially located within the culture of the academy.

Productivity and issues of workload and responsibility

Issues of productivity and workload are interrelated in the academy. It was shown that by the measures of assessing productivity in the academy, that is research and publications, academic women are not as 'productive' as academic men. The question is why? There are two interrelated issues. The first concerns the definition and measurement of 'productivity' in the academy. A formal measure of productivity is the number of publications. There is a disparity between the levels of productivity of academic women and men using this yardstick. Academic women publish less than their male colleagues and are thus seen as less productive. The second issue is the fact that academic women frequently carry heavier teaching, administrative, and counselling responsibilities than their male colleagues. Further, women academics are asked to accept many non-scholastic responsibilities which detracts from the time needed to publish. There are clear areas of responsibility which are shared by all academics, for example, administration, tutoring/ pastoral function, and postgraduate supervision. However, beyond these, there is a wide range of additional areas of responsibility (see list below) identified by academic women which, while not seen as exclusively carried by academic women, are seen as an important dimension of being fully participatory within the academic community.

Many of the responsibilities identified by academic women are clearly seen as part of good general academic practice within the academy, e.g. postgraduate supervision, career advice, course review and validation. Other areas of responsibility identified could be seen as contributing significantly to the quality of academic life and advancing the position of women in the

academy, but would generally be unrecognized and unrewarded by traditional definitions of productivity in the academy, e.g. sexual harassment
adviser, and women in computing role.

List of responsibilities identified and carried by women academics at universities and polytechnics (UK)

1. Administration
2. Personal tutor/pastoral function
3. Postgraduate student supervision
4. Postgraduate committee convenor
5. Fundraising for research
6. Liaison with schools/teachers
7. Directing studies
8. Examination officer/chair of examining board
9. PhD student supervision
10. Graduate recruitment
11. Convenor of first year (science) field course
12. Modularization of degree courses
13. Organizing conferences/seminars
14. Grantholder – three research projects
15. Deputy HOD
16. Sexual harassment adviser
17. Executive of AUT
18. Policy and administration of research; student affairs; staff policy, planning at university level (pro vice chancellor)
19. Director of centre concerned with consultancy, research and national seminars (senior lecturer)
20. Chair of undergraduate teaching committee
21. Laboratory directorship (administration, financial, management)
22. Head of research centre
23. Careers advice (subject specialism)
24. Chair of board of studies and graduate executive committee
25. Women in computing role
26. Tutor for admissions (subject specific)
27. Academic management
28. Staff development
29. Admissions
30. Course review and validation
31. Researcher involved in teaching
32. MA coordinator

There was a high level of agreement among academic women regarding the issue of workload/responsibilities carried by academic women and the lack of translation of these responsibilities into something more tangible, such as promotion or extra pay. While it is difficult to define a typical workload and to quantify this in terms of academic women and men there was clearly frustration among the academic women regarding the lack of recognition for the level of responsibility carried. A lecturer in the human sciences commented: 'I basically manage and run the whole undergraduate teaching programme and have no official title for this, nor official recognition nor extra pay, nor compensation by less teaching.' Another lecturer stated: 'I've brought and designed major innovations to our degrees and degree structures, single handedly. I tried for promotion on this basis . . . no luck.' A senior research officer commented on one of the informal and 'invisible' roles she played: 'I supervise a proportion of undergraduate projects, plus like many other researchers I have an "informal" pastoral role with students who tend to talk to researchers precisely because they are *not* staff.' A senior research assistant highlighted the level of responsibility involved in defining 'client led' research: 'Senior research assistants are largely responsible for identifying funding possibilities, preparing and submitting research proposals. Because the process is "client led", it is not always easy to control the scope and focus of research programmes.'

Both the range of responsibilities and the comments from women academics at different levels, and in different areas of academic life, indicate some of the reasons why fewer women academics than men are in senior positions, and why they publish less than their male colleagues. In addition, universities/polytechnics would argue that on grounds of equity, the need for women to be represented in all areas of academic life, requires that they serve on a number of university/faculty and departmental bodies. Academic women are, as a result, left with less time for research and publishing. Further, women academics frequently take on a wide range of responsibilities which are frequently unrecognized and unrewarded, as indicated by the responses of academic women.

A second issue with regard to responsibility and workload is the level of representation women have on a range of departmental and university wide committees. Women are drawn on heavily for committee membership, due to the need for balance and equity in representation on committees. However, when it comes to decision-making bodies, are academic women represented and getting their voices heard in the academy? Academic women were seen to serve extensively on departmental/faculty committees: 71 per cent served on either departmental or faculty committees; 26 per cent said they did not; 3 per cent did not answer. However, only 37 per cent of academic women served on university/polytechnic committees/decision-making bodies; 59 per cent did not; 4 per cent did not answer. The range of committees identified by academic women in which they are involved are listed below:

Research findings showing the number and range of committees on which academic women serve at universities/polytechnics in the UK

Departmental/Faculty Committees
Planning Committee
Timetabling Committee
Board of Medical Studies
Staff/Student Liaison
Teaching Committee
Dental Board
Admissions Committee

Progress Committee
Curriculum Committee
Working Party on Postgraduate
  Training in History
Faculty Board of Law
Education Committee
Student Committee
Research Committee
Board of Studies
Women's Studies
Postgraduate Committee
Finance and General Purposes
  Committee
Teaching Committee
Computing Facilities Committee
Faculty Committee
Cost Centre Committee
Policy and Administration of
  Research Committee
Staff Policy Committee
Special Committee on Caribbean
  Studies
Athletics Committee
Undergraduate Teaching
  Committee
Graduate Student Committee
Research Steering Committee
Computing Committee
Staff Development Committee
Committee of Centre for Research
  in Health and Safety Committee

University (Polytechnic) Committees
Senate (high level membership)
Council
Academic Women's Committee
Technical Staff Training Committee
Computer Users Committee
Central Purchasing Committee
Non Professorial Assembly for
  Senate
College Governing Body
UFC subpanel
UFC Review

AUT representative
Senate Disciplinary Committee
Women's Affairs Committee
Staff Committee
Social Policy Board
Research Committee
Policy and Planning Group
Academic Planning

University Moderators
Academic Board
Promotions Committee
Board of Studies
School Administration

Teaching Committee
Board of Educational Studies

Library Committee
Audit Committee

Discipline Committee
Professorial Board
Sexual Harassment Network
Management Review Committee
Disability Committee
Academic Appraisal

European Humanities
Board of Arts Committee
Final Year Board of Studies
   Committee
Curriculum Committee
Workloads Committee
Research and Staff Develop.
   Committee
Faculty Review Group
Humanities Research Centre
   Committee
Faculty Executive and Academic
   Standards Comittee

Women academics gave the following responses to the issue of how membership of university/polytechnic committees is decided: 'Good question'; 'By invitation from VC'; 'Patronage'; 'By policy advisory group'; 'Increasingly by appointment from above rather than election from below'; 'As far as I can tell mostly by relevant chairs, although some positions are elective. Depends on the committee. I suspect, however, that a great deal of personal networking is involved.'

As a result of the smaller number of women academics in all areas of the academy, women academics tend to serve on departmental/faculty committees more than university/polytechnic decision-making bodies. The issue of women academics' membership of committees is not a straightforward matter. Membership of committees can signify an important set of factors for academic women, including: visibility, role modelling, decision-making, equity and representation. It can also be seen as helpful in terms of career development, because of the 'prestige value' attached to decision-making bodies. However, there are two negative factors for women academics: membership of committees is an additional area of responsibility for women already carrying considerable administrative and teaching workloads; secondly, involvement in departmental, low level servicing committee work does not assist women in terms of official definitions of productivity and must detract from the time given to research and publishing.

Discrimination

The *Report of the Hansard Society Commission on Women at the Top* (1990) states that discrimination against women across a number of institutions including universities was both wide-ranging and resilient. Within academic institutions the Report identifies both direct and indirect patterns of discrimination including: selection procedures; 'old boy networks'; age barriers; and a range of discriminatory attitudes and practices. The Report maintains that such attitudes and practices included a refusal to take women seriously through to sexual harassment.

Academic women's responses showed unanimity around a range of issues or areas of discrimination in the academy. However, issues of 'subjectivity' and 'difference' around age, nationality, ethnicity, class, caregiving and feminism, among others, were shown to be important in their specific experiences or awareness of discrimination. Academic women identified the following as significant issues or areas of discrimination in the academy. Many of the issues were identified by a large number of respondents:

ability to publish	unequal pay
rights of authorship	recruitment
initial appointment	sexual discrimination
promotion	low pay
maternity leave	job tenure/temporary contracts
admissions/appointments	selection criteria
responsibility allocation	imbalances in staff/student gender ratios
political outlook	creche facilities
disability	

In addition, there were some more specific issues identified by respondents: 'Allocation of pastoral and administrative tasks to women' (multiresponse); 'Lack of job share facilities' (senior lecturer); 'Prevalence of patronage' (professor). One lecturer identified class and ethnicity as an aspect of discriminatory behaviour by certain male academics: 'Discrimination against non-white, non-middle class students, the result of government policies as well as covert classism on the part of white male dons' (lecturer). Academic women's experience of discrimination showed that 30 per cent had experienced discrimination in their present post; 57 per cent had not; 8 per cent did not know; 5 per cent did not answer the question. Of the 30 per cent who had experienced discrimination, subjective factors, as well as more generally experienced patterns of discrimination, were important. In many cases academic women found it difficult to identify discriminatory practices because of their implicit character.

Several academic women identified discriminatory practices around caregiving/parenting. A lecturer noted that: 'It's far too implicit and elusive to call it clear "discrimination". I got accidentally pregnant within a month of taking my job. The HOD was not happy, when I returned from maternity leave I was given an enormous admin job . . . plus full teaching. I consider that outrageous for a new mother with a baby.' A senior lecturer stated that she has experienced discrimination 'directly in the sense that my promotion was delayed because I took time out of research to have children'. A lecturer identified a general discriminatory attitude: 'That which arises from childcare problems and lack of understanding about family commitments – late timing of meetings and lectures and refusal to see "career" women with children as "serious" academics.' However, a senior lecturer, while acknowledging the difficulties of identifying discrimination, noted the fact that childcare and familial obligations seem to operate in reverse for male academics: 'Difficult to say. Possible delay in promotion from lecturer to senior lecturer due to priority being given to male colleagues with families to support, etc.'

A senior lecturer had experienced discrimination based on 'age' in her present post. Another woman academic, while maintaining that such discrimination was not direct, had experienced discrimination based on nationality: 'Not formally, but indirectly, the culture of academic life is male dominated and British dominated so as an Irish woman I constantly question my position here in a way I believe my male counterparts never do.' Two academic women identified feminism and feminist issues as forming dimensions of more subtle discriminatory patterns: 'Yes, the general sort whereby it is assumed that because you are a feminist you should be excluded from any decision making meetings' (lecturer). A senior research fellow saw anti-feminism as part of a more broad-based pattern of discrimination: 'Very hard to say. All staff are imposed upon here. The structure is so complicated that anti-feminism forms only a strand of putting down of more junior colleagues.' Finally, a lecturer saw the issue of academic men not treating academic women seriously as part of a larger pattern of discriminatory pressures imposed upon academic women in the academy: 'Male academics do not treat women academics seriously in many cases, which since so much depends on opinions formed, personal appraisal, nominations to jobs, etc., is a discriminatory pressure.'

'Violence' in academic life

Male academics' attitude to and treatment of academic women has been framed within a broader discussion of violence in academic life outlined by Caroline Ramazanoglu (1987). She identified a range of masculinist practices within the academy as symptomatic of the threat posed by academic women to male academics and to their power base in the academy. A range of practices can be identified which Ramazanoglu argues act 'to manage' academic women. Academic women's responses appeared to confirm Ramazanoglu's argument. A professor in the humanities reported on the following experience of being 'labelled' by academic men: 'It was extremely difficult from the beginning to get serious attention, support, high grade teaching, promotion . . . I was "shrill", "strident", etc., if I spoke at all' (professor in humanities). Another academic woman in a professorial post had also experienced discrimination from her male colleagues: 'Only the usual threats that (some) male colleagues seem to feel when women are successful' (professor). At the other end of the scale, two female lecturers had experienced verbal and physical harassment from senior academic men: 'Yes. Verbal and physical harassment and attempts to remove me from my position and knowledge that promotional prospects are zero. The physical harassment has been the least of the problems' (lecturer); 'Verbally attacked by professors for not adhering to their perceived "dress code"; expected to play flirting game even with crusty old family men; done down when not cooperating; promotion held up on above grounds (implicitly)' (lecturer).

Academic women were frequently reluctant to describe their own experience as discriminatory. Fifty-seven per cent of academic women maintained they had not experienced discrimination. However, their comments belied their own reluctance to designate their experience as a product of discrimination. A lecturer at Cambridge commented on her experiences at Cambridge: 'No. No direct "discrimination" but constantly meet patronising and belittling attitudes from senior male colleagues and feel alienated by "Gentleman's Club" atmosphere. Also much male resentment of any attempt at organising socials for women in the faculty' (lecturer, Cambridge). A senior research associate described her experiences of being 'diminished' both by her male colleagues and by Union (AUT) Officers: 'Not blatantly [discriminatory]. However as a woman and a contract researcher, I am frequently made to feel that I am of inferior status to my male lecturer colleagues. Some of the worst offenders are members/officers of the local AUT executive committee' (senior research associate). A lecturer described her experience of returning to work from maternity leave and to the attitudes of some of her male colleagues: 'Some male staff are difficult to get on with, perhaps they do it deliberately. I've returned from maternity leave back to full time work, some male members have gone out of their way to make me feel guilty – "you should be at home looking after your little one".' A professor described her experience prior to promotion and subsequent to being appointed to a chair: 'Not since promotion. Considerable discrimination previously – largely in attitudes and perception.' A reader in sociology gave her explanation of why she had not experienced discrimination: 'No – I'm too clever, publish too much and am too stroppy for anyone to dare.'

Discrimination is frequently covert and often results from the application of 'male' standards, priorities and practices. As much discrimination is 'implicit', many respondents had difficulty defining discrimination. The matter was compounded by the fact that 'discrimination' was frequently not defined by universities in terms of a possible source of grievance, unlike more specific issues, of sexual and racial harassment. Academic women's experiences of discrimination reflect issues of 'subjectivity' and 'difference' around academic status/position, age, nationality, parenthood and feminism.

Sexual harassment

Sexual harassment has become one of the most clearly identified and defined areas of discrimination in academic life. From data collected in this research 58 per cent of academic women were aware of issues of sexual harassment arising in their present institution and 32 per cent were not.

Some women had experienced sexual harassment personally. Real attempts by universities to monitor and remove sexual harassment often had the effect of driving the practices underground. As one professor noted: 'Sexual practices have on the whole simply gone underground. Harassment of female students continues and male lecturers have trouble with older women in authority – so things continue as ever.' Harassment can take different forms and as Stanko (1985) notes, the form of 'sexual intrusion' is immaterial in terms of the distress experienced. A senior lecturer had experienced sexual harassment: 'In minor form; I am the only female member of teaching staff. Sometimes groups of male staff will talk about women with reference to their sexiness in front of me which I object to.' Not all academic women who had experienced sexual harassment had experienced it from a male colleague. As another senior lecturer commented: 'Please do not assume that sexual harassment is a matter of male harassment of female. My own experience is of being harassed by a female student.'

On the issue of sexual harassment, 59 per cent of academic women were aware of information circulated by university and polytechnic on the existence of procedures for dealing with issues of discrimination, and 58 per cent were aware of issues of sexual harassment arising in their present institution. Academic women's subjective perception of sexual harassment as discriminatory varied depending on their experiences. There is a general movement towards an explicit recognition on the part of academic institutions of the need for both policy and procedures for dealing with issues of sexual harassment.

Role modelling/mentorship

Role modelling and mentorship as concepts are more familiar in the USA, Australia and New Zealand, where they have been the subject of considerable debate as mechanisms for breaking down traditional patterns of gender stereotyping. Mentorship is widely employed within equal opportunities policy within the USA and Australasia. However, role modelling as a concept, and mentorship as a strategy, are less well-established as areas of academic research and 'as practice' in the UK[3]. The issues of mentorship and role modelling are seen as problematic in terms of feminist theorizing and have been largely discounted as effective strategies for change. Academic women identified many of the problematic aspects of mentoring, however they were far from unanimous in totally rejecting the concept. A large number of academic women felt that informal role modelling and mentorship patterns were already in existence, so that no formal policy was needed or could be implemented.

Other general issues raised by academic women included 'patronage' or 'favouritism' which some respondents thought might result. A professor in the humanities outlined some of her concerns around the questions of role modelling and mentorship: 'I think it is extremely important that students should see successful women around them but "imitation" sounds to me a bit unhealthy. As for being a "mentor", I'd offer support but I'm not sure enough of my own strategies to pass them on wholesale.' A lecturer also had worries around the question of 'imitation': 'Role modelling seems fraught with problems to me. I wouldn't want any of my students to feel they had to imitate me.' A senior research officer, while not giving reasons, was extremely negative about the usefulness of role modelling and mentorship: 'I can't see how they [role modelling/mentorship] could be positive or break down stereotypes. My view of "mentorship" is exploitative and bad.' Academic women were asked what areas of academic life they thought role modelling/mentorship most lent themselves to. The following areas were identified: research; teaching; new academic staff; publishing; and 'nearly every aspect' of academic life. Other more specific areas mentioned included: black students; career development; students with disabilities; and postgraduate supervision. Two academic women identified the application of role modelling/mentorship as having a more specific value for women in the academy, and it seemed to be a generally held assumption that same sex mentoring was preferable. A teaching fellow saw the ideas as having importance for: 'Collegiate life: female students can see that women can succeed against male competition. Hence the importance of women's colleges with predominantly female fellows.' A senior lecturer understood the ideas to have a more general relevance and application: 'Anywhere where there is a hierarchical structure with women under-represented at the top.'

Fifty per cent of academic women thought that the idea of role modelling/mentorship was useful in breaking down gender stereotyping in academic relationships; 17 per cent did not; 11 per cent did not know; and 22 per cent did not answer. A teaching fellow saw role modelling/mentorship as useful: 'In the teaching relationship, especially supervision; good for men and women students.' A senior research fellow highlighted one of the difficulties of implementing role modelling/mentorship: 'Of course but how is this done without senior female academics for junior academics.' A very positive response came from a lecturer in women's studies: 'As I work with women more or less exclusively this isn't a problem. I have a surplus of wonderful role models.'

Academic women's experience of mentorship was limited. Fifty-six per cent of academic women stated that they had no experience of mentorship; 19 per cent had some experience of mentorship; 25 per cent did not answer. Two respondents indicated that their experience of mentorship had involved mentoring from male academics. A reader commented: 'All my life I have had active sponsorship in my research and teaching from male colleagues almost never by a woman and not because there have been very few on the staff.' A research assistant stated: 'I'm afraid to say that the greatest support I've had has been from male tutors (as a student) and colleagues now.'

The experience of one woman academic of mentorship in the USA highlighted some of the problems in the 'practice' of mentorship: 'When I worked in the USA mentorship was the one grievance most brought up by women PhD students. They said that even if they did better than men students in exams, when it came to choosing research assistants, professors always took male students; not because they were actively sexist but because they felt more comfortable working closely with male students. Since all the professors were men (economics – male dominated) this meant women students were excluded from opportunities to "learn by doing"' (lecturer).

Fifty-seven per cent of academic women thought that mentorship was a good idea to extend to tutor/student relationships, although a large number thought that it was most appropriate for postgraduate level only. Fourteen per cent did not think mentorship was a useful idea to extend to tutor/ student relationships; 15 per cent did not know; 14 per cent did not answer. A research assistant highlighted another difficulty associated with mentorship: 'Maybe, but if a tutor is good at their job they should surely give the student the support they need. Maybe the mentorship role could be seen as intrusive to a student.' A reader noted the views of women students: 'I'm quite wary of this although I have been told by women students that they find it important.'

Fifty per cent of academic women thought that role modelling was useful for postgraduate supervision. However, there were differences of view on this issue. A research associate thought that role modelling was a good idea: 'But I think to an extent this is inevitable, with a good supervisor.' A teaching fellow maintained that on the contrary it was a very bad idea: 'No – it's very important for the postgraduate to become his/her own person not a "clone" of the supervisor.'

When the above issue was related to the question of choice in the gender of the supervisor, 41 per cent of academic women said they would prefer a choice; 38 per cent said they would not; 14 per cent did not know; 7 per cent did not answer. Many academic women noted that although ideally there should be a choice, in reality the current situation made this impossible. As a lecturer commented: 'Yes, though it is only one factor in the equation and the reality is there are so few women around, the choice may be fairly theoretical.' This point was reinforced by a senior research associate: 'Ideally yes, but given the present under-representation of women this may not be practical. However, access to a senior female member of staff should always be available – even if not in the same subject area.'

Fifty per cent of academic women said they would support mentorship if adopted as an aspect of a university/polytechnic equal opportunities policy; 19 per cent said they would not; 12 per cent did not know; 19 per cent did not answer. One of the academic women in a professorial post commented: 'I fear that neither of these have an easy relationship with equal opportunities so I would be very cautious.' A senior lecturer thought it could act as a counterweight to the 'old boy network'. Two academic women argued against their formal application within a policy framework. A lecturer stated: 'I think this is artificial. Using it as a deliberate strategy will undermine those cases where it occurs naturally.' Similarly, a reader commented: 'No. I would oppose a formal incorporation of this policy.' Finally, another lecturer made an important point: 'Yes, only if the structures were there to support it, otherwise it becomes another tokenistic statement where the onus is put on the participants.'

The area of mentorship and role modelling is a problematic one in terms of the theoretical implications and practical problems of implementation. Academic women reflected many of the issues which make the concepts problematic. The relative lack of women academics means that those who are available carry considerably more than their male colleagues in terms of a supervisory role. Issues of diversity and difference emerged among academic women who had specific experience of mentoring and those who opposed some of the conceptual implications.

Equal opportunities policy and practice in the academy

The *Report of the Hansard Society Commission on Women at the Top* (1990) made the following recommendations regarding universities in the United Kingdom: 'We recommend that all universities should appoint equal opportunities officers and that they should monitor and publish information about women's progress' (Hansard Society, 1990: 11).

Many universities and polytechnics in the UK have introduced an equal opportunities policy (EOP) as a result of pressure from women academics, the findings of the Hansard Society Commission Report, and the need to recruit larger numbers of students, particularly from groups traditionally under-represented in higher education. While the result is by no means uniform, universities and polytechnics have made considerable advances in this area.

Despite advances in this area a large number of questions remain regarding the effectiveness of equal opportunities policy and practice. The current implementation of these strategies is still very uneven, although increasing competition within the tertiary sector will demand increasing flexibility of provision, and require a greater commitment to equal opportunities practice as well as policy. Despite the very real effort by a number of institutions to consider 'positive action'[4] strategies to enhance the opportunities of academic women (among other groups), the academy remains overwhelmingly defined by a culture which disadvantages academic women. To what extent the implementation of equal opportunities policy impacts on the institutional climate of higher education needs to be set against academic women's experiences of the discourses and practices of the academy. It is only in this context that the real impact of policy on practice can be assessed.

There was unity among academic women on the importance of an equal opportunities policy within the academy. Sixty-eight per cent said that an equal opportunities policy was very important, 17 per cent said that it was important; 9 per cent said that it was not very important; 6 per cent did not answer. Despite the large number of academic women who regarded this as an important issue, a large number of respondents made the distinction between policy and practice, and were disillusioned with the lack of effectiveness of equal opportunities policy within the academy. A professor in the humanities commented: 'In principle very important, in practice we barely have one.' Similarly, a professor in the social sciences made the following point: 'Symbolically important – in practice I don't know.' Three other academic women made the following comments: 'It should be extremely important but in practice isn't' (lecturer); 'Here at . . . we are at the lip service stage' (senior lecturer); 'Very. It should be but there is little substance to it in this institution' (lecturer). The 9 per cent who argued that it was 'not important', in the main felt that it did not change the situation for women and many academic women saw the process of implementation of EOP as institutionally managed and controlled.

There was less agreement around the question of the impact of EOP on academic relationships: 42 per cent of academic women said they thought it had an impact on academic relationships; 24 per cent said it did not; 21 per cent said they did not know; 13 per cent did not reply. Many academic women, while maintaining that EOP could have an impact on academic relations, again made a distinction between policy and practice. Some academic women saw EOP as fulfilling a consciousness raising function: 'Yes – awareness raising' (lecturer); 'Yes, it makes colleagues stop and question their assumptions and makes them aware of unconscious bias and institutional discrimination' (senior lecturer); 'Yes. Influences perceptions of academic staff and opportunities for women, blacks, etc. Doesn't solve problems but makes discrimination more difficult' (professor).

Other academic women saw EOP as a benchmark towards off-setting some of the worst excesses of the academy and towards the establishment of good practice. A lecturer maintained that EOP 'sets standards, goals and parameters, establishes good practice re academic relations, legal and constitutional implications. Confidence to alter academic relations, as a woman.' Another lecturer maintained:

> 'Yes, it can be helpful in changing attitudes amongst all those but the most bloody minded . . . I was the only woman to apply for my present job – society filtered out the others long ago. If you look at the social profiles of members of the department it's interesting to note that the women don't have young families and the men do. One woman works part-time to accommodate her family life. Put simply, men are able to work full-time and have children without suffering social disapprobation, women are not. Equal opportunities policies are vital of course since no action at all is indefensible, but I fear it is cosmetic.'

A senior lecturer was succinct in her view: 'Yes, it can help counter the overwhelming dominance of white heterosexual males in academia.'
Several academic women made distinctions between policy and its effective

translation into practice: 'Policy and practice are different things, we have a draft policy with no practice and no funding of initiatives to raise awareness' (lecturer). A senior research associate made the following comment: 'Policy on its own probably has little impact. In the long term I would hope to see some changes in academic relationships. In the short term people (men) may appear more sympathetic to equal opportunities, but I suspect this is more a matter of changing what they say openly rather than changing attitudes.' A similar point was made by a lecturer: 'Yes. It alerts people to the existence of discrimination and generates discussion about the problems. There is unfortunately a huge gulf between having a policy and practising it. But at least the existence of a policy brings the problems of practice to the fore. It has made people distinctly more sensitive about language.'

A proportion of academic women (24 per cent) felt that equal opportunities policy often masks discriminatory practices or at best does little or nothing to improve the quality of academic relationships. Some of the respondents explained their position as follows. A lecturer in social work claimed 'the policy often masks appalling practice'; a lecturer maintained that: 'The status quo carries a huge amount of inbuilt self protection and inertia, very difficult to overcome.' A research fellow commented: 'Not really. There is a great deal of rhetoric which does not get translated into policy or practice if it costs e.g. full replacement costs for maternity leave.' A senior lecturer commented that EOP had barely scratched the surface of the power base of the academy: 'No. The question requires a paper to answer it. Universities have a long, long way to go here. Just look at the composition of any University Board.'

From the vantage point of administration, another academic woman commented on the nature of academic relationships within certain disciplines. The assumption being made by this respondent was that EOP was unlikely to change this problem: 'Many academic staff (men) genuinely do not wish to work with women. It is particularly a problem in physical sciences and engineering' (administrative officer). A further 21 per cent of respondents said that they did not know whether EOP would have an impact on academic relationships.

There was a clear awareness among women academics that the mere existence of an equal opportunities policy had a limited impact on the culture of the academy and the quality of academic relationships. While there was a general unity among academic women around the question of how important an equal opportunities policy was, there was diversity and differences in views on the impact of EOP on academic relationships. Many 'old' and 'new' universities have only recently introduced equal opportunities policy, statement and committees. While there was no clear cut division between groups of academic women on the basis of seniority or academic position, many of the responses highlighted the gulf between policy and practice. Many respondents feel that the existence of an equal opportunities policy conceals unfair and discriminatory practices, and that the existence per se of an equal opportunities policy without an accompanying set of practices is merely a public relations exercise. Other respondents seemed unclear or unprepared to comment on the implications of equal opportunity policy and practice for academic relationships.

When asked to identify what they regarded as the most important equal opportunities issues, academic women were unified in identifying as most significant three issues: promotion, childcare/parenting (caregiving), and maternity and pregnancy issues. A wide range of other issues were also identified by women academics as significant, many of these issues being supported by a number of respondents. These included: sexism; recruitment; harassment; lack of women and ethnic minorities among academic staff; pay; working hours; teaching and curriculum issues; research staff; racism; representation; disability; equal opportunities procedures; positive discrimination; awareness of the potential for disadvantage; treatment of part-time and temporary staff; increasing numbers of politically active women; training; mismatch between policy and practice; career breaks; discriminatory work practices.

On the question of how significant an EOP is in the recruitment of students currently under-represented in the academy (black students[5], women returners and students with disabilities) there was significant diversity of view. Forty-four per cent of academic women felt that an equal opportunities policy was very important for students currently under-represented in the academy; 25 per cent thought it was important; 16 per cent felt that it was not very important; 15 per cent did not respond. Those who thought it was important gave the following reasons. One senior academic woman argued that it had a 'symbolic significance' (professor in social science). A senior lecturer felt that: 'A policy which actively promotes change is essential.' A senior research associate argued that: 'With sufficient commitment and financial backing, potentially very significant.' And a lecturer saw the benefits for the specific groups involved: 'I would say it is very significant, because disadvantaged groups need positive encouragement.'

Differences of view also emerged within the 16 per cent of academic women who maintained that EOP had little impact. A senior research officer maintained that: 'Policy alone doesn't mean much if there are no facilities.' A lecturer had a similar response: 'Not very, given that such policy does not translate into appropriate action.' A senior lecturer pointed out that: 'Under-representation does not automatically equate with absence of equal opportunities.' In addition, a lecturer who had spent a year as a visiting assistant professor at a university in California maintained that to establish a policy, in this case of positive discrimination, to encourage the recruitment of students under-represented in the academy can be problematic without significant additional resources and backup. She commented: 'I was shocked to discover after the exam that almost all the people who failed were black mainly women, admitted under a positive discrimination policy; the reason they failed was their standard of basic maths, statistics, English, etc., was far below the average and there was no way they could keep up with the course. So I think this kind of admissions policy can harm the students involved . . .

unless there is a specific programme of remedial teaching to give them an equal starting point.' Academic women's views on this issue showed both difference and diversity based on their experiences in the academy and again reflected the problem of policy and practice in the effective implementation of EOP. Academic women were asked whether the university/ polytechnic with which they were associated had adopted an equal opportunities statement: 79 per cent of respondents said yes; 3 per cent said no; 16 per cent said they did not know; and 3 per cent did not answer. There were some qualifying comments made in terms of the current status of equal opportunities policy, for example, 'In process'; 'Yes but no supporting policy'; 'Just approved'. Academic women were further asked whether the university/polytechnic had an equal opportunities committee (EOC): 53 per cent said yes; 17 per cent said no; 25 per cent did not know; 5 per cent did not answer. Findings indicated that in a number of cases, the formulation of an equal opportunities policy or statement had not been accompanied by the establishment of an equal opportunities committee. In other cases, an equal opportunities officer had been designated. On the issue of whether the aims of the equal opportunities committee were available to all academic staff and students and if so in what form, the results were as follows: 41 per cent of respondents said yes; 5 per cent said no; 45 per cent said they did not know; 9 per cent did not answer.

Issues concerned with how regularly the EOC met, the type of issue addressed by the EOC and how membership of the EOC is decided, showed a considerable lack of information on the part of women academics of these matters. Seventy-two per cent of respondents did not know how often the EOC met; 54 per cent were not aware of the types of issue addressed by the EOC. In terms of how membership of the EOC is decided, 73 per cent did not know how membership was decided.

There appears to be an incongruity between the significance attached to equal opportunities issues and their relevance within the academy as viewed by academic women and a knowledge of equal opportunity procedures within tertiary institutions held by women academics. One of the reasons for the lack of familiarity with equal opportunities procedures could be the recent establishment of EOP within universities and polytechnics. In addition, it may be the result of the distinction between equal opportunities policy and practice identified earlier and in some cases (as some academic women made clear) a general disillusionment with the operation of equal opportunity policy and practice and its inability to significantly change the culture of the academy and the position of academic women within that culture. The institutional character of equal opportunity policy and procedures reinforced the sense of disillusionment as shown in the following comments. A senior lecturer commented: 'Unfortunately this body (EOC) seems remote from the majority of women and doesn't have an effective position in the University committee structure.' An administrative officer outlined the position as follows: 'The staff working group has focussed on training, consciousness raising and the issue of monitoring. But the university has given it very little money.' While a lecturer in women's studies made the following comment: 'We have policies on sexual harassment and are developing one on racism. Not sure how equal opps works at a personal level.' Two academic women also commented on appointments to equal opportunities committees. A lecturer made the following observations: 'The Deputy VC selects people from a list of nominations but it is extremely hard to find out when and how nominations can be made.' A professor in the humanities commented: 'Yes, but so constituted as to consist largely of people indifferent to the issues.'

Conclusion

The difficulty of generalizing about women's experience as if it were a coherent and unified whole has already been established as problematic in feminist theoretical and methodological debates. Academic women's experience of the academy is diverse, reflecting issues of age, nationality, class, race, ethnicity, parenthood and academic position. The lack of a shared experience among academic women around issues of sexism in the academy, and of feminism and feminist issues, was expressed over a range of issues.

On the subject of the gendered nature of power in leadership positions within the academy, academic women in different academic positions reflected a range of views. Academic women generally understood that women were both under-represented in positions of leadership in the academy and that their under-representation was the result of a mixture of power, patronage and prejudice which resulted in the promotion of the white academic male to positions of control and leadership in the academy. However, there did appear to be a failure on the part of a number of academic women to translate this in any systematic way to the operation of sexism or patriarchy in the academy.

Academic women's views on the opportunities for promotion within the framework of the academy revealed a number of issues. While academic women showed a high degree of unity with 76 per cent seeing themselves as having access to and experiencing promotion, academic position was an important factor in terms of how promotion was viewed.

On the issue of career structure and appraisal, academic position was again significant in understanding the varied responses within different groups of academic women. In terms of career structure, promotion opportunities and even the opportunity to discuss professional development (appraisal), academic women are differentially positioned. The subjective perception of academic women was related to whether posts were contractual or permanent. Academic women in research posts are disadvantaged by the structure of research funding and by the contractual nature of posts. The career structure for those in teaching/research provides the opportunity for career development and promotion in theory, if not in practice, in contrast to women in 'contractual positions'. The nature of contract research effectively locates different groups of academic women outside the career and promotion framework. Thus, the experience of academic women is characterized by diversity and difference and related to their position within the academy.

Academic women's productivity and ultimately promotion is directly related to issues of workload and the number and range of responsibilities held. Women academics are involved in an enormous range of additional responsibilities, which in many cases do not enhance their career prospects or facilitate promotion. These responsibilities detract from the time and energy needed for publishing and research, these being the main criteria on which productivity is assessed in the academy.

Similarly on issues of committee membership, academic women are overburdened, due to the demand for equity, in terms of representation, and the lack of women academics to serve on committees. Further, women academics are frequently involved in committee work at the departmental or faculty level undertaking necessary, but essentially 'housekeeping' functions. They are less frequently found on university decision-making bodies.

On the issue of discrimination, the responses from academic women showed that discrimination is frequently implicit and results from the application of masculinist standards, priorities and practices. Fifty-seven per cent of respondents stated that they had not experienced discrimination, although a large number stated that they had difficulty in defining discrimination. Age, nationality, ethnicity, parenting (caregiving) and feminism were significant factors in the perceptions and experiences of academic women. The covert nature of much discriminatory behaviour frequently makes women reluctant to designate behaviour and attitudes from their male colleagues as discriminatory. The more explicit definition of, and criteria for, assessment of sexual harassment makes it a more straightforward matter to identify than discrimination. Fifty-eight per cent of academic women were aware of issues of sexual harassment in their universities. Both the form of sexual harassment and the subjective experience of academic women varied. There is recognition on the part of academic institutions of the need to implement policy and procedures for monitoring issues of sexual harassment and discrimination more generally.

Issues of mentorship and role modelling are problematic, conceptually in terms of feminist theorizing and in terms of practical implementation. The responses of academic women to these concepts reflected these debates. The support shown by some academic women to the general principle was qualified by the reality that the lack of women in academic life makes its effective implementation difficult. Differences emerged in the subjective perceptions of different academic women which were often related to their experiences of mentorship and role modelling.

The introduction of an EOP within universities and polytechnics in the UK is important in the establishment of equity within the academy. Some universities have made advances in the direction of implementing equal opportunities policy. However, considerable doubt remains about how effectively this is being translated into practice. Academic women were united in their support for equal opportunities policy within the academy; 68 per cent said it was important. However, a large number of academic women expressed concern about the gulf between policy and practice. Many respondents indicated that the existence of an EOP may conceal unfair and discriminatory practices, and, without an accompanying set of practices, may merely be a public relations exercise.

Many academic women identified promotion, childcare facilities and costs, and maternity and pregnancy issues, as the most important equal opportunities issues. Academic women showed a wider degree of disagreement and difference around the impact of an EOP on academic relationships. Subjective perceptions around issues of seniority, workloads, promotion opportunities, were significant factors in establishing a wide range of responses among academic women on the effectiveness and impact of EOP. There does appear to be a discrepancy in terms of how women academics view equal opportunities policy in the academy and their knowledge of, and involvement with, equal opportunities procedures. This could partly be explained by the recent implementation of EOP and procedures in the academy. There appears to be a fairly high level of disillusionment among academic women with the operation of EOP and practice within the academy.

Academic women's experience is characterized by diversity reflecting issues such as academic position, age, nationality, race, ethnicity and parenthood (caregiving). This chapter establishes links between the issues of diversity and difference as identified in feminist theoretical and methodological debates and as articulated by academic women in their experiences of the academy.

3

Academic Women in Aotearoa/New Zealand, 1970–1990

This chapter seeks to investigate the 'discourses' of the academy in New Zealand/Aotearoa.[1] The emphasis of the analysis of the New Zealand academy has as its focus the contemporary history (1970–90) of the academy. The primary aim is to provide a review of a range of literature in the form of reports and studies, as well as a limited statistical profile of the New Zealand academy, to show how academic women are located within the academy in New Zealand. There is scant empirical research of a national kind on gender differentiation in universities in New Zealand and, as is the case in the academy in the UK, data collection by universities on gender breakdown of academic staff is a recent development and in many cases is still being compiled.[2] While there can be no direct comparison between New Zealand and UK data, the New Zealand findings do parallel some of the findings from the UK.

Some of the reasons behind the lack of research into the operation of the academy and the position of women academics in New Zealand are similar to the reasons that have inhibited research in the UK. Of central importance is the ideology of egalitarianism which characterizes higher education, and which has been so central to the growth and development of the nation state in New Zealand and the UK. As O'Neill maintains, 'such myths and the liberal rhetoric through which educational discourse is conducted, should be understood and analysed as having the effects of a material force within education. They are constitutive of an ideology that has worked to mask and hide from critical enquiry deep-seated contradictions within the system' (O'Neill, 1992: 10).

Academic women, feminist research and the academy in Aotearoa/New Zealand

The tradition of research into the position of academic women within the academy in New Zealand is limited. In addition, the significant international character of the 'academic community' in New Zealand, which some would argue is part of a post-colonialist heritage, has been one of the reasons which has led to a 'fragmented identity' for women as an academic group. The interests of many academic women in New Zealand are concerned with the analysis of their own particular history and position in the New Zealand academy. Further, many academic women, particularly feminist academics, are specifically interested in issues which intersect with gender issues in the academy, particularly race and ethnicity, and the specific character that it takes on in a New Zealand context. More precisely, they are interested in the bi-cultural context of Maori and Pakeha[3] relations and the position, and representation, of Maori women as part of an indigenous group in the academy in New Zealand. Issues of colonialism and post-colonialism, bi-culturalism and multi-culturalism, as well as issues of national identity are critically important dimensions in addition to gender in understanding the operation of the feminist research in New Zealand. Feminist politics has to be set in the context of a range of contradictory discourses in the New Zealand academy. The interests of academic women, and of feminist research into the position of academic women in New Zealand, articulate and reflect many of these conflicting pressures.

Feminist research in education in Aotearoa/ New Zealand

Feminist research into the position of academic women in the wider 'academic community' in New Zealand confirms many of the obstacles facing feminist researchers in the UK and elsewhere. As O'Neill comments: 'academic analyses of the university as an organisation and the particular marginality of women university teachers are virtually non-existent' (O'Neill, 1992: 59). Issues of importance to feminist research in education such as questions of feminist epistemology, methodology and pedagogy have generally been focused at the level of schooling in New Zealand. Analysis of these issues has not happened in any substantial way at the higher education level. In commenting on the experience of feminist research in New Zealand, O'Neill mistakenly assumes that there exists an international literature documenting the position of women academics in the academy. In fact, international feminist research on the operation and practices of the academy and on the position of women academics in the academy remains scant.

It is not intended here to provide a history of academic women in the university sector in New Zealand, but simply to reflect briefly on some of the work that has been undertaken in this area. In New Zealand, just as in Britain, research into the position of academic women has been promoted by a few significant women academics. A number of women academics in New Zealand have, over the years, campaigned on a personal basis and written widely on the marginalization of academic women. More recently,

the work of Morris-Matthews (1993) at the University of Auckland has con-
solidated a more indigenous feminist critique of the academy in theoretical
and historical terms. Further, the work of Hughes (1980) and Irwin (1988,
1992) has developed the argument for greater numbers of women in the
professions in New Zealand and for Maori women academics. The tradition
of feminist research into the position of academic women in New Zealand
has emerged mainly from Departments of Education in New Zealand universities. Particularly important has been the work of Sue Middleton at the
University of Waikato, Alison Jones and Linda Smith at the University of
Auckland, and Dorothy Page at the University of Otago.

Morris-Matthews' (1993) doctoral thesis, 'For and about women: the
development of women's studies in New Zealand universities, 1973–1990',
charts the history of women's participation in New Zealand universities as
students and as academics. She notes the absence of academic women in
the histories of New Zealand universities:

> To gain an overview of women's participation in New Zealand univer-
> sities I read the jubilee and centennial histories of the universities of
> Auckland, Victoria, Canterbury and Otago. In all but two, women were
> rendered invisible; 'women' were not even listed in the index. The
> histories were examples of what June Purvis has described as 'main-
> stream' research which 'operates within a male-centred paradigm where
> man and man's experiences are taken as the norm'. I then turned to
> conventional historical accounts of the higher education of women,
> again written by men. These depicted a gradual opening up of educa-
> tional opportunities and steady progress towards an eventual victory
> for 'equal opportunity'.
>
> (Morris-Matthews, 1993: 62)

Morris-Matthews states that it took over 30 years for the first women to be
appointed to the staff of a New Zealand university.

Middleton's work (1984, 1987, 1989, 1993) is better known internation-
ally. Middleton (1984) notes a similar pattern to the UK in the emergence
of a feminist literature in education. She observes that because education
departments remain male dominated, feminist education theory and feminist critiques more generally, are not reflected in the content of education degrees. She goes on to note that the majority of education students
are women, either trainee or practising teachers, and 'issues of gender and
power, structure their personal and professional lives' (Middleton, 1984: 42).
Middleton engages with issues of feminist epistemology, methodology and
pedagogy. She highlights the disjuncture between feminist theory and practice characteristic of feminist literature in education in the early 1980s in
New Zealand. Middleton (1984) notes that questions of feminist epistemology, pedagogy and methodology in education tend to be published in the
feminist press and generally outside mainstream textbooks and journals in
education.

An indigenous feminist methodology[4] for research in education in Aotearoa/New Zealand

The concept of an indigenous feminist methodology in New Zealand is central to the work of Sue Middleton and highly relevant to the level of political awareness of academic women in New Zealand. It is also important in understanding where feminist debates are located in relation to the academy in different countries.

Middleton's work on the analysis and application of feminist theory to education in New Zealand was, even in 1984, drawing on a more indigenous framework, for a more authentically Aotearoan (New Zealand) feminist methodological context for her work. In her critique of a liberal feminist perspective in the sociology of education, Middleton states that 'with respect to Maori society, Rose Pere (1983) has shown that at least for the Tuhoe and Ngati Kahungunu tribes (of which she is a member) the passive "feminine" stereotype of ideal womanhood portrayed in sex role research did not exist before the coming of the pakeha (European) – she sees it as an import of the missionaries' (Middleton, 1984: 46).

Further, Middleton's critique of radical feminism, recognizes much that is valuable in this perspective for the evolution of feminist epistemology and methodology generally, and more specifically in its application to educational analysis. While recognizing the limitations of a radical feminist perspective, Middleton argues that one of its strengths is its understanding and exposing of the cultural biases of knowledge. As Middleton (1984) maintains 'knowledge', within a radical feminist perspective, is 'grounded' in the specific experience of oppression, of being a woman in a patriarchal (male-dominated) society.

Middleton recognizes many of the conceptual and theoretical criticisms of radical feminism particularly the questions raised by women of colour regarding the essentially white, middle-class conception of experience. However, much of her attempt to define an authentic Aotearoan feminist methodology through her oral history or life history research can be critiqued for its acceptance of women's experience as 'absolute' and 'true'. As Middleton notes in 'Researching feminist, educational life histories' (1988), 'these adult memories and interpretations were accepted as "valid" since it was the women's adult feminist interpretation of their experiences which were the centre of interest in the study . . . In my study I assumed that women were telling the "truth" about their lives insofar as they understood and remembered the events' (Middleton, 1988: 130). In her text *Educating Feminists Life Histories and Pedagogy* (1993), Middleton reflects on the critiques of feminist models, particularly by women of colour and by poststructuralist and postmodernist challenges. Her latest text considers the intersection of feminism with poststructural and postmodern critiques reflecting of the current position of feminist theorizing in New Zealand and more generally, focusing on the concept of 'difference' and its application to a more 'local', culturally specific and politically sensitive set of feminist methodologies. This brief summary of Middleton's research is included here, as the development of the debates within her work mirror the larger debates occupying feminist academics in New Zealand.

The challenge posed to feminist theory by wider theoretical debates has, in some respects, moved the direction of the debates within feminist theory and practice away from the development of an indigenous feminist method-ology, and back towards mainstream feminist epistemological debates. How-ever, the demand by feminists and others for an increasing recognition of an authentically Aotearoan scholarship and community has been reflected particularly in the development and establishment of educational curricula as shown in the development of new courses. A typical example is the development of a bi-cultural feminist educational history course in New Zealand in the Department of Education at Auckland University.

Participation of academic women and students in the academy in Aotearoa/New Zealand, 1880–1990

Morris-Matthews (1993) indicates parallel trends to those in the UK. Morris-Matthews notes:

> My surveys of the numbers of graduates from 1877 to 1958, not surpris-ingly showed steadily increasing numbers of women graduating. How-ever, there was little change in their fields of study. To 1958, when the University of New Zealand listing of graduates ceased, there were still few women with degrees other than those in the arts, few with higher degrees and correspondingly, few women academics. All New Zealand's first 143 women graduates between 1880 and 1900 graduated in Arts except two in science and one each in medicine and law. Between 1900 and 1914 most women students continued to be arts students although a small number were in science, medicine and law.
>
> (Morris-Matthews, 1993: 82)

Table 3.1 and Figure 3.1 drawn from Morris-Matthews' (1993) research show the number (and percentage) of women students enrolled in New Zealand universities for the period 1890–1990. Women students constitute 31 per cent of all students enrolled in 1970 and 55 per cent of all students enrolled in 1990, the numbers of women students at universities in New Zealand had increased from 10,664 in 1970 to 40,513 in 1990.

As shown in Table 3.2, most women university students in New Zealand study in the social sciences, arts and humanities areas. However, they have, in recent years, made significant inroads into law, medicine, veterinary sci-ence and pharmacy. According to O'Neill (1992), this is due to the practices

Table 3.1 Women Enrolled in New Zealand universities, 1890–1990

Year	Number of women enrolled	Percentage of all students enrolled
1890	211	37
1900	294	33
1910	714	39
1920	1345	37
1930	1284	43
1940	1357	28
1950	2783	24
1960	3877	25
1970	10664	31
1980	22653	44
1990	40513	55

Sources: *New Zealand Year Book*, 1891, 1901, 1911, 1923, 1932, 1942, 1951/2, 1962, 1977, 1982, 1991. (Cited in Morris-Matthews, 1993: 88)

Figure 3.1 Women enrolled in New Zealand universities, 1890–1990

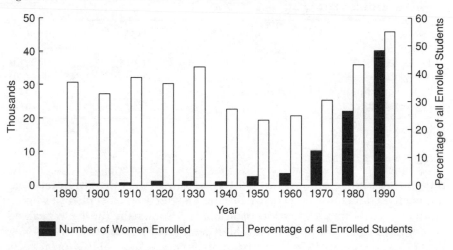

■ Number of Women Enrolled   □ Percentage of all Enrolled Students

Source: Morris-Matthews, 1993: 88

that middle-class families now engage in, to secure careers for their daughters as well as their sons, and in part to the recruitment policies of these faculties.

The numbers of women participating in all undergraduate and graduate courses have risen over the decade, as Table 3.3 shows, and as Morris-Matthews (1993) notes, participation rates of women in New Zealand universities indicate that progress is being made within all fields of study in terms of numbers and range of subjects studied at the undergraduate level. However, given this general increase in the number of women students, Morris-Matthews notes that the statistics for women graduates, and post-graduates are disappointing (see Table 3.3).

Table 3.2 Courses taken by all internal university students (including degree, diploma and certificate courses) showing percentage of females for each course, New Zealand, 1987

Engineering	7	Parks and recreation	47
Forestry science	13	Law	48
Agriculture	21	Medicine	49
Architecture/building science	28	Physical education	54
Divinity/theology	32	Veterinary science	51
Surveying/town planning	32	Music	59
Technology	34	Pharmacy	63
Science	36	Social sciences	65
Commerce/business admin.	36	Arts and humanities	66
Dentistry	37	Education	78
Horticulture	39	Social work	79
Resource planning/management	44	Home science	98

Source: O'Neill, 1992: 62.

Table 3.3 Courses taken by internal university students showing percentage of females at each level, New Zealand, 1977 and 1987

	1977	*1987*
PhD degrees	19.7	31.0
Masters degrees	31.4	43.0
Postgraduate diplomas and certificates	34.5	51.0
Bachelors degrees	35.7	51.9

Source: O'Neill, 1992: 62.

As has been the case in the UK and USA, the overall increase in the numbers of women undertaking university courses over the last decade has not been accompanied by a corresponding increase in the number of women academics. It is to the position of academic women in the New Zealand academy that we now turn. Morris-Matthews (1993) states that in the New Zealand academy, in 1975, International Women's Year, of 363 professors, only 7 (1.8 per cent) were women; of 1322 associate professors, readers and senior lecturers, 90 (6.8 per cent) were women; of 803 lecturers, 87 (10.8 per cent) were women; and of 220 junior or assistant lecturers, 63 (28.6 per cent) were women. Studies examining the status of women in academia in the USA, UK and Australia show that women continue to be under-represented among university academic staff and concentrated in the lower ranks (Finkelstein, 1984; Simeone, 1987; Smith, 1991). Recent New Zealand statistics confirm this picture: 'Statistics on the percentage of female academic staff in New Zealand Universities during the period 1986–91 show very little change in this pattern of female under-representation in the senior ranks (Smith, 1991)' (Vasil, 1993: 143). Statistics from the Ministry of Education

Table 3.4 Academic staff by gender and method of employment at universities in New Zealand, 1980

Positions	Full-time staff			Part-time staff		
	M	F	Total	M	F	Total
Filled teaching posts						
Full professors	380	9	389	35	–	35
Senior lecturers, associate professors, readers, lecturers-in-charge	1530	123	1653	347	16	363
Lecturers	614	114	728	75	17	92
Junior lecturers	144	75	219	86	15	101
Instructors, demonstrators engaged in teaching	109	45	154	813	233	1046
Total	2777	366	3143	1356	281	1637

Source: Adapted from MoEdNZ (1980).

Table 3.5 Academic staff by gender and method of employment at universities in New Zealand, 1991

Designation	Full-time staff			Part-time staff		
	M	F	Total	M	F	Total
Academic staff						
Vice-Chancellors	14	1	15	1	–	1
Professors	352	14	366	40	1	41
Associate professors	384	31	415	40	4	44
Senior lecturers	1205	193	1398	409	78	487
Lecturers	635	417	1052	57	70	127
Assistant lecturers	86	84	170	129	109	238
Teaching fellows	1	–	1	6	7	13
Teaching assistants	–	–	–	135	120	255
Total academic staff	2677	740	3417	817	389	1206

Source: Adapted from *Education Statistics of New Zealand* (MoEdNZ, 1992).

(New Zealand) bear out these facts. Tables 3.4 and 3.5 show the numbers of academic staff by gender and method of employment (full-time and part-time) for the years 1980 and 1991 at universities in New Zealand.

In making comparisons between figures for 1980 and 1991, significant increases can be seen in the proportion of posts held by academic women at almost every level. Table 3.6 shows the number of academic men and women holding full-time professorships for the period 1980–91. The numbers

Table 3.6 Academic staff at professorial rank by gender and method of employment (full-time) at universities in New Zealand, 1980–91

Gender of post	Year		% increase
	1991	*1980*	
Men	352	380	−7.4
Women	14	9	55.5
Total	366	389	−5.9

Source: *Education Statistics of New Zealand* (MoEdNZ, 1992).

Table 3.7 Academic staff at associate professor/reader/senior lecturer (and lecturer-in-charge) grade by gender and method of employment (full-time) at universities in New Zealand, 1980–91

Gender of post	Year		% increase
	1991	*1980*	
Men	1589	1530	3.9
Women	224	123	82.1
Total	1813	1653	9.7

Source: *Education Statistics of New Zealand* (MoEdNZ, 1992).

of academic men can be seen to have fallen from 380 in 1980 to 352 in 1991, a percentage decrease of −7.4 per cent. However, while the actual numbers of academic women holding chairs is very much lower, 9 in 1980 and 14 in 1991, the percentage increase in academic women holding chairs is much greater at 55.5 per cent.

The pattern of increase is not dissimilar for academic women at other levels (as shown by Tables 3.7, 3.9 and 3.11) but the increase is particularly marked for part-time posts (Tables 3.8 and 3.10).

Table 3.10 shows that the number of academic women holding part-time lecturer grade posts has increased from 17 in 1980 to 70 in 1991, a percentage increase of 311.8 per cent. The number of academic women holding part-time lectureships in 1991 actually exceeds that for academic men. Thus the only grade of post where academic women out-number academic men is the part-time lecturer grade.

In the years between 1980 and 1991, the proportion of women academics in all grades based on method of employment can be seen to have increased. Throughout the grades the percentage increase for women in both full-time and part-time positions is greater than that for men, in some cases far outstripping men. There are real increases for women including an

Table 3.8 Academic staff at associate professor/reader/senior lecturer (and lecturer-in-charge) grade by gender and method of employment (part-time) at universities in New Zealand, 1980–91

Gender of post	Year		% increase
	1991	*1980*	
Men	449	347	29.4
Women	81	16	406.3
Total	531	363	46.3

Source: *Education Statistics of New Zealand* (MoEdNZ, 1992).

Table 3.9 Academic staff at lecturer grade by gender and method of employment (full-time) at universities in New Zealand, 1980–91

Gender of post	Year		% increase
	1991	*1980*	
Men	635	614	3.4
Women	417	114	265.8
Total	1052	728	44.5

Source: *Education Statistics of New Zealand* (MoEdNZ, 1992).

Table 3.10 Academic staff at lecturer grade by gender and method of employment (part-time) at universities in New Zealand, 1980–91

Gender of post	Year		% increase
	1991	*1980*	
Men	57	75	−24.0
Women	70	17	311.8
Total	127	92	38.0

Source: *Education Statistics of New Zealand* (MoEdNZ, 1992).

improvement in full-time and part-time positions. This is despite the fact that throughout the grades, the numbers of academic women remain relatively small. The greater gains being made by women in full-time positions in particular, must be set against the lower base from which they started. As mentioned above, the only grade at which, in absolute numerical terms, women out-number men is at the level of part-time lecturer grade. There are

Table 3.11 Academic staff at assistant (junior) lecturer grade by gender and method of employment (full-time) at universities in New Zealand, 1980–91

Gender of post	Year		% increase
	1991	*1980*	
Men	86	144	−40.3
Women	84	75	12.0
Total	170	219	−22.4

Source: *Education Statistics of New Zealand* (MoEdNZ, 1992).

striking parallels in the patterns of distribution of academic staff by gender and method of employment for the period 1980–91 for universities in the UK (see Chapter 1) and New Zealand. Despite the overall figures and the real increases for academic women in the New Zealand academy, the numbers of academic women compared to academic men remain small. Academic women still lack parity with academic men in the New Zealand academy and the reasons for this lack of parity that will now be explored.

Research on the status of academic women in universities in Aotearoa/New Zealand

During the 1980s, the academy in New Zealand decided to investigate its operation and practices. This happened partly in response to international trends, particularly in Australia and the USA, for the establishment of equal opportunities programmes, partly as a result of AUSNZ (Association of University Staff of New Zealand) pressure and partly because of the demands for equity by feminist women academics. Various universities, including the Universities of Auckland, Otago and Massey, undertook internal investigations. The largest and most comprehensive of the resulting reports was prepared for the Association of University Staff by Margaret Wilson[5] entitled *Report on the Status of Academic Women in New Zealand* (1986). A major finding was that the democratic egalitarian ethos of universities makes it difficult to introduce equal opportunities programmes, as there is no perceived need of them. Discrimination is both difficult to detect and rarely acknowledged. Wilson commented that it is important and necessary to define and identify discrimination within specific institutions.

Making direct comparison between reports based on different universities, using different profiles of the academic community and using different criteria is clearly problematic. A range of general categories has been selected from the reports which together present a wide-ranging summary of the position of academic women in the university sector of higher education in New Zealand by the early 1990s. These criteria include:

1. Academic status (i.e. position on lecturer scale)
2. Academic status at first appointment
3. Tenure (now called continuance)
4. Publications/research
5. Promotion
6. Discriminatory practices
7. Committee membership

General profile of academic women in Aotearoa/New Zealand

Margaret Wilson, in her 1986 *Report on the Status of Academic Women in New Zealand,* provides a general profile of academic women at universities in New Zealand. Wilson cites figures from the Department of Education Statistics publication 'Profile of Women' (1985) indicating that there were 2999 academics employed in New Zealand universities in 1983. Of this number, 404 (13.5 per cent) were women. Wilson goes on to note that the majority of women, 61.6 per cent, were born in New Zealand; the next biggest group, 17.5 per cent, were from the United Kingdom; and 5.7 per cent from the USA. Only 1.3 per cent described themselves as Maori. These findings are supported by the research undertaken on behalf of Massey University and published as the *Report on the Status of Academic Women at Massey University* (1989), which reports that in terms of the nationality and ethnicity of academic women in the survey, the majority, 59 per cent, of respondents were born in New Zealand. Those born overseas included 11.5 per cent from the United Kingdom, 8.6 per cent from the USA, 7.9 per cent from Australia, 5.8 per cent from other European countries, and 7.2 per cent from elsewhere. Eighty-five per cent of respondents described themselves as European or of European descent, 4 per cent as Maori and 6 per cent as Asian. There was no representation from the Pacific Islands.[6]

Although there is slight variation between the reports, the general description given by Wilson of an average New Zealand woman academic holds good for the later reports. Wilson states that a general description of an average New Zealand woman academic would include the following characteristics: aged 40 (38 in the Massey University Report, 1989); employed in a full-time tenured position as a lecturer in the Arts or Social Science faculty; and likely to be married or to have once been married. Wilson notes that in terms of marital status, 59.1 per cent indicated that they were married, while 22.7 per cent indicated they had never married and 3.8 per cent stated that they had been but were no longer married. A feature of these statistics is the marked difference in marital status between female and male academics (Wilson, 1986: 9) while the *Report on the Status of Women Academics at Massey University* notes that 'perhaps it is no coincidence that the three women professors at Massey in October 1988 were not married' (Massey University, 1989: 24).

Table 3.12   Gender differences in marital status, New Zealand

Marital status	Males		Females		Total	
	N	%	N	%	N	%
Married	168	85.3	110	55.8	278	70.6
Divorced/separated	11	5.6	38	19.3	49	12.4
Widowed	2	1.0	2	1.0	4	1.0
Never Married	16	8.1	47	23.9	63	16.0

Source: Vasil, 1993: 150.

Table 3.13   Gender differences in caregiver status, New Zealand

Have children	Males		Females		Total	
	N	%	N	%	N	%
Yes	165	83.8	121	60.8	286	72.2
No	32	16.2	78	39.2	110	27.8

Source: Vasil, 1993: 150.

A more recent study by Latika Vasil published as 'Gender Differences in The Academic Career in New Zealand Universities' (1993) profiles the distribution of male and female academic staff by marital status. Table 3.12 shows the distribution of male and female academic staff by marital status. The proportion of male academics who were married was 85 per cent compared to the proportion of female academics at 56 per cent. A higher proportion of female than male academics were divorced or separated, and a higher proportion had never been married. In addition, Vasil reports that significantly more female than male academic staff reported not having any children (Table 3.13). These figures correspond with and update the findings of the *Report on the Status of Academic Women in New Zealand* (1986).

Status of academic women in Aotearoa/ New Zealand universities

Statistics on the percentage of academic women holding posts at universities in New Zealand since the 1970s (see Table 3.14) indicate a similar pattern to the position in Britain. There has been a steady increase in the percentage of university positions occupied by women, but these have been at lower status levels, that is at the lower rungs of the lecturer scale.

These findings outlined by the *Report on the Status of Academic Women in New Zealand* (1986) are confirmed by a number of subsequent reports. The

Table 3.14 Females as percentage of total university staff by academic rank, New Zealand, 1970–83

Teaching post	1970	1976	1979	1981	1983
Full professor	1.3	1.6	2.1	2.6	2.9
Senior lecturer, associate professor, reader, lecturer-in-charge	6.5	7.3	7.6	7.2	7.7
Lecturer	12.9	13.4	17.2	20.0	20.4
Junior lecturer, assistant lecturer	28.3	23.5	32.0	33.0	45.4
Instructor and demonstrator engaged in teaching	28.9	13.2	24.0	36.6	45.2
Percentage of total teaching posts	10.7	9.5	11.4	12.3	13.5

Source: Wilson, 1986: 8.

Report on the Status of Academic Women at Massey University (1989) states that, in the senior ranks, men outnumber women 12:1. Fifty-two per cent of the total academic staff are senior lecturer or above. However, only 18 per cent of academic women are senior lecturer or above. The Report considers a breakdown based on gender across the grades; one in every 11 men but only one in every 44 women is a professor; one in every eight men but only one in every 59 women is a reader; one in every three men but only one in every seven women is a senior lecturer; one in every three women but only one in every six men is a lecturer; one in every seven women but only one in every 17 men is an assistant lecturer; one in every eight women but only one in every 24 men is a graduate assistant. As Worth (1992) notes, in commenting on the figures in the Massey Report, there is no doubt that women academics as a group are differentially located in levels of status within Massey University.

The situation is clearly closely linked to the appointment and promotion policies adopted by universities and supported by departments. Worth notes, in the *Report on Issues Affecting Academic Staff at Massey University* (1992), that this issue affects both women and Maori: 'Respondents in the present study reported that criteria for appointments and promotions were often inappropriate and at times culturally insensitive. Some academics reported tokenism in the way that women and Maori staff were called on to be on certain committees or perform certain functions without the "real" rewards for these such as promotion' (Worth, 1992: 34). The crucial variable appears to be academic status at first appointment.

Academic status at first appointment

Wilson's Report (1986) notes that it is clear from the figures that academic women were appointed at a lower level to academic men (see Table 3.15). This is particularly obvious at the level of lecturer, where 26.3 per cent of

Table 3.15 Academic status at time of first appointment to a university position, New Zealand

	% Female	% Male
Professor	–	1.1
Reader/associate professor	–	1.1
Senior lecturer > bar	1.5	2.1
Senior lecturer ≤ bar	0.8	5.6
Lecturer	26.3	40.8
Junior lecturer	32.9	30.3
Research fellow	8.7	6.0
Tutor	15.6	5.6
Other	13.5	6.7

Source: Wilson, 1986: 18.

Table 3.16 Academic status of women at first appointment to a university position, New Zealand

Position	Massey frequency	%	% Wilson Report (all universities)
Junior lecturer/assistant lecturer	39	28.0	33.0
Graduate assistant/demonstrator	34	25.0	–
Lecturer	27	19.0	26.0
Tutor	10	7	16
Research officer	5	4	–
Senior lecturer	3	2	2
Other	18	13	–
Not applicable	1	0.7	–
No response	1	0.7	–
Total	139	100.0	

Note: Some categories are not compatible with those used by Wilson.
Source: Massey University, 1989: 16.

first appointments at this level were women and 40.8 per cent were men. This situation is further amplified at the level of tutor, where 15.6 per cent of first appointments at this level were women, and 5.6 per cent were men.

The situation is reflected in statistics for Massey University (Table 3.16), which shows that the largest single group of women, 28.0 per cent, were appointed at junior lecturer/assistant lecturer level. The second largest group, 25.0 per cent, were appointed at the graduate assistant/demonstrator level. The Report shows more than half the women indicated in these statistics, 52.6 per cent, started their university careers in low level, untenured positions.

Table 3.17 Highest qualifications gained by academic staff, New Zealand

Category	% Female	% Male
Diploma	1.7	1.0
Degree	11.2	5.9
Honours	11.4	8.4
Masters or equivalent	33.8	19.9
PhD or equivalent	35.6	58.0
Other	6.2	6.6

Source: Wilson, 1986: 16.

Table 3.18 Gender differences in highest degree obtained, New Zealand

Highest degree	Males		Females		Total	
	N	%	N	%	N	%
Masters	39	20.3	84	44.2	123	32.2
PhD	153	79.7	106	55.8	259	67.8

Source: Vasil, 1993: 150.

Academic status at first appointment is frequently (but not always) related to the level of qualification previously gained. Wilson's Report (1986) notes that only 35.6 per cent of women had obtained a doctorate compared with 58.0 per cent of men, and that this clearly had important implications for the level at which women were appointed and also for their promotion prospects (see Table 3.17). Recent research by Vasil (1993) shows that significant differences remain in the highest degree held by academic staff (see Table 3.18).

Wilson's Report shows that controlling for other variables, women with PhDs were appointed at a lower level to men (see Table 3.19). Wilson notes that, 52.6 per cent of men with doctorates were appointed as lecturer or above, compared with 39.5 per cent of women with PhDs. No women were appointed above senior lecturer level. Wilson further notes that 21 per cent of women with a Masters qualification were appointed as lecturer or above, compared with 50 per cent of men with the same qualification. Wilson (1986) states that a total of 60.4 per cent of women with a PhD qualification were appointed at levels below that of lecturer and mainly to non-tenured positions, while only 47.4 per cent of men with the same qualification were appointed at these levels. The conclusion reached is that while the appointment of academic women to lower grades on the scale may be attributable to their lower qualifications, this cannot explain why women with the highest qualifications (PhD) are also appointed to lower levels than their male colleagues with the same qualification.

Table 3.19 Relationship between highest qualification held and status of first appointment, New Zealand

	Diploma	Degree	Honours	Masters	PhD	Other	Total
Males							
Professor	–	6.3	–	–	0.6	5.6	1.1
Reader	–	–	–	–	1.3	5.6	1.1
Senior lecturer > bar	50.0	6.3	4.2	–	1.9	–	1.9
Senior lecturer ≤ bar	–	–	–	1.9	7.1	16.7	5.9
Lecturer	–	50.0	29.2	48.1	41.7	16.7	40.4
Junior lecturer	–	18.8	45.8	40.7	27.6	33.3	31.5
Research fellow	–	–	–	–	9.6	5.6	5.9
Tutor	–	6.3	12.5	5.6	3.8	5.6	5.2
Other	50.0	12.5	8.3	3.7	6.4	11.1	7.0
Females							
Professor	–	–	–	–	–	–	–
Reader	–	–	–	–	–	–	–
Senior lecturer > bar	–	–	2.4	1.7	0.7	4.0	1.4
Senior lecturer ≤ bar	–	–	–	1.7	–	4.0	0.8
Lecturer	14.3	9.8	19.0	17.6	38.8	44.0	26.4
Junior lecturer	28.6	26.8	47.6	38.7	26.9	20.0	32.6
Research fellow	–	4.9	2.4	5.0	16.4	12.0	9.2
Tutor	42.9	26.8	9.5	26.1	5.2	8.0	15.8
Other	14.3	31.7	19.0	9.2	11.9	8.0	13.0

Source: Wilson, 1986: 19.

Tenure[7]

The *Report on the Status of Academic Women at Massey University* (1989) found that 'under half the respondents 58 (41.7%) had tenure (career positions). If tenure is considered the norm such a high number of untenured women should be cause for concern' (Massey University, 1989: 7). Wilson (1986) maintains that the problem for women may be that they are too willing to accept non-tenured positions. However, it is clearly difficult for women to refuse academic positions even if untenured in a limited and competitive market (see Table 3.20). There is a growing pattern of appointment on a contractual basis in New Zealand, and this trend is likely to continue given the financial stringencies within which universities in New Zealand are operating.

Publications, research and conference papers

Once established in an academic post, the usual criteria for promotion are publications, research/teaching and contribution to the university. However, a key factor for women academics, given their low status at first appointment, is completing doctoral research. The *Report on the Status of Academic Women*

Table 3.20 Relationship between university of employment and percentage of tenured staff, New Zealand

University	Tenured staff	
	% Female	% Male
Auckland	57.3	87.9
Waikato	55.6	81.0
Massey	49.4	72.2
Victoria	71.7	83.7
Canterbury	57.4	100.0
Lincoln	43.8	86.4
Otago	62.5	79.7

Source: Wilson, 1986: 20.

at Massey University noted that 60 per cent of the respondents considered the time available for research to be inadequate. Some respondents tried to keep a balance between teaching and research. 'Two women respondents gave their PhD research priority while another was torn between teaching and PhD research' (Massey University, 1989: 19).

Because of the importance of publications to the success of a promotion application, respondents in Wilson's Report were asked about the number of publications they had. Wilson found that 76 per cent of women had published no books, 53 per cent had published no part books and 22 per cent had published no journal articles (see Table 3.21). In the *Report on the Status of Academic Women at Massey University* similar conclusions were found. Eighty-seven per cent of respondents had published no books, 65 per cent had published no part books and 37 per cent had published no journal articles.

Wilson states that since promotion is largely dependent on publication it is a matter of concern that women have a lower publication rate than men. Wilson's *Report on the Status of Academic Women in New Zealand* (1986) maintains that academic women are generally found in lower status positions which often carry heavier teaching loads. In addition, women in lower status positions may not be ready to publish their research. Additional reasons cited by Wilson for the low publication rate of academic women include: the lack of funding for areas in which women research; that women sometimes research in areas not well understood or accepted by male colleagues, for example, women's studies; and the fact that many women prefer to work and publish collectively. A final reason cited by Wilson for the low publication rate of academic women is the fact that women often write and publish in journals that are not considered 'academic' and are, therefore, not counted for promotion.

A third related area, and one frequently linked to publication, is presenting papers at conferences. The *Report on the Status of Academic Women at Massey University* (1989) found that half the women respondents had not presented

Table 3.21   Number of publications (academic women and men), New Zealand

Number	% Female	% Male
Whole books		
Nil	75.7	64.2
1–3	20.1	25.9
4–9	4.1	10.1
10+	–	–
Part books		
Nil	52.9	41.4
1–3	37.2	45.0
4–9	8.9	10.4
10+	1.0	3.2
Journal articles		
Nil	21.9	7.3
1–3	29.9	15.4
4–9	27.9	24.5
10+	20.3	52.8

Source: Wilson, 1986: 23.

any papers in the previous three years. This compares with 42 per cent in Wilson's Report. In the Massey Report, 14 per cent had presented one paper, 14 per cent two papers and 9 per cent three papers, with 11 per cent presenting more than three papers; this compares with 20 per cent, 10 per cent, 13 per cent and 16 per cent respectively in Wilson's Report. The overall rate of conference papers given by Massey women academics is thus lower than that reported in the Wilson's Report for women academics at universities in New Zealand generally (see Table 3.22).

Promotion

Some of the obstacles that face women academics in attempting to gain promotion have been outlined. Women respondents in the Massey Report were asked about past lack of success in gaining promotion. The respondents gave the following details: ten women had been unsuccessful once in getting double increments, one unsuccessful on three occasions, and another on four occasions. Five women were unsuccessful once in promotion from lecturer to senior lecturer, one woman was unsuccessful twice in attempting to get above the bar at senior lecturer level. In attempting promotion from senior lecturer to reader, one woman was unsuccessful once, one twice, and one three times.

As significant as the lack of success in gaining promotion for women academics is the lack of confidence felt by academic women at the prospect of gaining promotion. The *Report on the Status of Academic Women in New*

Table 3.22   Academic papers presented in the last three years, New Zealand

	Massey University %	Wilson Report %
No papers	50.0	42.10
1 paper	14.0	19.50
2 papers	14.0	9.50
3 papers	9.1	13.31
More than 3 papers	11.0	15.60

Source: Massey University, 1989: 20.

Zealand asked respondents how they rated their chances of promotion in the next five years; they were asked whether they were confident, optimistic, uncertain or pessimistic: 'The results indicated that 16.8% (28.2%) were confident, 28.1% (20.8%) were optimistic; 26.4% (27.3%) were uncertain and 28.7% (23.7%) were pessimistic. These results show that the women were less confident than their male colleagues about promotion' (Wilson, 1986: 21).

Discrimination

Discrimination is frequently difficult to define, can be direct or indirect and can manifest itself in individual behaviour and in institutional practices. Some discrimination can be legislated against, while other forms of discrimination of an attitudinal or behavioural kind are more difficult to identify and remove. The *Report on the Status of Academic Women at Massey University* (1989) in elaborating on the ways in which university structures discriminate against women identifies the following areas: 'the failure of the university as a whole to respond flexibly to responsibilities that women had beyond the university, the extension of the salary scale, the position of men in senior positions and the power of the Heads of Department' (Massey University, 1989: 28).

Discriminatory attitudes and behaviour

In terms of experiencing discrimination, Wilson (1986) asked women respondents if they had encountered any discrimination with respect to their employment; 35 per cent stated yes and 65 per cent said no. Male respondents were asked whether they thought the university discriminates against women in any way; 41 per cent said yes. When asked if they knew of any instance of discrimination against a female colleague 19 per cent said yes, while 83 per cent stated no. One respondent from the *Report on the Status of Academic Women at Massey University* noted that 'some of the discrimination against women is so insidious that it may not be possible to diagnose it immediately as gender based' (Massey University, 1989: 27).

   A number of respondents over the Reports identified a range of discriminatory attitudes and behaviour. In Wilson's Report several women

Table 3.23   Positions of authority held within the university by academic staff, New Zealand

Position	% Female	% Male
Dean	1.2	5.7
Sub-dean	1.9	4.0
Head of department	6.1	17.1
Director	3.1	1.0
Other	14.8	11.7

Source: Wilson, 1986: 24.

Table 3.24   Positions of authority that have been or are held, New67 Zealand

Position	N	%
Dean	1	0.7
Sub-dean	2	1.0
Head of department	3	2.0
Director	4	3.0
Other	15	11.0
Not applicable/none	101	73.0
No response	13	9.0
Total respondents = 139		

Note: Positions are not exclusive: more than one may have been held.
Source: Massey University, 1989: 11.

respondents commented on the sexism of the environment within which they worked: 'One woman also coupled this sexist environment with a racist environment as being a double barrier created for Maori women' (Wilson, 1986: 34). Another woman respondent commented on the superior attitude of some men towards women. This type of attitude is clearly reinforced by the lack of women in decision-making positions, and positions of authority.

The *Report on the Status of Academic Women in New Zealand* (1986) found relatively few academic women who had held positions of authority (see Table 3.23). 'The respondents were asked to state if they felt it is more difficult for a woman to achieve a position of authority in a university than it is for a man. In answer to this question 77.6 per cent stated 'it was more difficult for a woman' (Wilson, 1986: 24). The *Report on the Status of Academic Women at Massey University* (1989) found that only 17 per cent of respondents held a position of authority (e.g. associate dean, sub-dean, head of department, director) though 62 per cent were willing to take such responsibilities (Massey University, 1989: 2) (see Table 3.24). The same Report notes that as a consequence of the low number of women at senior levels there were few women in decision or policy-making positions.

Committee membership/administration

Committee membership is seen as an important way to contribute to the life of the university. Both the *Report on the Status of Academic Women in New Zealand* (1986) and the *Report on the Status of Academic Women at Massey University* (1989) show that women academics served extensively on university committees and bodies. However, the conclusion of both Reports is that participation by women academics is limited as far as decision-making bodies/committees is concerned and that women academics are more likely to be found at departmental and faculty level committees. The *Report on Issues Affecting Academic Staff at Massey University* (1992) confirms the findings of the two earlier reports in noting that 'many women interviewed were on numerous committees and often felt obliged to be because there were so few women represented in the university structure' (Worth, 1992: 17).

From these reports on the status of academic women in universities in New Zealand, what conclusions can be drawn about the position of women academics? Wilson commented on the hierarchal and undemocratic way in which decisions are made within the university. More specifically, Wilson notes that 'for most women the head of department is an all powerful figure not only on questions of appointment and promotion, but also on allocation and support' (Wilson, 1986: 36). The *Report on the Status of Academic Women at Massey University* confirms the significant role of the head of department, and in its recommendations states: 'The power of heads of department over appointment and promotion processes may advantage some women and disadvantage others. There is a need for the power and influence associated with these positions to be demystified. Rules should be acknowledged and applied consistently and without recourse to personality' (Massey University, 1989: 32).

A second area to emerge was the level at which academic women are appointed. The *Report on the Academic Status of Women at Massey University* recommended that 'all departments review their policies regarding the recruitment, appointment and promotion of all women staff' (Massey University, 1989: 2). Allied to this issue is the third area of supporting and promoting research by academic women. A final point is the worth of academic women's careers. The *Report on the Status of Academic Women at Massey University* notes that 'while women themselves may be serious about academic careers, they are likely to meet with opposition. Some stated that women's careers were not taken seriously and that this considerably disadvantages academic women at the level of appointment and in terms of promotion' (Massey University, 1989: 13).

Conclusion

This chapter, in analysing the discourses of the academy, has reviewed a range of data; feminist theoretical debates in New Zealand have been

explored alongside a review of the literature in the form of academic reports on the position and status of academic women in the academy in New
Zealand. In addition, a limited statistical profile has been provided of the
New Zealand academy. While the conclusions that can be drawn show some
clear parallels with the findings from universities in the UK on the status of
academic women, there are also issues emerging which are more specific to
the academic community in New Zealand.

These issues include the fact that the career pattern for academic women
in New Zealand is rather distinctive. Morris-Matthews (1993), citing a study
by Lodge (1975), showed that women won first appointments at an older
age than their male counterparts. Only 7 per cent of all male academics
received their first appointment after the age of 34, while 28 per cent of
women did. In Morris-Matthews' (1993) own research, 19 per cent of all
academic women surveyed were first appointed over the age of 40. As Morris-
Matthews notes in her research, the age of appointment has implications
for the level of seniority which can be achieved in the university. Those who
start young have a better chance of attaining more senior positions than
those who start later in life.

In addition, this pattern of appointment is not accompanied by a more
supportive academic culture within the academy in New Zealand, as evid-
enced by empirical data and the findings of a number of reports. The position of academic women in relation to academic status, promotion, tenure,
publications, and to a range of discriminatory practices, is a disadvantaged
one. The *Report on the Status of Academic Women in New Zealand* (1986) maintained that the attitude that emerged from interviews with academic women
revealed that universities are seen as sexist by many academic women. The
Report argues that women feel alienated from the male/macho world of
the academy. Academic women stated that they found the 'constant sexism'
exhausting on top of heavy teaching loads and student demands. Academic
women also expressed pessimism at the prospect of universities changing.

The structure of academic career paths, the emphasis on traditional
definitions of productivity, and the prioritization of publications over other
criteria as critical for promotion, all play crucial roles in blocking the advancement of many women in universities in New Zealand, as they do in the
academy in the UK. The conclusion reached by Wilson and the other reports
is that although some of the areas of structural discrimination can be overcome in universities by adopting equal opportunities programmes, the problem still remains of the hierarchical, undemocratic way in which decisions
are made within universities. As Wilson maintains: 'To remedy this would
require a structural change independent of any equal opportunities programme' (Wilson, 1986: 37). Attitudes, prejudices and behaviour may be
even harder to monitor and change than structures and legislation.

4

Academic Women's Experience of the Academy in Aotearoa/New Zealand

This chapter investigates and reflects on the experiences of academic women at universities in New Zealand. It is recognized within contemporary feminism that the use of 'women's experience' raises conceptual problems and needs to be understood within a critical feminist theoretical and methodological framework. The experiences of academic women as reflected in reports and literature on the position and status of academic women in Aotearoa/New Zealand were described earlier. These are characterized by diversity and difference, fractured along the lines of age, nationality, race, ethnicity, class, marital status, parenthood and academic position. This chapter contextualizes the experiences of academic women within this framework. Statistics on the position of academic women in New Zealand show gendered patterns across a range of factors, including academic status, productivity, promotion opportunities, career development and advancement, security of tenure, discrimination, sexual harassment and workloads. In this context, there are parallels with the situation of academic women at universities in the UK.

Women academics in New Zealand universities – issues of confidentiality

> In this . . . much has to be left out because the issues of confidentiality had to be a prime consideration. In a country the size of New Zealand this can pose particular difficulties. To reveal someone as a Maori, a lesbian and a kindergarten teacher for example would readily identify her to many people.
>
> (Middleton, 1988: 142)

The issue of confidentiality and anonymity as identified in this quote from Middleton, when applied to the experiences of academic women at universities in New Zealand is problematic. There are seven universities in

New Zealand and the academic community is an 'intensely intimate' one in an academic sense. Academic positions, publications, disputes and crises are well known throughout the academic community in New Zealand. For these reasons the profile that is presented of New Zealand academic women goes to considerable lengths to provide confidentiality and anonymity.

Thirty women academics at three universities in New Zealand were originally selected to take part in the research.[1] Of the 30 academic women initially selected 23 interviews were eventually undertaken. There was no precise breakdown of ethnicity, but the participants included European/ Pakeha, Maori, North American and Canadian academic women. There were no Pacific Island academic women in the sample.[2]

The academic women involved in the research were distributed across different disciplines. As a result of the need to maintain confidentiality, it was not possible to link grade of post with subject area/department. This was significant across the grades, as identifying an associate professor or assistant lecturer in a particular subject area is frequently to identify the person due to the size of the academic community in New Zealand.[3] Academic women from the following subject areas and departments were represented:

Law	Women's studies
Physics	Sociology
Maths and statistics	Business studies
Psychology	English
Education	Economics
Maori studies	Social anthropology

The following profile of academic status emerged from the academic women interviewed. There was 1 assistant lecturer, 12 lecturers, 5 of whom were currently below point 9 on the lecturer scale (see Appendix 3) and 7 were on point 9 or above; there were 4 senior lecturers (one of these appointments was half-time); there was 1 associate professor and 1 professor. Outside of the formal lecturer scale, the senior tutor was on a separate scale but was at the equivalent of point 10/11 on the lecturer scale. In addition, three academic women (administration) were outside the lecturer scale.

The following analysis considers the experiences of academic women within the New Zealand academy. The analysis is framed around the following areas: the gendered nature of power in leadership positions; academic status (including an analysis of academic status at first appointment); issues of tenure; issues of promotion and appraisal; productivity; workload/ responsibility; committee membership; issues of discrimination and sexual harassment. In addition, academic women's perceptions and experiences were sought on the questions of mentorship and equal opportunities policy and practice.[4]

Evidence from research undertaken by feminist researchers (Morris-Matthews, 1993) and by reports emanating from universities in New Zealand (Massey University, 1989; University of Auckland, 1988; Wilson, 1986;

Worth, 1992) indicate that, although there has been an increase in the number of women academics appointed to university posts, both the level of the appointment and nature of the post remain disproportionately disadvantaged by comparison with academic men. The positions occupied by academic women are largely at the lower rungs of the lecturer scale. This is partially related to qualifications gained but, as Wilson (1986) has shown, even when this variable is held constant academic women were still appointed to lower points on the scale.

Evidence cited earlier on the position of academic women in the academy in New Zealand (Chapter 3) shows the continued under-representation of academic women at every level except that of assistant lecturer. Vasil (1993) argues that 'striking disparities in rank were . . . found, suggesting that women move up the academic hierarchy more slowly than men' (Vasil, 1993: 143). Statistics drawn from the Ministry of Education (MoEdNZ, 1990) show that in 1989 academic women accounted for only 4.5 per cent of professors, 6.9 per cent of associate professors/readers, 10.8 per cent of senior lecturers and 37.8 per cent of lecturers in New Zealand universities. However, 47.7 per cent of all assistant lecturers were women.

A number of factors have been identified in the literature and within the empirical data as contributory factors in the under-representation of academic women at senior levels in the academy. They include: the attitudes of academic men in positions of power and decision-making in the academy; the lower productivity level (in terms of research and publications) of academic women; the heavier administrative and teaching workload carried by academic women; and the greater likelihood of academic men holding a doctorate. Additional factors identified in the literature include the fact that fewer academic women are involved in professional networks and have, 'fewer opportunities for co-authoring and fewer mentors' (Vasil, 1993: 144).

When academic women are appointed to senior positions the experience can frequently be an isolating one in academic terms, particularly given the extensive demands accompanying appointment to the position of 'chair'. When asked about the areas of academic responsibility that the position (chair) carried, a professor at the University of Waikato gave the following response:

> Well, it's specified in the chair descriptions here that the chair is supposed to provide academic leadership. I'm talking not of the administrative chair, but of the professorial chair. That leadership takes a number of different things. As a very minimum it involves advice and guidance to other members of staff with respect to their own research, publication, career opportunities, promotion, etc. It also involves a considerable amount of advice to intending postgraduate students. Rethinking on a regular basis and trying to plan ahead financially as well as academically for what we want to do to develop a research programme, for example, that will be focussed on Waikato which has been singularly absent in the social sciences up till now. Trying to develop a much

stronger postgraduate research function than we have in the past. These, as I see it, are all areas of academic responsibility that are subsumed under the rubric of academic leadership – and they're why I get the salary I do.

(Professor, University of Waikato)

The situation for academic women in positions of authority is clearly a highly problematic, and frequently isolating, one in terms of both the university as an institution, but also the lack of empathy from more junior academic women. This latter view is shown in the views expressed by an assistant lecturer at the University of Waikato:

I think, looking at the women who have succeeded in this university who are in senior posts has actually made me feel more committed to my family and less committed to a career, because I think they've paid enormous costs in terms of the people that they are. I don't want to be that single-minded as the women that I see here who have made it, so to speak. So, it could be just the particular women in this university who are in senior posts, I don't know. It could be just something of the nature of how you have to be to get ahead in universities in general, I don't know. But, personally for me, they have been more of a negative than a positive role model.

(Assistant lecturer, University of Waikato)

Academic status at first appointment

The academic profile of those interviewed reveals a disproportionately large number of academic women at the higher levels of the lecturer scale and in senior lecturer positions compared to the national average. Despite the fact that a large proportion of academic women were on higher points on the lecturer scale than might have been expected, many had taken seven or eight years (in some cases considerably longer) to reach their current position. This is related to their academic status at first appointment. Reports cited earlier (Wilson, 1986; Massey University, 1989) show that academic women were overwhelmingly appointed at a lower level than academic men at first appointment.

Many academic women confirmed their appointment to lower points on the scale than their qualifications warranted. However, their subjective perceptions and experiences varied, as did their decision to accept or contest their 'positioning'. The majority of the academic women interviewed had been initially appointed well below point 9 on the lecturer scale; this was despite the fact that the majority held a PhD on appointment. One academic woman at Massey University had had the following experience:

I was appointed on the lecturers' scale at point 8 and I didn't query it at the time. Then, after being employed here for some time, some new members of staff were appointed and, although their qualifications weren't superior to mine and their experience I didn't think was any greater than mine, they were appointed at a higher grade and that was apparently because they asked the institution for more money and the institution gave them more money and I think that's fair enough and it's great that they are able to do that, but I was amazed that the institution could then continue to ignore the fact that I was appointed at a point on the scale which means that even to get an increment, I have to go for promotion . . . It is possible to argue that I could have been appointed at senior lecturer level and I wasn't appointed at that level because the department was advertising for a lecturer when I took the post . . . so I assumed I wouldn't be eligible for a senior lecturer post.

(Lecturer, Massey University)

The same lecturer went on to argue that market forces as well as issues of gender intervene in decisions about appointments within universities:

When I came here, after a while it became obvious that people were employed in other departments without PhDs, without any academic experience, without publications and they were employed at senior lectureship level because they have come from industry or from government and they had salaries which are higher than the salaries they were offered at that lectureship level. So it seems that market forces rather than academic criteria seem to determine salary levels within the institution.

(Lecturer, Massey University)

This academic woman proceeded to contest her position and was eventually upgraded.

Relevant professional experience outside the academy was frequently 'genderized' in terms of appointment, as the experience of a woman academic at Waikato University illustrates. In considering whether academic women are appointed to lower positions on the scale even with relevant professional experience, she stated that:

It would be difficult, but I think one would find that women are generally appointed lower . . . some of my male colleagues who were roughly my age, were appointed to senior lecturer (there are three senior lecturers with fewer degrees than I have and two of them less experienced in private practice) and there are three other people who were appointed to the same rank to which I was promoted who, I think, have the same [qualifications] and they are ten years younger than me. So I was really kind of annoyed.

(Lecturer, Waikato University)

The relatively large number of academic women interviewed above a point 9 on the lecturer scale (see Appendix 3) conceals the fact that a fairly high proportion of women academics had taken years to work their way up the lecturer scale from very low starting points. As one woman academic commented:

I'm at level 10 of the lecturer scale and the lecturer scale has 11 levels
at the moment. I was appointed at level 4 which means that I'm now
in my seventh year.

(Lecturer, University of Auckland)

This was despite the fact that this academic woman had gained her doctorate some years previously. Another woman academic had experienced
an even longer wait and had spent almost fifteen years being employed on
an annual contractual basis:

Well I have a half-time position as a senior lecturer in the department
. . . I was initially appointed as a half-time lecturer, temporary, one year
at a time, it must be twenty years ago . . . it was made permanent in
1986 after a rather long struggle.

(Senior lecturer, University of Waikato)

The experience of another woman academic at Massey University shows
that contesting 'discursive positioning' through negotiation over appointment
does work:

In my department I'm the only woman . . . with a PhD . . . I was offered
a very low level in contrast to a man who came in at the same time with
an MA . . . not a PhD, who is now dead. I'm sure he won't mind me talking about it. He was something like 53 or 54. He was offered a senior
lectureship . . . What I learnt to do . . . and I'd never learnt as a woman
before, but . . . I was offered a low step . . . I negotiated to double that
and I got half way between, but it's still a long trail up that thing.

(Lecturer, Massey University)

One of the factors that might influence level of appointment for women
academics is that many women academics in New Zealand enter academic
life at a later point than has been the case with women academics in the
UK or the USA. There are a number of reasons for this. First, universities
in New Zealand appear less discriminatory in terms of age at first appointment. Secondly, many women in New Zealand enter academic life having
had a profession elsewhere, either in law or psychiatry, and are thus entering at a later point in their careers. It appears to be the case that, although
there is less discrimination in universities in New Zealand on the basis of
age, there is also less recognition of the skills and experience women academics in this position bring to the post, hence the frequency of low level
appointments of women, many of whom have PhDs and/or professional
qualifications. Academic women's experiences of and response to their discursive location within the academy is variable and related to factors such
as age, qualifications and professional experience.

Tenure (continuance)

Wilson's *Report on the Status of Academic Women in New Zealand* (1986) states
that there was a clear pattern of tenure along gender lines in New Zealand

universities and that women academics were disadvantaged in that, on most occasions, they did not get tenured positions. Of the academic women participating in the research, 17 held tenured posts. It had frequently been a very long process to move from untenured to tenured positions, and many women defined promotion in terms of gaining tenure. The remainder were in short-term contractual posts. These included three academic women (administration) and two contractually based lectureships. The contracts were usually of two or three years duration. The term tenure, as indicated earlier, is no longer used in universities in New Zealand although in negotiations between the Association of University Staff of New Zealand (AUSNZ) and New Zealand universities, there is some question as to what tenure really means. One academic woman noted:

> Well nobody has any kind of definite tenure (in the sense that there's always the scope for things to be changed) but the understanding at the moment is, I think you are here until retirement unless something drastic happens.

> (Lecturer, University of Auckland)

Academic women's responses to whether tenureship in the academy is strongly gendered were varied and related to their own discursive position within the academy. A senior lecturer at the University of Waikato observed:

> It is true that most . . . a lot of untenured positions are sort of peripheral positions and they're frequently filled with females.

An assistant lecturer at the University of Waikato was in just such a position and her response was strongly resistant. The assistant lecturer was on a four-year fixed-term appointment and did not see any hope of extending it beyond that term:

> Usually when a junior lectureship [assistant lecturer] is created within a department the money is allocated to turn it into a lectureship which means at the end of the four-year contract or the junior lectureship, the lectureship is publicly advertised but usually the junior lecturer gets it, because they are already part of the structure of the department and they know what's going on, they're teaching the courses that have been developed along with the whole programme within the department, so usually we just move on into that. Whereas for me that's not the case, that's it when I finish.

However, a lecturer at the University of Auckland felt that the situation had changed since the mid-1980s as she stated:

> I think things are probably changing, in that more women are kind of going above the 'glass ceiling' and getting into tenured posts.

The position as far as 'tenure' is concerned is clearly closely related to the political changes being experienced by the university sector in New Zealand. These changes are similar to those already experienced in the UK, and this position was noted by one of the women academics interviewed. She had experienced both university systems. Her view of New Zealand universities' attitude to tenure, was as follows:

My impression is that it is actually more generous than the way British institutions have started to go recently . . . that might change with higher education policy changes in this country. But it is a lot more secure once you actually get into the system here. It was clear that in the last five or ten years [in Britain] it was women really who were marginalised in temporary positions and who found it increasingly difficult to get offered permanent contracts. I'm not sure about New Zealand.

(Lecturer, Massey University)

The response from this academic woman was partly related to her own experience of attempting to gain 'tenure' in the academy in the UK. However, another lecturer from Massey University, who had more experience of political pressures on universities in New Zealand over the longer term, was not optimistic about the issue of 'continuance':

I would suggest that tenure is something that's under threat in New Zealand and I think the National government are giving it a rest at the moment but we've already had indications . . . in the . . . faculty where they didn't want to offer any new tenured appointments, they wanted to keep them as contractual.

(Lecturer, Massey University)

The economic and political pressures being faced by universities in New Zealand appears to bear out these views.

The findings of Wilson's Report still hold good as far as an academic woman from the University of Auckland was concerned. Her view was based on her own doctoral research on the history of women's participation in New Zealand universities. Her response to the issue of whether tenured appointments at universities in New Zealand remained 'gendered' as Wilson had claimed in the *Report on the Status of Academic Women in New Zealand* (1986) was as follows:

I know that's the case here. One chapter of my thesis deals with the history of women's participation in New Zealand universities – as students, and as academics – and the graphs and statistics that I've collected in there, support Margaret Wilson's thesis and the statistics are very high. In 1990 (and this is just from memory) of the women employed as academics in New Zealand universities, half had untenured posts, and most of those were for two years or less. So that even those women who were appointed to the lecturer scale, even though when you look at the graph you say, ooh, gosh, you know, the number of women lecturers has really increased, what was actually happening was a lot of those women, at least half of those women, were on limited-term appointments . . . What you could make from that is that the figures are artificially inflated, because, sure, they can say we've got more women. But the actual fact is they've got more women who're on limited-term appointments. So I think what Margaret Wilson was saying remains pretty true. There's certainly been an increase in the number of women who have got senior lectureships and associate professorships, but interestingly enough, in the last 18 months, a lot of those women have actually retired, and they're not . . . being replaced, not by women.

(Lecturer, University of Auckland)

The experiences of academic women on the issue of the gendered nature of tenureship show some differences in experience and perception. The views of those academic women who were themselves experiencing the reality of an 'untenured' position or who had undertaken research into the position of academic women, were less optimistic than those in tenured positions, or with less experience of the academy in New Zealand.

Promotion and appraisal

Reports emanating from universities in New Zealand (Massey University, 1989; Wilson, 1986) show that promotion for women academics was the source of greatest discontent. Lack of success in gaining promotion was matched by the lack of confidence felt by academic women at the prospect of gaining promotion. Academic women's responses to the issue of promotion, as reflected in the findings of this research, confirmed the findings of the reports.

Whereas a large number of the academic women interviewed felt that they had gained promotion in their current post, promotion was defined in most cases as the process of gaining tenure in their current positions. In the case of those who had moved from a lecturer position to senior lecturer, the process had frequently been very slow, very long and drawn out and fairly demoralizing, resulting in bitterness and feelings of discrimination. However, within this more general sense of frustration and injustice towards the process of promotion, academic women were divided in their identification of the cause.

A lecturer at the University of Auckland felt thwarted in her attempt to gain promotion and felt that while she had been encouraged to apply for promotion by her colleagues she had not been encouraged by her head of department. In addition, while well published within a New Zealand context, she felt that her allegiance to an indigenous cultural context disadvantaged her promotion opportunities:

In terms of my own personal experience, I personally have been very frustrated in trying to get promotion. I've got a very good CV, I've got four books that I've either written or been very involved with and I think my publications are reasonably good, but there's been a kind of consistent resistance towards people who are locally published in New Zealand. And I can understand it, but it's very frustrating, and I suppose that's outside of gender in some ways, although that's not outside of the whole kind of issue of the local and being indigenous and so on, and if I see myself as communicating with this particular audience down here, in New Zealand, I think that there are enormous disadvantages. Not for me as a woman, but for me as a kind of member of the group Pakeha, if you like. Which is problematic, but that's something that's on the edge of some of these arguments, because I'm not a Maori. But I write within the local, just as the Maori writers do as well, and that can be disadvantaging.

(Lecturer, University of Auckland)

A lecturer from Massey University felt annoyed that the university did not address the issue of promotion more systematically, as is clear from the following:

Q. Have you been encouraged to apply for more senior posts in your present institution?
A. I haven't been explicitly encouraged. I have begun to raise the issue myself, but it wasn't forthcoming from the hierarchy of the institution.
Q. What are your feelings about that?
A. I'm furious. The assumption is, I suppose that we probably do all that ourselves but that begs a lot of questions. That sort of assumption tends to suit the institution's interests. I don't know whether it is an explicit strategy – I'm sure it's not. But in practice it works to the institution's benefit that people don't know what the possibilities are and how to go about them.

(Section from interview with lecturer, Massey University)

This view that the culture of the academy in New Zealand was not one that encouraged promotion for academic women was shared by a lecturer from the University of Auckland who notes:

Nobody has actually ever said to me, you should go for promotion. But then I don't think in general that that's part of the culture in the department that people go around encouraging other people to go for promotion.

These views did not reflect the experience or perception of other academic women. A lecturer at Massey University had found that her department did encourage staff to apply for promotion as she said, 'I think our head of department, in the last couple of years, has certainly pushed us to apply for promotion and I think he's quite unusual in that way.' However the same lecturer notes that:

being encouraged to apply for senior posts still works better for men than women. And certainly I don't think I've been encouraged to think too high and that was the thing when I went along and I said well how much do I need to do. I've got a book out now, I've got a PhD and I'm still stuck (with a very good Head of Department and a very good Dean) and that kind of attitude well you know maybe next year or there's only so many of these to go around and yet on the basis of the principles that they're saying promotion is for . . .

(Lecturer, Massey University)

Some academic women clearly felt that the experience of promotion for academic women was a different experience from that of men and that the attitudes and some of the practices surrounding promotion were potentially, if not actually, discriminatory for women academics at universities in New Zealand. A lecturer from the University of Auckland who had researched the history of women in the academy in New Zealand as students and as academics relates a view from her own research experience:

From the experiences of the forty women that I spoke to, a lot of them mirrored . . . my personal experiences in terms of really having to lobby very hard when they applied for promotion. That whereas blokes might put in their application, the women seemed to spend a lot of time checking out whether what they'd done seemed okay, in terms of you know the written presentation, whether there were things that they might emphasise more. That they felt that when they were asked to appear in front of promotions committees that they were quite often asked trivial kinds of questions about what they'd done in their past. I mean of course you'll be aware that a lot women academics in New Zealand have come into academic life much later and so a lot of us have been teachers, a lot of us have had other careers, sometimes have had several careers, and that that has been a focus, particularly by the scientists, engineers, and so on and it's kind of been like, well you haven't always been an academic, therefore what do you think you're doing applying for promotion now, kind of thing. And there seemed to be some really strong messages coming out from the women that I spoke to, about, just really feeling really vulnerable and marginal. And I mean I've certainly experienced that, coming from a very much better-paid job before, into the university where that feeling of vulnerability and marginality had kind of never occurred. I mean I'd never experienced that, so I found it really quite shocking.

(Lecturer, University of Auckland)

The views of this academic woman highlight some of the issues raised earlier in the chapter, that many academic women move into the academy from a well-established career or profession elsewhere. The appointment of professionally skilled, older women does not automatically mean a recognition of these skills within the academy, or the translation of these skills into tangible promotion criteria.

The ritual practices surrounding promotion was not something that appealed to some academic women. As a lecturer from Massey University notes:

I think there's one aspect of promotion which I find a little alien. That promotion is also linked with high profile . . . very apparent in the . . . faculty . . . But I think that this high kind of profile thing works in terms of connections . . . being seen talking to the right people, connecting up, being on the right committees . . .

Q. Well that also applies in other departments . . .

A. Yes and I imagine it's university-wide too. I think that's alien to a lot of women . . . men are more conditioned . . . their conditioning helps them to put themselves forward more readily where women and I would say this also applies to Maori – wait to be chosen. I know there are exceptions, some really strong women here, but there is still that kind of reluctance to push themselves forward in quite that way.

(Section from interview with lecturer, Massey University)

Although this view of academic women was confirmed in one case, the general experience of academic women as far as promotion was concerned, was that their expectations were continually being redefined by the experience of applying for promotion and being disappointed. However, whereas the responses of some academic women show a resistance and contestation of their discursive location within the promotion process – the response of other academic women was to accept their position. This was the case with a lecturer at the University of Waikato. She had gained her doctorate ten years ago, had published and was at the top of the lecturer scale but had no immediate plans to apply for promotion. Her reasons were as follows:

Well it's just the way things are at the moment with funding. It is very difficult to obtain promotion. Nothing to do with being female or anything . . . the usual expectation is that you would hang around for a couple of years before being promoted . . . No I just couldn't be bothered going through when I knew I wouldn't get promoted. Possibly by the end of next year I'll have a few more publications. They tend to want quite a lot before they will consider it. I mean I think I could have done a reasonable amount but probably not enough for senior lecturer.

(Lecturer, University of Waikato)

Different academic women define promotion in different ways. In addition, issues of subjectivity and identity are important factors in understanding 'difference'. Subjective perceptions of promotion for different academic women have to be set in the context of other academic factors, as well as personal and situational factors. This was shown in the views of the same lecturer:

Q. Have you been encouraged to apply for more senior posts?

A. I don't think that really applies to my situation. With regard to funding, the whole structure of the university, I mean, there's just a fixed amount of people they want to be senior lecturers and professors, so it's not just automatic.

Q. Aren't you ambitious for those positions?
A. Not really, no. You don't believe me?
Q. No, it's not that I don't believe you.
A. You mean, do I want to be a professor before I'm 40 – no.
Q. Yes, or certainly an associate professor. It doesn't matter to you . . . ?
A. It doesn't matter to me at all. What matters to me is that I do my job to my satisfaction, which is teaching correctly and also that . . . my real love, if you like, is the research I do and as long as I can do that and have the opportunity to get funding for it and travel if necessary, then it doesn't really matter to me.
Q. Right.
A. Does that sound too noble?
Q. No, it's certainly different . . .
A. Well, I mean. I still want to be involved in publishing but not for promotion so much as just making a contribution to the scientific work I do. That's really . . . I mean it sounds appalling, but it's true.
Q. No, it doesn't. It's refreshing.

(Extract from interview with lecturer, University of Waikato)

While some academic women appeared apparently disinterested in promotion, for other academic women at the top end of the scale, promotion was still an issue. A professor at the University of Waikato, who had worked her way up (outside New Zealand) from junior research fellow to a personal chair, spoke from the vantage point of a professorship:

In New Zealand both associate and full professorships do not carry automatic promotion with them. You move slowly and painfully, if at all, so I'm told, from one informally recognised notch within the range to another. And the range for professors is large – its nearly $20,000 in the range, so if you start toward the bottom, or even half way up, there is still a fair amount of extra money which you can get, if you work your butt off. But, I suppose a recognised career structure involves them thinking about deanships, and vice-chancellorships and that sort of thing.

(Professor, University of Waikato)

Where posts did not carry a career structure in promotional or salary terms, there is a disincentive to academic women. A senior tutor at the University of Auckland had clearly grown out of her current post but had no opportunities within the career structure of the post for promotion. She had instead taken on a number of other positions, including a senior administrative position, to enhance her career profile. She also raised the issue of the decisions that academic women have to make in negotiating a balance between career/promotion and family commitments:

I guess promotion's always tied to salary, and I think it's a shame that there's like a ceiling on the career structure that I'm in at the moment, for senior tutors. Because I do know that I'm continuing to grow and I know that my performance this year is better than what I did last year. But there isn't any way in which that can be financially rewarded, and . . .

Q. It's not reflected?

A. It's not reflected. And so there is a concern in my mind about where am I in ten years from now. And you have to sort of say, well here I am now, I mean I haven't wasted any time in my career, because I've continued to work right the way through it and I've continued to grow and develop and I've always given my best. But now my kids are of the age that they are, where they're dressing themselves and doing everything else, I now have more energy left to sort of start off again, and pick up again. We talk about people coming back at a mature age. Well I'm starting to feel now, I'm in a career-building phase and I have to ask the question what can I do to build my career? And I just have to hope that there will be opportunities. I don't really want to narrow my opportunities down into something that doesn't involve lecturing and teaching because I enjoy that so much. But, at the same time, if something came up that was more of a sort of director of programmes, or sort of academic administration, then I would look at that, because I think I've got strengths and skills in that area.

(Senior tutor, University of Auckland)

Vasil's (1993) work on gender differences in academic careers in New Zealand universities shows the distribution of academic staff by marital status. Her findings show a larger proportion of male to female academics married, more female academics divorced or separated, or never having been married. In addition, she found significant differences in caregiver status with substantially more female than male academic staff not having children.

The issue of balancing the demands and commitments of family in relation to meeting the demands of promotion and an academic lifestyle was outlined by a lecturer from the University of Auckland:

I think its harder for senior women. The other thing I would comment on (though not from personal experience) is that I think there's still a problem for women who devoted a fair bit of time to bringing up families, because I think it's harder for them to have an academic record with lots of publications on it, compared to a man of the same age who is applying for promotion. And I think that's very double-edged because you could run the argument that in fact in families the husband should be spending as much time looking after the children as the wife, so that it shouldn't be a factor, but my impression is that in practice that doesn't happen. One of my closest friends in Australia has children and is in a very male-dominated academic department and has had a lot of trouble with getting promotion, despite the fact that she's got a terrific record in all areas and she attributes that partly to the fact that she's got children – if the children are sick and she has to

take time off, that isn't treated in the same way as if one of the guys
has a rugby injury and he takes time off.

(Lecturer, University of Auckland)

Three academic women, involved in academic administration as opposed
to teaching and research were appointed on a contractual basis so the issue
of promotion did not apply directly to them. However, all three were either
directly or indirectly concerned with issues such as promotion opportunities for academic women. One of the women served on all appointment and
promotion committees and had access to 'returns' from the university to the
Ministry of Education. She made the following comment about promotion
opportunities for academic women:

What I have discovered from last year's figures to the Ministry of Education was that by a small majority, most men were senior academics –
senior lecturer and above, and by a small majority, most women were
junior academics.

(Academic woman, University of Auckland)

The subjective perceptions and experiences of academic women to promotion were thus influenced in part by academic position, age, ethnicity,
marital status, parenthood (caregiving) and by a range of personal and
situational factors. Academic women can be seen to resist, contest and
accommodate their discursive location within the academy.

Appraisal

The appraisal process is generally understood to be an important aspect
of career development, as well as an integral element in the promotion process. The use of appraisal, which is becoming more a feature of academic life
in countries such as the UK, remains relatively under-used in New Zealand.
Some academic women had no experience of an appraisal, other than during the formal process of applying for promotion, although most expressed
the fact that they would benefit from the appraisal process. While academic
women's experience of appraisal differed, being related to a number of
factors including academic position, there was a general sense of dissatisfaction at the way the appraisal process operated.

A lecturer at the University of Waikato had not really found anything very
positive in her experience of the appraisal process despite her sense of carrying considerable academic demands in a newly established department:

I think a number of us throughout the whole year tried to do everything we had to do to offer the programme, and we went and had this
little meeting and I didn't want to say anything really negative because
it just didn't seem to be appropriate in this little meeting we had, and
then I got a letter back from them saying something along the lines,

'Thank you, your performance was satisfactory last year and we look forward to your publications.' I thought 'beam me up!'

(Lecturer, University of Waikato)

A lecturer at Massey University, who had had three appraisals in New Zealand and elsewhere, was also fairly unimpressed with the process as providing any sense of 'real' professional development for the lecturer involved:

I've never found them that useful. I've had three appraisals, two here and one at . . . , and, apart from saying 'how do you feel about the job?' and, 'oh, you've done a good job this year' – stuff like that – it's never been an in-depth look at ways forward, how to develop. I think, to achieve that sort of thing, it might need some sort of professional development or more professional development on the part of the person who is appraising you, because I think it is often fairly informal and ad hoc. It's not really part of career development.

(Lecturer, Massey University)

One of the issues raised here is the need for 'training' for those who undertake an appraisal, particularly heads of department (HOD). The role of the HOD was seen as a crucial one in the appraisal process, thus perceptions of the success or otherwise of the appraisal process were often directly related to the relationship between HOD and the member of staff as the following comments from lecturers at the Universities of Auckland and Waikato reveal:

Well, I guess that I could only really feel as though I could benefit within the context of a head of department taking my work seriously. So, I guess it's not just saying I want an appraisal, but I want him to talk with me in an ongoing way about how, you know, how my career might develop, what I might do next, and so-on and so-forth.

(Lecturer, University of Auckland)

The issues of both the power relationship involved in an appraisal process and the masculinist discourses operating in the academy, in this case between a male HOD and a 'junior' female academic, are highlighted here. This academic woman's perceptions are clearly influenced by the sense that as an academic woman, her work is not being treated seriously by her male head of department. The implications of the appraisal process for the relationship between HOD and a junior member of the department is shown in the following comments from a lecturer at the University of Waikato:

Yes, I think there were very serious negative aspects to that. The employee is continually aware that she is dependent upon the Head of Department's positive rendering of her efforts during the year and, while she has access to that report and can actually make application if she doesn't agree with it, that in itself appears to me to demonstrate an inability on the employee's part to get on well with her head of department, rather than any shortcoming in terms of the departmental head. My second concern about its negative impact is that since the employee wants to continue, and the departmental head wants to show that everything's working smoothly in the department, there seems to be an implicit agreement, no matter what their personal approach to each other has been, to present a report that achieves both objects. Which can often mean that quite serious and worrisome aspects for that employee are not attended to. For example, if there were serious concerns in the department, and particularly in relation to the head of that department, they may not be addressed because there is no opportunity. My third concern about the negative impact of it is that the interview itself at the end of all this lasts no more than ten minutes.

(Lecturer, University of Waikato)

These comments highlight some of the implied power relationships involved in the appraisal process. While the nature of the power relationship is not always a 'gendered' one, the likelihood is, given the differentiated gender imbalance at senior levels in the academy, that it will be a male HOD and a female 'junior' lecturer. Academic women were generally not enthusiastic about the benefits of the appraisal process, their perceptions clearly shaped by their experiences of the discourse of power involved in the appraisal process.

Productivity

The relationship between levels of productivity and the workloads academic women are expected to carry has been established as a problematic one and is reasonably well documented. Vasil comments, 'Studies suggest that women academics invest more time in teaching and less in research and hence publish less than their male counterparts (Helmreich et al., 1980; Over, 1982; Schoen and Winocur, 1988; Simeone, 1987; Vasil, 1992)' (Vasil, 1993: 144). Vasil also notes that some of the factors involved in gender differences in the amount of time spent teaching versus research, include the less 'well-established' process of networking for academic women and the greater likelihood of not holding a doctorate. Vasil (1993) relates levels of productivity with achieving doctoral status:

A significant finding in the present study was that a greater proportion of female than male academic staff reported not holding a doctorate (44% vs 20%). Furthermore, results indicated that academic staff who held doctorates were significantly more productive than those who did not. This is not surprising given the opportunities provided by doctoral training for establishing research skills, developing mentoring relationships and gaining access to professional networks, all of which are critical factors in academic success.

(Vasil, 1993: 151)

There are two major implications of Vasil's research. The first is the relationship between possessing a doctorate, productivity and what is identified by Vasil (1993) as 'self-efficacy'[5]. The second key implication is the gendered differences in levels of productivity for female and male academics and the implications of this for teaching and workloads more generally and for promotion. Vasil (1993) maintains that 'the greater prevalence of female academic staff not possessing a doctoral degree is likely to have contributed to observed gender differences in both productivity and research self-efficacy' (Vasil, 1993: 151). Further, Vasil notes that completion of a doctorate would enhance perceptions of self-efficacy for research purposes. In examining the concept of self-efficacy as a potential contributory factor to gender differences in research productivity, Vasil found that male academics were significantly more confident than female academics in their ability to perform research activities, and further, that self-efficacy beliefs were positively correlated with productivity. As Vasil notes: 'It is likely that perceptions of confidence would play a critical role in academic performance given the often rigorous standards of evaluation academic scholarship is subjected to. For example, strong self-efficacy beliefs would be needed to ensure persistence in performance in the face of setbacks such as publication rejections' (Vasil, 1993: 144).

The second implication of Vasil's work is related to levels of productivity (research and publication) for female and male academic staff. The results of Vasil's study shows that female academic staff may be disadvantaged in their career development due to their lower research productivity and more specifically their lower rate of publication. 'For example, male academic staff reported publishing significantly more articles in refereed journals over a 3 year period than did females' (Vasil, 1993: 151). Further, Vasil found differences in research productivity in different academic disciplines with female academic staff significantly less productive overall than their male colleagues in areas such as commerce, social sciences and mathematics/computer sciences.

Reports from universities in New Zealand (Massey University, 1989; Wilson, 1986; Worth, 1992) all refer to the fact that women academics tend to be concentrated on lower level courses with more administration and heavier workloads than their male colleagues. Vasil (1993: 151) notes that implicit in this argument is the assumption that female academics are more heavily involved in the teaching, as opposed to the research, function of the university. Vasil contends that:

Empirical findings including the present study would support the contention that female academic staff spend greater time in teaching related activities than do males. A multiplicity of factors have been identified in the literature as contributors to this difference including anecdotal accounts of discriminatory practices whereby female academic staff are assigned more time-consuming teaching responsibilities, such as running large undergraduate courses; female academic staff being assigned or assuming greater student advisory and counselling functions; and female academics actively choosing the role of teacher (Simeone, 1987; Wilson, 1986).

(Vasil, 1993: 151)

Women academics, as a result, have less time to write and publish, undertake research and present papers at conferences. They are, as a result, less able to compete with male academics in terms of promotion as measured by research and publications.

Academic women's responses in relation to issues of productivity and workload were related to academic position. A senior lecturer from the University of Waikato maintained that it was partially related to 'gendered' perceptions of the nature of teaching and academic relationships:

> Women do it themselves because I think a lot of us are more interested in people than just in our subject and so our interests . . . we are easily diverted into doing these things that we actually enjoy doing, but it does mean that it probably does affect publishing and that, in turn, affects promotion because in spite of what people say, that they do look at your teaching and whatever, I still think there's still a lot of promotion and advancement of various kinds that occurs because you've . . . been assessed by counting papers.
>
> (Senior lecturer, University of Waikato)

The following excerpt from an interview with a lecturer at the University of Auckland highlights the implications for workload of the 'gendered' nature of academic relationships. This academic woman's perceptions were informed by her own feminist analysis of the nature of academic power relationships and her own experience of being a feminist academic interacting with women students. Despite extensive publications, a PhD and a track record of scholarly endeavour, she had been turned down for promotion to senior lecturer in the annual promotion round. In the following comments she reflects on these issues as they impact on her experiences.

Q. Have you experienced any gender bias/weighting in the delegation of responsibilities?

A. That's an interesting question. Yes, I have, in the sense that the (this may be a tenuous connection) but because our senior people are all males, I don't think they do very much as far as leadership and administration is concerned, in terms of departmental committees. But I think they get away with it because they're men. And they say, oh, you know, I can't possibly do that. I'm away for a third of the year, or I've got 16 conferences to go to this year, or I've got 49 books I'm writing and can't possibly do that and I'm not interested in doing it. So everybody kind of nods sagely and goes to the next one down the line, you know. So there's a sort of interesting link with gender, and I think that if there were women who were senior . . . I think it would be easier to have expectations of women. I think they would bow more easily to those expectations, in terms of responsibility to their colleagues.

I think a lot of the senior men, you know, are very busy as academics and they just see the administrative responsibilities and the committee responsibilities as beneath their time and effort. And they often are, because they are so busy. I mean, they are all rushing off, you know, with book contracts, and going to conferences, but it's all self-perpetuating, of course. But it tends, in this department anyway, to not happen for women.

Q. Is there any aspect of areas of responsibility which I haven't covered, which you'd like to develop further? You made the point about women in the department carrying additional responsibility.

A. Well I think that in terms of the way in which we tend to see our relationship with students, for example. This is to do with teaching, you know, and our teaching load. And ways in which teaching loads and so on are often calculated are to do with numbers, how many students do you have, how many hours do you lecture, and so on. But it makes totally invisible the kind of work I do. Last week I had a student in my office, she was talking about how she needed me to help her to escape from home and as a professional person she wanted me to sign a piece of paper so that she could get money, you know, a special allowance to be able to leave home because her father's been abusing her, etc., etc. Now, I'm the only person she's ever told about this, and I spent a lot of time, both talking to her, then following it up . . . So I ring up another woman in this department who's involved with counselling, she puts me . . . in touch with another person, and so it goes on. I mean that's just one example, but I could multiply . . . you know, I could tell you that over and over and over, about the ways in which women academics get involved with their students. Whether it's to do with the student's kind of personal situation which flows into their ability to operate as students, or just in terms of giving them encouragement, following things up, finding references, or whatever. I'm not saying that men don't do this, but I do think that women in my experience tend to do it more, and students expect that from them more as well. So the students would be more likely to come and see me. If they've got a problem with . . . I can give countless instances of that sort of thing, and particularly when you're involved with Pacific Island students. This morning, one woman who rang is Maori, the woman who came to the door was a Pacific Island student. And I see a disproportionately high number of Maori and Pacific Island students who need assistance. I mean they're struggling, these women, to complete their course work and I didn't spend much time with either of them, but I know I will, in getting that work out of them, you know, and giving them extra feedback and so on, because I really want them to succeed. And I think that, on the whole, women staff often do that, and I think that that is an enormous area of responsibility that's completely under-recognised.

(Lecturer, University of Auckland)

The involvement of academic women, and specifically feminist academics, with students, as highlighted by this lecturer, and the implications for workload was mentioned by a number of contributors. An example of a fairly extensive delegation of responsibilities to a junior woman academic from the University of Waikato who had only been recently appointed, and whose position was untenured, was illustrative of this point. She had course team leadership of a compulsory first year paper (218 students), with team leadership of four team members, pastoral care for 10 designated students and responsibility for organizing the department's staff timetables (10 staff members). Her workload could have in part been explained (but not justified) by the fact that she was a Maori academic woman. The lack of academic women with Maori and Pacific Island backgrounds means that considerable burdens of a teaching and counselling nature are imposed on these women. Another fairly junior lecturer, also from the University of Waikato, had been involved in producing new courses, clearly undermining her opportunity to undertake research and to publish. She commented:

I've developed 3 new courses in the last three years . . . Purely for internals, but we don't have the library resources . . . I actually had thought when I got here that effort would be rewarded but it's only rewarded if you put a lot more effort into it.

(Lecturer, University of Waikato)

Additional areas of work were identified and outlined by another lecturer from the University of Waikato. The maintenance of professional skills, professional involvement in the community, meeting student needs and addressing departmental commitments produced a formidable workload profile for this lecturer:

I have committees that help the department run, for example, the curriculum committee . . . I've just left that for the research committee, but the subject committee is where I listen to students' concerns, then canvass lecturers with a view to changing aspects that are of concern to the students, and feeding back to the students major developments within the department that might impact on them or their progress through the department. That's one of the things I do. I provide lecturing to other universities and schools of medicine. I do community work that heightens the profile of the university in a positive way. And I have to engage in work to keep my professional skills sharp in order to maintain credibility within the training programme. What else do I do? I'm on various school committees as well, and I work long hours on promoting the application for the expansion of clinics within the training programme. Handle the staff meetings, mark theses, examine at other universities.

(Lecturer, University of Waikato)

It was apparent from the responses of the academic women interviewed that for a variety of reasons both personal and institutional, academic women carried considerable workloads and some organized their family life fairly strictly around their work life, as was the case with a senior tutor at the University of Auckland. With very little career structure potential within the role of a senior tutor, this academic woman went to extraordinary lengths to prove her competence over a range of skills. The following section from the interview illustrates the point:

Q. In terms of areas of responsibility, what areas of academic respons- ibility in addition to those of lecturing do you have?
A. I am sub-dean. I was admissions and enrolment coordinator last year, which is, you know, sort of three or four months absolutely full- time, right over summer. I did that the previous year, but with very little recognition.
Q. Right over the summer, did you say?
A. Yes.
Q. So you didn't have a holiday?
A. No. Oh, I had about three or four days. It's very difficult to fit holidays in if you're actually trying to do things well, and combine a couple of roles. I'd say that's probably one of the costs of actually trying to prove yourself. I think that it's very difficult to plan to take proper breaks. On average, I would probably find I would take, say, two weeks a year. I often take a week in August. I might take a couple of long weekends . . . I think what it is, in order to get on, you've actually got to do your job, but you've also got to take on lots of other tasks as well, in order to show what other skills you have. And I'm very conscious of that . . . Well, I've learned now that you can sort of say well, if I'm going to do this, I want a supplementary payment for it, and I think we've got to be more insistent that there should be scope and flexibility within salary structures to reward those extra activities. Because there's a huge cost involved, to me. I'm involved in enrolment over summer, it costs me a lot of money. If I took four weeks leave and I took my children out of childcare, I save myself a lot of money. Because to pay for full-time childcare for two children is very expensive. So there is a cost involved in not taking holidays, and I think that has to be recognized by people. I also go, when I'm recruiting, to Singapore and Malaysia and Indo- nesia, and I'm going up on the sixth of June to Hong Kong and China for a fortnight. And again, you're just working seven days a week, with very long hours. And I think it's recognition by the uni- versity that you can undertake that sort of role. But again, I mean

I'm putting pressure on my husband to do that . . . when I do that. I've got to go away and leave him to cope and manage . . . I'm lucky really that he's prepared to do a 50/50 deal on these things.

Q. Have you experienced any gender bias or weighting in the delegation of responsibilities?

A. I don't think it comes from the delegation of responsibilities, but the willingness to take on extra responsibilities. There's sort of a subtle difference there. I've got male colleagues who would be in a same position as I am (probably also females, to be fair) but who have not put themselves forward as being prepared to take on these extra responsibilities, and that's been their personal choice. Mainly they feel they're doing enough. Whereas I don't work for money, really. I work because I enjoy the job that I do. And I'm very lucky to have that. So therefore, I'm willing to do these extra things. But my attitude's always been, well my contract is sort of for 35–40 hour week for 48 weeks of the year. I don't know whether it's part of a female . . . I'm not a workaholic, but women do tend to take on more. And I'm not sure whether it's sort of this guilt thing, this sort of having to sort of prove yourselves to be better than or equal to, or whatever else, which is probably what your research is getting at . . . And I think women too have got . . . women have got skills in being able to juggle a dozen things at once, which I don't see very often in men.

(Senior tutor, University of Auckland)

A number of issues are raised by these comments. The first is the lengths this academic woman was prepared to go to, and felt that she had to go, to prove her competence over a range of areas of skill. This was by means of offsetting the fact that her professional background was that of a senior administrator in a school and differed from the conventional academic profile of doctoral research and publishing. Her perceptions and identity led to an interesting response to her position within the academic discourses of the academy. Rather than accepting a career framework circumscribed by the position of senior tutor, she had extended her workload and area of responsibilities which had resulted in her appointment to the position of sub-dean, carrying considerable additional responsibilities.

Secondly, the framing of family life and parenting around academic life is one which shows considerable points of difference from the findings which have emerged from a number of studies. Findings from Vasil's (1993) study show that:

female academic staff reported spending significantly more hours per week than male academics on housework/childcare . . . Thus, despite a greater proportion of male academics being involved in family roles, this involvement did not result in as great a time investment as for female academics. The potential for greater role conflict and overload among female academics is likely to have implications for research productivity.

(Vasil, 1993: 152)

Vasil raises a question which is relevant to the case outlined, she asks whether female academics perceive greater difficulty in attempting to combine career and family roles, frequently 'sacrificing' the latter (i.e. not having children) to concentrate on the former or, she asks, 'is there greater attrition from the profession by women strongly committed to family roles?' (Vasil, 1993: 152).

Academic women's responses to the issue of productivity and workload showed considerable variation, highlighting the fact that differences in perception and identity are significant factors in understanding the experiences of academic women in relation to productivity and workload. Women's subjective perceptions were seen to be related to academic factors, for example possession of a doctoral thesis; involvement in academic/professional networks; academic mentoring; level of seniority; and to factors such as ethnicity; feminist perceptions; professional commitments; marital status and parenthood (caregiving).

The issue of productivity *vis-à-vis* workload is also problematic when it comes to committee membership. Reports on the status of academic women at universities in New Zealand which emerged in the 1980s and early 1990s found that while academic women were expected to serve on a range of departmental and faculty committees, few had an opportunity to serve on prestigious university decision-making bodies. The same pattern emerged in the current research. Only one of the lecturers below the level of senior lecturer served on a university decision-making committee, although all served on a variety of departmental and faculty committees. Three academic women served on university wide, decision-making bodies, however their representation was frequently nominal. A number of specific issues surrounding the position of academic women *vis-à-vis* committee work did emerge. The first of these involved the delegation of responsibilities within a committee and the 'politics of committee work' as noted by a lecturer from the University of Waikato:

> I've observed it in the sense that, on a committee comprised of one woman and three men, the woman seems to be doing all the work, seems to be doing all the preparing and collating and putting together, while the men make the decisions about how that will be used. I've experienced that the 'team' which includes male and female is represented only by the male and therefore seen as that particular male's committee, even though the females on it may have been working extremely hard to produce what it is that that male reports. So, I guess my experience is consistent with my observations. And the harrowing thing is that because the woman's doing the work, the students approach the woman, which provides her with more work and that is not reflected in the reports about the committee's work. The committee is seen to have

achieved this and that . . . collectively. And the committee is often referred to in terms of the male. Yes. The surname of the male is synonymous with the committee as a whole.

(Lecturer, University of Waikato)

A second issue to arise from the nature of committee work is the timing of committee meetings, particularly for academic women who are caregivers, as indicated by a senior tutor at the University of Auckland:

So something involves . . . for instance, meetings at eight o'clock in the morning, so therefore you didn't have an opportunity to be part of it, because of that. Eight o'clock meetings . . . I mean, I can cope with them. I just have to juggle my diary with my husband's diary. If not, we pay some childcare centre to be there at half past seven, but for people with family commitments, eight o'clock meetings, if you don't know in advance, if it's just sprung on you then, you know, it's a bit difficult. I think that that's sort of something that a male usually doesn't face and people without family commitments don't face. Those sorts of things are issues people need to be aware of. They need to be flexible in setting meetings times.

These examples show how the 'normal' practices of the academy discriminate against academic women.

A senior academic woman, holding a chair at the University of Waikato, experienced committee work from the position of one of a minority of academic women in positions of leadership. As she notes:

I have been warned that every committee at the University of Waikato must have a woman on it and there are not enough to go around, so I expect to find myself appointed to committees mainly because I happen to be a female in a senior position . . . But as far as I am concerned, as a professor with what I interpret to be primary responsibilities in the area of academic leadership, I regard those responsibilities as more important than committee work.

(Professor, University of Waikato)

Representation on committees is an important element both in the 'visibility' of academic women and as an aspect of the promotion process. However, academic women frequently find themselves serving on 'low level' 'housekeeping' committees which are time-consuming, detract from research and publishing, and are at the departmental as opposed to the university 'decision-making' committee level.

Discrimination

Research on the position and status of academic women in universities in New Zealand points to the difficulty of identifying and defining discrimination. The *Report on the Status of Academic Women at Massey University* (1989) identifies some of the ways in which university structures discriminate against women. Those factors include the failure of the university to respond flexibly to women as caregivers; the attitude of men in senior posts; and the power of the HOD. Academic women identified a number of areas of discrimination which are experienced by all academic women. However, beyond this, more specific areas of discrimination and discriminatory practice emerged related to the academic status of different academic women.

One of the key areas of discrimination identified by academic women at universities in New Zealand was the issue of women applying for permanent (tenured) positions and applying for promotion. Issues included women being expected to have achieved the same degree of academic status as a male colleague of the same age, despite the fact that she may have taken time out to have children. This was seen to be a factor in discriminating against academic women in terms of their productivity.

The culture of the academy defines its practices in ways which discriminate against the academic woman, particularly the academic woman who is a 'late starter' and who has parenting (caregiver) responsibilities. As a lecturer from Massey University notes:

> I was also getting another message and I think it's a message that says quite a lot. That I had done everything the wrong way. That I had looked towards a university career and I should have started as all good people start, but particularly good males start, and gone through and had scholarships, etc. . . . there is one pattern to follow and it seems to be the traditional male pattern and much easier for males of course because even if they do get married and have children they tend to have been able to pursue their careers more easily whereas it's much more difficult for women.
>
> (Lecturer, Massey University)

Another factor already identified by a number of academic women was the timing of meetings and committees, particularly for academic women with young children. It was felt that academic women with parenting (caregiver) responsibilities were discriminated against because they could not attend committee meetings at particular times because of caregiver responsibilities. As a result they were not seen as available for taking on such responsibilities as their male colleagues.

The practices of the academy are experienced as discriminatory by academic women who also define these practices in terms of power. A lecturer from the University of Waikato describes what she regards as discriminatory practice:

> Yes, I think that some of the unequal practices I have observed and experienced in relation to the management of women in academia, it certainly sets the scene for the male academic to feel more powerful in any conflict. Now, that's rather obtuse, what am I trying to say here? Women are not heard and listened to on the same basis as their male

counterparts. And their concerns are not always addressed, and if they are addressed, they're very often seen as a reflection of some shortcoming in the female rather than a product of the situation. For example, if a woman is having some difficulty with a student, it's not unusual to hear someone say 'is she having an off day?'

(Lecturer, University of Waikato)

There were other more specific experiences of discrimination mainly associated with the process of appointment. A senior lecturer at the University of Waikato had experienced discrimination in the length of time she had to wait before gaining a permanent contract:

I suppose you would call it discrimination. You know, the long performance about whether I was permanent or not and the fact that I actually had a position that was renewed annually for about 15 years and that is really a totally unsatisfactory sort of situation to be in. That it really was permanent, but it wasn't. So I would call that discrimination. I was discriminated against as a part-time employee when I asked for maternity leave because at that stage only full-time employees could actually get the payment.

(Senior lecturer, University of Waikato)

A lecturer at the University of Auckland felt she had experienced discrimination in gaining a permanent appointment as a result of her politics – her feminist politics:

Q. Have you experienced discrimination in your present post?
A. I don't know. At the very beginning when I applied for the job, there was a lot of opposition in this department to my getting the job.
Q. Because you hadn't completed your PhD?
A. No, because I was a feminist, and because I was interested in the whole area of women in education. In 1987, believe it or not, there was nothing in this department on women and already by 1987 there was a significant scholarship on women in education . . . I instituted, when I was a tutor here (the year before I got the job) a group called Women in Education, which was a group of senior students who were interested in women and gender, and wanted to read stuff on women and gender, but there wasn't any opportunity to do that within the papers that they were studying. So we got together, and we gave each other references, and generally encouraged each other to make gender an issue in the various papers that we were in. Now that was seen as a strategy for me to put pressure on the department to appoint me and . . . to at least appoint a woman anyway, appoint a feminist or someone who would teach in this area. So that was seen very, very negatively. And I say that as discriminatory, because it was seeing women as a kind of category, again, rather than seeing women . . . as an area of scholarship, a

legitimate area of scholarship, and I thought that was discriminatory, because it was seeing all the writing on women and . . . as
either not existing, or as not being of any value.

(Lecturer, University of Auckland)

Attitudes towards feminist academic women were also seen as an aspect
of discriminatory attitudes by a lecturer at Massey University. As she noted:

I think organizations are very wary of . . . organizational culture is
very wary of any cry of discrimination and there is a lot of resistance to
that and people like to bury those kinds of problems . . . Discrimination
is linked with attitudes and attitudes are often underground . . . just
teaching a gender issues course . . . I do think there have been certain
attitudes to me as a feminist . . . I find that extremely frustrating and
I notice that I do not get the opportunities for some of the graduate
teaching which I think I should be doing . . . it is very subtle and difficult
to pinpoint.

(Lecturer, Massey University)

Many of the 'normal' discourses and discursive practices of the academy
within which academic women are located are experienced as discriminatory by academic women. Further, the 'normalization' of a masculinist culture
within the academy frequently makes discrimination difficult to identify. As
a lecturer from the University of Auckland comments:

It's difficult to tell. It is usually possible to attribute suspected incidents
to another factor.

(Lecturer, University of Auckland)

Academic women identified a number of areas of discrimination including: promotion and gaining 'tenure'; as well as definitions of productivity.
Additional factors related to more specific subjective experiences of discrimination including: age; parenting; feminist politics; and academic status.

Sexual harassment

While only one of the academic women had experienced a degree, albeit
minor, of sexual harassment, most knew of, had acted as mediator in, or
had advised on issues of sexual harassment. It was generally felt that the
mechanisms were in place for dealing with cases of sexual harassment.

Mentorship

A great deal of interest has been shown in the area of mentorship by those
involved in equal opportunities policy and issues in New Zealand, and the
issue of mentorship has been widely researched in Australia and the USA.
Some feminist academics tend to see mentorship as both redundant and

passé as a mechanism for assisting academic women, and as being politically problematic because of the implications of patronage. Findings from this research show that academic women were generally positively disposed to the idea of mentorship although the idea of a formal policy, where mentors are allocated was one which was resisted by a large number of academic women. A lecturer at Massey University expresses her concern about the implications of mentorship:

> I think there is something about mentorship which bothers me and that is the whole issue of patronage and power within institutions. If you are mentored or your mentor is a more senior academic than you, what does that mean for your own position within the institution in terms of allegiances and freedom and autonomy of operation. So although I think it can be a very positive thing, I think it also potentially can be quite constraining so I have mixed feelings about it really.
>
> (Lecturer, Massey University)

However, other academic women were very positively disposed to the idea of mentorship, as is illustrated by this comment from a lecturer at the University of Auckland:

> I reckon that I, like most women, or most people probably, would really like an academic mentor. I would really like, preferably a woman, or it doesn't have to be a woman, but preferably a woman who's successful academically, who's wise, who can talk to me about my work, why I can't write, why I'm not writing or why I am writing, and what I'm writing, where I'm publishing. All that just to talk about academic and intellectual issues. Not just to do with the ideas specific to my area of interest, but the whole kind of craft, if you like, the whole work of being an academic and having a career as an academic, and making decisions about conferences overseas, and a whole range of issues . . . you have to make decisions all the time about what you're going to write, who you're going to write for, whether you're going to put yourself up for conferences, whether you're going to go to conferences, which conferences. I mean, it just goes on and on, and I find it very hard to do that by myself, and I don't have other people teaching in similar areas in the department with whom I could discuss it. I'm always just desperately keen to have that kind of guidance and encouragement.
>
> (Lecturer, University of Auckland)

A lecturer from Massey University indicates that her passage from being an extramural student to assistant lecturer, then lecturer would have been considerably assisted by the guidance of a mentor:

> I would have loved a mentor when I started – as I moved into the university from being an extramural student. If I'd had someone I could go along to and just ask a few things about, in terms of being an assistant lecturer, and where do I go from here and is it really like

this? Rather than getting those other messages that, you know, I'd done everything the wrong way – that would have been good. And in a kind of a way, I think that my . . . I only came back into the university because of a couple of women mentors, or they didn't set themselves up as mentors. It was sort of . . . pulled me back in.

(Lecturer, Massey University)

The question to what areas of academic life, mentorship lends itself to met with a very positive response. A lecturer at the University of Auckland stresses that mentorship is valuable in a range of areas:

I think that every area of academic life in terms of organizing . . . right from organizing your time when you come in in the morning, right through to making decisions about which academic journals to contribute to, what kind of research is going to be most useful to you. I can't think of any area of academic life that wouldn't benefit from either of those.

But the thing is, I guess when I think about the mentoring or role modelling relationship, I'm not thinking of something that's onerous. It has to be something . . . you can't say, right you have to be a mentor for this person. It has to spring naturally out of an enjoyable relationship between two people. Now it might just involve me having lunch with another woman once a month, or it might involve me just seeing her in operation with students, or going into her office and watching how she organizes her time. I mean I don't have to formally go, I want to watch you for a day or anything. But it has to . . . I mean I find I learn a terrific amount about how to be an academic from watching other women do it. Not from watching men do it. And I think that it's really good when we can actually spend time with each other, just watching how the other person operates.

I see it very much as a kind of entering into the life of another woman, or getting somehow a window into it. And I think a lot of women like to talk about themselves, so I don't think that that is the problem. And when I say I'd like to (it sort of sounds contradictory to what I was saying before) but in a way I'm not seeking specific advice, you should do x, you should do y – but I do x and I do y and it works for me in these kinds of ways.

I suppose the only thing that I feel, is that for me, personally, role modelling and encouragement or mentoring or whatever it is, from other women in the university is just a key to my success and my survival. I'm not the sort of person who can just sit and beaver away in my office totally independently of any kind of local support. And I think some people can. I think they do, and some of the people have sort of colleagues in America, and they get to them on e-mail or fax or whatever, and they can get it out of a sort of an intellectual excitement, with ideas or writing or publishing, but I'm not like that at all. I need, and I want to have that kind of constant feeling that I'm operating all

right as an academic, you know. And you can only get that from looking at other people doing it, and that you're feeling good about it.

(Lecturer, University of Auckland)

Academic women were, in the main, united in their view that mentorship,
and the practice of mentoring could act to support and reinforce their
sense of identity and academic scholarship in the academy.

Equal opportunities policy and practice in the academy in New Zealand

Equal employment opportunities policy (EEOP)[6] is a relatively recent
development in universities in New Zealand, as it is in the case in the UK.
It would appear that despite the introduction of equal opportunities policy (EOP) in New Zealand universities, the situation of academic women
has not dramatically improved. As Vasil notes: 'While the lack of improvement should not be attributed to the ineffectiveness of equal opportunity
staff, the question remains why the rhetoric of equal opportunity policies
as defined in most university charters is so much at variance with the reality
of unequal opportunity and progress as exemplified by the statistics' (Vasil,
1993: 143).

Many academic women articulate a general concern that the existence of
an EEOP should not in itself be seen as adequate without an accompanying
commitment to the implementation of policy at the level of practice. However, beyond that, differences emerged as to the 'real' value or importance
of equal opportunities policy. A senior academic woman at the University
of Waikato notes that:

> Policy alone is insufficient. I've been struck here by the importance of
> people at the executive levels to the ethos rather than the policy – their
> own personal behaviour is as important as the policy itself. If you have
> a water-tight policy but no commitment to it at the top then it can sit
> on the table for a long time.
>
> (Professor, University of Waikato)

However, the response of two academic women at the University of
Auckland was to maintain (quite separately) that 'it was tokenism'. One of
the respondents outlined her reasons as follows:

> I think it's tokenism, because I've never seen any evidence in this
> institution of there being any real attempts to come to terms with
> the implications of the policy at all. I mean, we do things like on the
> front of our annual review, we've got a lovely glossy cover, which has
> always got plenty of Polynesians in wonderful kind of ethnic gear, being
> scholars at the university, but it's rubbish really, in terms of what you
> know, happens, in terms of practice, I think. In terms of commitment
> to putting resources where the problems are, and to changing practices

within the committee structures. Which is really where it happens, you know, if you're talking about appointments committees or promotion committees, you could have the committee sitting about it, but unless you've got people who are prepared to say, okay, let's implement this policy, or let's look at how this policy is implemented here, in those committees, it's not going to make any difference. And I really severely wonder at whether the EEO officer has any effect at all. I mean, presumably she goes to most of these meetings, but I've got little confidence in her . . . and I'm not talking about in terms of her personal competence, I'm talking in terms of her ability to intervene.

(Lecturer, University of Auckland)

The second respondent recalled the time:

When I went to sign up, the Registrar of this university apologized for having to make me sit through while he read out a paragraph about them [EEOPs] and I took him to task and said, it has taken a lot of people a long time to get this policy established in this university do not apologize for it . . . But I think the attitude of the Registrar was highly significant . . . And actually apologizing to me, who was a woman, what would he say to a bloke, so that troubled me.

(Lecturer, University of Auckland)

These responses reflect the different experiences of academic women differentially positioned in the academic hierarchy to equal opportunities policy and practice. Secondly, both academic women from the University of Auckland had been involved in feminist scholarship and feminist politics – their perceptions and experiences informed by and reflecting feminist issues and values.

At Massey University, an academic woman involved in the formulation and implementation of EEOP responded as follows:

A. I think many academics would argue that an equal employment opportunities policy has been in existence for a long time and they would argue that people are selected to positions on the basis of the 'best person for the job'. So I think many people would believe that it's already in place.

Q. Do you agree with that view?

A. No, I think all we have to look at are the statistics.

(Academic woman, Massey University)

Academic women's response to the question of whether the existence of an equal opportunities policy and practice has an impact on academic relationships was generally positive with some reservations. A lecturer at Massey University comments:

I think it could do. It certainly makes institutions and individuals within those institutions more aware of the issues, but my experience in other institutions that I've worked for, although such policies might have been in place, whether or not they are actually adhered to is a different matter.

(Lecturer, Massey University)

A lecturer from the University of Auckland was convinced that it had impacted on her experience of academic relationships:

Yes, I'm just thinking about my own experience. I think it has had an impact. And it's had an enormously positive impact for someone like me who's operating . . . in a gender area. And when I first came to the department, there was nothing on gender in the department. Now, I could have argued for those . . . But now I don't need to do that any more – all I need to do is cite the policy and say we have a policy of blah, blah, so . . . and so on, you know. So in meetings when we've got this list of people applying for a job and we get a short-list and there are no women on the short-list, I can say let's look at the whole issue of why women aren't . . . why we haven't put women on the short-list, and that just isn't me being a wacky feminist. It's actually . . . I can legitimately say, you know, we're operating the university policy here, and I can preface everything with that statement, which gives it a kind of formal power.

(Lecturer, University of Auckland)

The majority of academic women knew that the University in which they were situated had an EEOP, although very few had actually seen or read the policy. Most knew of the existence of an equal employment opportunities officer, but few, if any, knew who the relevant officer was, whether there was an EEO Committee or how to go about putting items on the agenda of an EEO Committee meeting.

While many of the academic women who participated in the research recognized the fact that women, Maori and Pacific Islanders were all identified as 'target groups' by EEOP for 'positive action', very few respondents discussed the intersection of sexism and racism within the context of equal opportunities policy and university culture. One woman academic outlined what she saw as the impact of EEOP on the behaviour and practices of academic life:

I guess I have a rather cynical viewpoint on this. Certainly, it's been much better in terms of things like sexist language and people being much more aware . . . I always feel that there's a big relationship between sexism and racism. But in New Zealand at least no one wants to be racist . . . but the sexist jokes still go on in the university, and sexist practices in many ways.

(Lecturer, Massey University)

The introduction of EEOP into the academic culture of New Zealand universities has been a recent development paralleling the situation in the UK, and the shortfall in terms of policy and practice has been characteristic

of both cultures. EEOP in New Zealand has gone further than equal opportunities policy in Britain in introducing a stronger element of affirmative
action or 'positive action' as it is called in New Zealand. In the UK 'positive action' within equal opportunities policy is simply what is legislated
for, that is, there is an awareness of there being an inequity in the past,
whereas affirmative action is the adoption of a policy which will set out to
redress the balance. In New Zealand although the phrase affirmative action
is avoided, and while 'affirmative' and 'positive' action are not synonymous,
'positive action' implies the use of strategies to redress past inequities and
to establish 'target groups'. It is argued by one of the academic women, interviewed, that the existence of a policy as a written document is not just
tokenism, but that the next step of implementation was something different.
As she notes:

> I suppose it comes down first of all to morale which affects the entire
> university and the departments. And the other thing is people not
> being able to work to their full potential as academics. There's a lot of
> departments around here, which have very large numbers of women
> students, a reasonable number of women academics generally, but still
> all run by a little cabal of men, you know, in the same way as primary
> schools are – there's not really much difference really.
> (Academic woman [administration], University of Auckland)

Conclusion

Academic women's experiences of the academy in New Zealand reflect
diversity and difference. A range of factors intervene in these experiences
including social, political and academic factors. Academic women's experiences were assessed across a range of issues and areas which in part frame
the discourses of the academy. These include: the issue of power and leadership; academic status; promotion; productivity; workload; discrimination and
harassment; equal opportunities policy and practice and mentorship. Academic women's responses to the discourses of the academy in New Zealand
are varied, ranging from contestatory and challenging to accommodating
and supportive. What is perhaps most interesting in drawing conclusions
from this analysis are the points of similarity and difference that can be
shown in the experiences of academic women in the UK and New Zealand.

5

Gender, Power and the Academy: Patterns of Discrimination and Disadvantage for Academic Women in the UK and Aotearoa/New Zealand

It is apparent from the research findings that academic women's perceptions and experience are varied and reflect issues of 'identity' and 'difference' across a range of factors including: age; ethnicity; marital status; nationality; class; parenthood (caregiving) and academic status (seniority; doctoral status; position in relation to professional networks; level of productivity, i.e. research, publications; responsibility level/workload). The issue of the theorizing, 'difference' in feminist theoretical debates and more specifically through a feminist poststructuralist framework is an important element in understanding this process.

Feminist poststructuralism rejects the concept of a unitary model of subjectivity and 'experience' advocated by feminist theories and methodologies of the 1970s. Within a feminist poststructuralist model, subjectivity is understood as both fragmented and contradictory. Feminist poststructuralism posits a model of experience, which is variable, contestatory and resistant. The experiences of academic women are framed within an analysis of the discourses and discursive practices of the academy, and investigated within the context of understanding 'difference' around issues of 'subjectivity', 'identity' and academic position. Within this context feminist poststructuralism provides an analytical framework to investigate issues of 'subjectivity', 'identity', 'difference' and 'location', framed within an analysis of the differentiated experience of academic women within the academy. A feminist poststructuralist analysis of discourse was drawn on, to elucidate the nature of the relationship between gender, power and the academy and was reinforced through a process of systematic enquiry into the position and experiences of academic women within the academy.

The position of academic women within the academy was investigated through an analysis of patterns of exclusion, segregation and differentiation for academic women in the academy in the UK and New Zealand. Patterns of differentiation for academic women were investigated, in part through an analysis of statistical data drawn from universities. The statistical profile of the academy in the UK attempted to define the frameworks within which academic women are positioned. The position of academic women within the academy in New Zealand was also assessed by an investigation of patterns of discrimination and differentiation. A more limited statistical profile of the New Zealand academy was provided.

It was established at an early point in the text that empirical data drawn from universities in the UK and New Zealand were not directly comparable. It was recognized that there are difficulties in terms of comparability in relation to the findings themselves and the claims that could be made regarding the data. Considerable caution has to be exercised in making claims from the findings based on direct comparability. However, where appropriate, parallels can be drawn in patterns of differentiation, discrimination, and disadvantage in the position and experiences of academic women in universities in the UK and New Zealand.

Direct comparison between the empirical data from the UK and New Zealand cannot be made. However, there are parallels, comparable differences and similarities in patterns of discrimination and disadvantage based around the diverse and differentiated experience of academic women in the two countries which warrant some assessment of the two sets of findings. On the issue of the gendered nature of power in leadership positions in the academy, academic women in New Zealand and the UK reflected similar views. Academic women in both communities in the main understood their under-representation in senior positions and positions of leadership in the academy to be a result of power, patronage and prejudice, although academic women in New Zealand related these issues in a more systematic way to the sexist and patriarchal character of the academy.

A number of factors have been identified in the literature and empirical data from the UK and New Zealand as contributing to the under-representation of academic women at senior levels in the academy. The factors include:

- the operation of practices which privilege the white, male, middle-class academic;
- the attitude of academic men in positions of power and decision making in the academy (including the 'old boys network' and homosociability);
- the system of promotion which identifies and defines 'productivity' in terms which disadvantage academic women;
- the greater likelihood of academic men holding a doctorate;
- the lower productivity level (defined by research and publications) of academic women;
- the heavier teaching workload carried by academic women;
- the failure of the academy to recognize the primary caregiver status of many academic women;

- the lack of role models and an effective process of mentoring for academic women;
- the failure of equal opportunities policies to be effectively translated into equal opportunities practice.

The recognition of a range of seemingly parallel issues and problems for academic women in the operation of discourses of the academy in the UK and New Zealand does not mean that there were not specific cultural, national or political dimensions or 'differences' which altered the position and experiences of academic women within the culture of the academy in the UK and New Zealand. It is important to identify differences in patterns of discrimination and disadvantage in the two cultures.

In terms of academic status and the level of appointment of academic women in the UK and New Zealand, there are differences. In universities in the UK and New Zealand the number of academic women is increasing and in both countries academic women are still disproportionately located at the lower levels of the appointment scale. Academic status at first appointment (in relation to qualifications) is something which has been more systematically researched in New Zealand. The findings of the *Report on the Status of Academic Women in New Zealand* (1986) and the *Report on the Status of Academic Women at Massey University* (1989) as well as the *Report on Issues Affecting Academic Staff at Massey University* (1992) and the work of Vasil (1993) are in the main confirmed by the findings of this research into the experience of academic women at universities in New Zealand.

The lecturer scale in New Zealand[1] (Appendix 3) is a much wider one than in British universities with smaller variations between points on the scale and more formal steps in the promotion process. For example, point 9 (new point 5) on the lecturer scale in New Zealand is not normally gained without completion of a doctorate. In addition, promotion to senior lecturer, while seen as part of the promotion process, is not normally a consideration without a doctorate and publications. Thus, the formal criteria demanded for promotion in universities in New Zealand disadvantages academic women more systematically. Appointments and promotion policy discriminates against academic women, particularly women who are entering the academy after a first career (a very common pattern in New Zealand) and who are therefore older, and academic women who are primary caregivers.

This point highlights the different pattern of appointment in New Zealand. The New Zealand academy, while apparently less ageist in its policy on appointment, as reflected in the appointment of 'older' academic women, often with an established first career outside the academy, frequently appoints these academic women to a lower point on the salary scale, with little recognition of professional skill and experience previously acquired. The response of academic women to their position in the New Zealand academy in relation to appointment was varied and related to factors such as age, qualifications and professional experience. It was shown that these issues shape the experiences of academic women and play an important part in academic women's perceptions of and responses to their position in the academy.

The subjective perception of academic women in the UK and New Zealand was related to whether posts were contractual or 'tenured'. The *Report on the Status of Academic Women in New Zealand* (1986) maintains there is a clear pattern of tenure along gender lines in New Zealand universities. A high proportion of the academic women interviewed from universities in New Zealand held tenured posts (74 per cent) and their response to whether tenureship in the New Zealand academy is gendered, was varied and related to their own position within the academy. The situation around the tenured nature of posts in the academy in New Zealand remains somewhat uncertain and closely related to the political pressures the tertiary sector in New Zealand is experiencing. The perceptions of academic women who were themselves experiencing the reality of 'untenured' positions are less optimistic than those of women in tenured positions. The situation is compounded by an increasing tendency to move to short-term contractual appointments where contracts can be renewed on an annual basis for periods of up to ten years. This results in academic women finding themselves in untenured positions, lacking a career structure and with no opportunity for career development and advancement. This position is similar to recent developments in the UK.

Data drawn from the UK also show a high proportion of academic women (71 per cent) had job security. However, evidence from academic women in universities in the UK shows that it was those involved in research who were overwhelmingly employed on a contractual basis. The 'untenured' nature of contract research effectively locates this group of academic women outside the career structure of the academy and thus differentiates groups of academic women. The differentiated position of academic women in relation to 'tenure' had implications for the promotion process in the UK and New Zealand.

From the data drawn from academic women in New Zealand universities it was shown that, whereas a large number of academic women felt they had gained promotion in their current post, promotion was defined, in most cases, as the process of 'gaining tenure'. In addition, academic women in the New Zealand academy felt that the experience of promotion for academic women was a different experience from that for academic men.

The practices of the academy in New Zealand are discriminatory on the subject of promotion. On the issue of promotion, almost every academic woman interviewed had experienced what can be defined as discrimination. The exact form that discrimination took varied from the length and number of times suitably qualified academic women had applied for promotion and been turned down, to the position of academic women on contractual posts who have no opportunity to apply for promotion.

There is a clear pattern emerging in New Zealand universities which is that automatic promotion based on criteria of scholarship: doctorate; publications; and quality of teaching; appear no longer to be sufficient grounds for promotion. The increasingly limited funding regime within which the university system in New Zealand is being placed politically, is clearly resulting in fewer senior posts and increasing competition for those posts. It could be argued that the increasing 'democratization' of the promotion system, through the introduction on an informal basis of 'the peer review system' may be putting a gloss on an increasingly unpalatable system. Academic women are aware of the increasing demands being made on them in terms of gaining promotion. This position is confirmed by the comments of a senior academic woman in the post of professor at the University of Waikato. As she notes:

I think my impression of the past year is that promotion has been regarded more or less as axiomatic. If you didn't do anything terrible, you could expect to be promoted. You didn't actually have to do anything positive. That is going to change, is right now in the process of changing here in our school. Partly because the money is limited. It's going to go to those who can best justify a case for being promoted and that's going to lay much heavier emphasis than it's my impression has operated in the past regarding research and publication. That, then, potentially, is going to act against the interests of women with young families who are going to have to make that choice between career time and domestic time.

(Professor, University of Waikato)

Academic women in universities in the UK saw themselves as either having gained promotion and/or as having access to promotion opportunities. The position of academic women within the promotion framework of the UK academy revealed a number of issues. Seventy-five per cent of academic women saw themselves as having access to and/or experience of promotion. Academic women have differing experiences of and thus different perceptions of the promotion process. In terms of career structure, promotion opportunities and even the opportunity to discuss professional development, academic women are differentially located. The career structure for academic women in teaching provides for career development and promotion in theory, if not in practice, in contrast to women in contract research. Academic women undertaking contract research are disadvantaged because they are outside the promotion framework.

An important aspect of career development, as well as an integral element in promotion, is the process of appraisal. The appraisal process is more widely used as an aspect of career development in the UK than in New Zealand, where it is still a relatively new feature of university life and largely tied in a formal way to the process of promotion. Academic women's experience of appraisal was influenced by their academic position. There was a sense of dissatisfaction at the way the appraisal process operated in the New Zealand academy. Academic women raised the issue of the power relationship involved in the appraisal process and the masculinist discourses operating in the academy in cases of a male HOD and a junior female academic. Academic women in the New Zealand academy were not enthusiastic about the benefits of the appraisal process. In the UK the process of 'institutional' appraisal, as viewed by the academy, is an aspect of 'managed' career development and promotion for academic women and is frequently not seen as something that applies to academics on short-term or fixed contracts. It is an example of how academic women are differentially located within the academy.

The relationship between levels of productivity for academic women, based on the criteria of research and publications, set against the workloads that academic women carry has been shown to be problematic in the academy in New Zealand and in the UK. The results of wide-ranging and extensive empirical research and reports in New Zealand show that academic women are less productive than academic men in terms of a number of measures of research productivity including holding a doctorate, publications and presenting conference papers. Related to this point is the fact that academic women spend more time in teaching and less in research, have less well-established academic and publishing networks, and have less time to write and publish, undertake research and present papers at conferences. Further, academic women, as a result of their lower level of productivity are disadvantaged in terms of their career development and opportunities for promotion. Academic women's responses to the issues of productivity and workload show considerable variation. Academic women's experiences and subjective perceptions were seen to be related to academic factors such as: level of seniority; possession of a doctoral thesis; links to academic/professional networks; access to academic mentors; as well as to factors such as: ethnicity; feminist perceptions; professional commitments; marital status; and parenting (caregiving).

The same relationship between definitions and levels of productivity *vis-à-vis* workloads are apparent in the UK. There was unity among academic women regarding the issue of the workload/level of responsibility carried by academic women and the failure to translate these responsibilities into something more tangible such as promotion.

It has been maintained that given the differential performance of male and female academics there is an argument for re-evaluating the academic reward structure. Vasil (1993) argues, however, that this would reinforce:

the distinction between male academics as creators and shapers of academic scholarship and female academics as teachers disseminating an existing body of knowledge. Instead it is important that greater institutional support is given to female academic staff in their research activities. In particular academic staff need to be aware of possible gender biases in their departments in the allocation of teaching duties, whereby female academic staff are burdened with more time-consuming teaching.

(Vasil, 1993: 152)

Related to the issue of workload is the issue of the representation of academic women within the committee structure. Academic women in the UK and New Zealand are drawn on heavily for committee membership due to the need for balance and equity in the representation of academic staff on committees. Representation on committees is an important element both in the 'visibility' of academic women and as an aspect of the promotion process. However, academic women frequently find themselves serving on low level 'housekeeping' committees which are time-consuming, detract from research and publishing, and are at the departmental or faculty level as opposed to the university 'decision-making' level.

Academic women in New Zealand and the UK identified a number of areas of discrimination which are experienced by many academic women. However, beyond these, more specific areas of discrimination, related to the position of academic women in the academy, were identified. Academic women in New Zealand identified promotion, the issue of gaining tenured positions, as well as academic women being expected to have achieved the same level of productivity as academic men, if they had taken time out to have children, as general areas of discrimination. Other areas of discrimination included discrimination against 'late starters'; women with parenting (caregiving) responsibilities; and those who espoused feminist politics. In the UK, areas of discrimination identified by academic women included:

ability to publish	unequal pay
rights of authorship	recruitment
initial appointment	sexual discrimination
promotion	low pay
maternity leave	job tenure/temporary contracts
admissions/appointments	selection criteria
responsibility allocation	imbalances in staff/student gender ratios
political outlook	creche facilities
disability	

In addition, more general experiences of discrimination were identified including discrimination around: age; nationality; ethnicity; class; and parenting (caregiving).

Many academic women in New Zealand and the UK felt that discriminatory practices were difficult to define. One of the reasons for this difficulty in identifying discrimination is that many of the 'normal' discourses and practices within which academic women are located are experienced as discriminatory by academic women. As indicated earlier, the 'normalization' of a masculinist and patriarchal culture within the academy frequently makes discrimination difficult to identify as it is a normal part of academic culture.

Two additional areas were investigated as potential mechanisms for breaking down patterns of disadvantage and discrimination in the academy. The first was the issue of mentorship as a mechanism for breaking down 'gender stereotyping'; the second is the area of equal opportunities policy and practice.

Mentorship is frequently part of an equal opportunities policy in New Zealand and has been more widely researched and practised in Australia, New Zealand and the USA than in the UK. Academic women in New Zealand were generally positively disposed to the idea of mentorship on an informal basis rather than as part of a planned strategy, although there was a sense that the process of mentoring was too closely tied in to the issue of patronage and power in academic institutions. However, most academic women saw the practice of mentoring as a means of providing support and reinforcing academic women's sense of identity and academic scholarship in the academy.

Academic women in the UK saw the issue of mentorship and the practice of mentoring as more problematic than their colleagues in New Zealand, mainly for reasons of patronage. However, 50 per cent of academic women in the UK thought that mentorship was useful in breaking down gender stereotyping in academic relationships and 50 per cent said that they would support mentorship as an aspect of an equal opportunities policy.

In both New Zealand and the UK, the implementation of equal opportunities policy (EOP) in the UK and equal employment opportunities policy (EEOP) in New Zealand is a relatively recent development. The introduction of EOP and EEOP within universities in the UK and New Zealand has been an important first step towards the establishment of equity within the academy. However, concern was raised in the responses from academic women in the UK and New Zealand about whether equal opportunities policy is being effectively translated into practice. EEOP in New Zealand has gone further than EOP in the UK in introducing a stronger element of 'affirmative action' (positive action) which sets out to redress the inequities of the past and to establish 'target groups'. Academic women in the UK and New Zealand were united in their support for equal opportunities policy. However, academic women in both countries showed a wider degree of disagreement and difference around a number of equal opportunities issues, including: the effect of equal opportunities policy on academic relationships; on appointments; on the role of the equal opportunities officer; and on sexism in the academy. The different responses partly reflected the different experiences of academic women within the academy and partly the relative ineffectiveness of equal opportunities policies and practices in the academy.

Conclusion

In 1986, Margaret Wilson in the *Report on the Status of Academic Women in New Zealand* wrote of the need for both structural and attitudinal change in New Zealand universities. She also stressed the need for changes in the discriminatory practices in New Zealand universities as they were experienced by academic women (and Maori and Pacific Islanders). She argued that universities should develop 'a new set of criteria and practices that both acknowledge the position of women and endeavour to provide women with genuine equal opportunity' (Wilson, 1986: 6). In the mid-1990s, and on the basis of these research findings, and with the need for more thoroughgoing and extensive research on the workings of the academy in New Zealand and in the UK, Margaret Wilson and hundreds of academic women in the United Kingdom and New Zealand must remain both frustrated and disappointed.

Conclusion

The analysis of the position of academic women has been framed in this book within the context of contemporary feminist theoretical and methodological debates. In addition, feminist educational theoretical models have been drawn on to elucidate the specific cultural context within which the position of academic women in the academy needs to be understood. However, as is clear from the preceding analysis, 'feminist educational theories, although often produced within the ivory tower of academia, are nevertheless, also clearly framed within state discourses and structures' (Arnot, 1993a: 4). Feminist theoretical intervention, particularly in terms of influencing government policy on teritary education, has had a greater impact in some countries than in others, and this is particularly evident in terms of issues of equity and gender equality.

Acker notes that in the UK:

> Under the Conservatives, central government has intervened extensively in British higher education in recent years, for example by modifying the curriculum in initial teacher education, abolishing academic tenure, taking polytechnics out of local government control and later giving them university status, differentially, distributing funds so as to increase institutions accountability and dependence on market forces.
>
> (Acker, 1994: 145)

However, as Acker goes on to note, although the Conservative Government in Britain has pursued 'a number of aggressive higher education policies in recent years, none is concerned with gender equality' (Acker, 1994: 148).

Arnot (1993a: 188), in an article entitled 'A crisis in patriarchy? British feminist, educational politics and state regulation of gender', maintains that Conservative education policy in the 1980s was presented as a means of '"modernizing" gender relations (c.f. Weiner, 1989; Arnot, 1992a)', through its emphasis on equal opportunities and vocationalism. However, this polished technocratic veneer masked a reinforcement of patriarchal values with 'new distinctions . . . being made between the rights and responsibilities of male and female citizens in the public and familial spheres (Arnot, 1992b) and new forms of gender differentiation . . . being created within areas of knowledge' (ibid.). Elsewhere, Arnot (1992a: 52) notes with surprise how little opposition was shown by feminist educationalists and how little intervention was made by feminist theorists and policy analysts to Conservative education policy. She puts forward two reasons for this, the first being 'the legacy of social democracy as the main target of the sociology of education proved hard to break in all aspects of the discipline'. The second reason she identifies as the fact that in contrast to Reagan's aggressive Moral Right crusade in the US, 'the first Thatcher government made few explicitly "anti-feminist" statements' or made any attempt to repeal anti-discriminatory legislation.

Despite the limited intervention by feminists into government policy in Britain, Acker points to the continuing difficulties of being an academic feminist and David (1994) discusses the 'backlash' (Coward, 1992; Faludi, 1992) against feminism. David (1994: 6) points to some of the different strategies and solutions for transforming the academy, such as the development of 'feminist management and the recruitment of more women, particularly non traditional women students to study (Sperling, 1991; Riujs, 1993)'. However, there is no evidence that the recruitment of more women students has any impact on the representation of academic women in either specific subject areas or to the academy more generally. In addition, as David comments, 'These stronger political solutions of new styles of academic and educational management may, of course, contribute to the backlash to which I have already alluded against feminism in education and the academy (King, 1993; Ozga, 1993).'

David claims that attempting educational change through what she describes as 'feminist management strategies' is difficult. However, she notes the development of 'professional and senior management pressure groups such as "Beyond the Glass Ceiling"' (ibid.) which have been formed to 'develop strategies for women senior academics and/or managers in higher education' (ibid.).

While it is important that a range of strategies are adopted to address issues of discrimination and gender imbalance that face academic women, in order to confront gender and other divisions within higher education there also needs to be change at the level of policy making. In countries such as Australia and to a lesser extent New Zealand, feminist educational theorists have had a greater impact on the articulation of policy by national government and in their analysis of the relationship between feminism and the state more generally.

The work of a number of Australian feminist theorists has been influential in its development of the relationship between the role of the state and gender politics (Blackmore and Kenway, 1988; Eisenstein 1990; Franzway et al., 1989; Pringle and Watson, 1992; Watson, 1990, 1995; Yates, 1990, 1993; Yeatman, 1988, 1990). Kenway's (1988, 1990, 1993, 1994, 1995) work has been particularly important in these debates. Arnot summarizes her contribution:

> For Jane Kenway, the solution is to develop 'gender and educational policy analysis' as a new field of study. This field, she argues, already exists insofar as one can find a diversity of research literature which focuses upon state policy-making. Such literature includes, for example, analyses of the gendered assumptions behind government policies and studies of the impact of the women's movement and feminist struggles on state policy making processes. Contained within this new field are studies of the success and the limitations of legislation which attempt to promote equal opportunities for women.
>
> (Arnot, 1993a: 187)

Arnot goes on to point out that in Australia feminists are analysing 'state administrative apparatuses through which such equality politics are implemented'. In this context, reports on the ways in which feminists have been incorporated within the state bureaucracy as 'femocrats are especially instructive' (ibid.) (see Eisenstein, 1990 and Yeatman, 1990).

The work of Yeatman, Watson, Pringle, Kenway and Yates has done much to extend the range of feminist theoretical models in the analysis of the operation of power within state and institutional structures. The work of these feminist theorists has moved feminist theoretical models away from the traditional socialist, radical and liberal feminist framework analysis of state power. As Arnot (1993a: 190) observes: 'The result has been seen in the more sophisticated reinterpretations of the relationship between patriarchy as a political power structure and state formation.' Similar work has also been undertaken by Walby (1989, 1990) and Witz (1990, 1992) in the UK. The emerging theoretical frameworks within which feminism is operating in the 1990s has led to a deconstruction of 'monolithic' conceptions of power as being either 'patriarchal' or 'male'. Feminist theoretical debates have moved increasingly to a position where a critique of state and institutional framework and practices is framed within a broader analysis of 'gendered concepts of citizenship and male defined notions of democracy' (Arnot 1993a: 191) (see Connell, 1990; Pateman, 1980 and Watson, 1990).

Many of these Australian and New Zealand feminist theorists have drawn on poststructuralist and postmodernist frameworks to facilitate a broader based analysis of power. Yates (1993) examines the role of the Australian state in relation to feminism and policy formation. She explores the links between feminist discourses and policy debates and considers how the articulation of policy is sometimes a reflection of shifts in feminist educational theorizing in Australia. Yates outlines 'the historical shifts from a policy discourse around equality to that of "difference"' (Arnot, 1993a: 7). She also considers 'the ways in which feminist theory has been used and reinterpreted to construct new policy agendas by the Australian Labour government' (ibid.).

However, Yates goes on to show how feminist debates are 'managed' and 'contained' by the state. Yates (1993: 177) claims that a number of feminist writers 'have shown how the language of feminist politics is taken up but transformed and contained when it is made policy'. Yates argues that this is an element of the operation of state policy in liberal democratic societies which will 'continue to assert and "naturalize" the rule of law, the rights of individuals, the absence of structured conflict and inequalities of power, and will modify challenges to groups given political legitimacy (here, the Women's Movement) where they propose any fundamental challenge to these principles' (ibid.). In other words, in the framing of policies, the terms within which feminism is constituted in policy discourse are 'non-contestatory'. Equal opportunities issues, and affirmative action policy are coopted as an integral element in the democratic framework, as Yates (1993: 181) notes 'feminist issues, when they are taken as policy, are not located as part of "politics of contested discourse" . . . but as reforms achievable within the existing framework'.

The failure of the liberal democratic state to deliver real equality of opportunity has led to a shift in emphasis in feminist theorizing from equality to 'difference'. This shift presented challenges, as Arnot (1993b: 198) notes, to 'the liberal principles of individual rational autonomy and freedom'. In this context, Weiler provides an interesting analysis of the links between feminism, postmodernism, post-colonialism and theories of social justice. She claims that:

> Writing in the early 1990s, . . . feminist scholars have been influenced in varying degrees by the challenges of post-modernist feminist theory and by post-colonial critiques of racist and Eurocentric ideology and forms of domination. These theories have raised serious questions about the unexamined voice of authority in Western modernist theory, claims to universal truths set forth by a small and privileged group of theorists and the possibility of formulating theory or policy around concepts such as freedom, social justice or truth.
>
> (Weiler, 1993: 212)

This shift in emphasis has been described as 'the cultural politics of difference' (West, 1990) and has been incorporated into feminist, post-colonialist and anti-racist writing in the 1990s. It emphasizes the need to embrace 'multiplicity', 'heterogeneity' and 'diversity'. Weiler points out that it is an important part of the feminist project to highlight the fact that male theorists continue to ignore or sideline gender in their analysis. However, she goes on to note that:

> It is also clear that focusing on gender alone will not capture the realities of women's education. The challenge for feminist theorists is to try to take account of and comprehend the complexity of all forces of identity formation acting upon women in relation to educational institutions and policies in a rapidly changing world.
>
> (Weiler, 1993: 213)

What has become apparent in the 1980s and 1990s is that the underlying assumptions of white western feminism have been increasingly challenged on the level of privilege and power. There has been, as a result, a rethinking of feminist models with the emergence of more reflexive feminist theory and models which acknowledge and address 'the realities of women in different sites and with different histories' (Weiler, 1993: 215).

Thus, as can be seen from the research and findings outlined in this book and as has been noted by Arnot:

> Reassessing feminist politics in relation to education therefore clearly involves a complex narrative. It involves identifying different feminist visions, different strategies and tactics, and different types of research. But it also involves . . . understanding specificities. Historical and political specificities emerge in these accounts precisely because of their different national settings. So for example, the concepts of equity, equality, egalitarianism and equality of opportunity are defined differently in different social settings.
>
> (Arnot, 1993a: 3/4)

It is in this context of a more reflexive feminist theoretical framework which acknowledges historical and cultural specificity that the analysis of academic women in the UK and New Zealand academy has been presented.

Appendix 1: Researching the Academic Community – Methodological Issues

Methods of data collection and analysis

In the process of undertaking research on the position of academic women in the UK and New Zealand two types of empirical data were collected and analysed. Qualitative research methods (in-depth interviews and open-ended questionnaires) were used to collect data on the experience of academic women. In the UK, the research methods used were open-ended questionnaires, as the numbers of academic women involved, 200 in total, required a 'standardized questionnaire format'. In addition, 30 'in-depth interviews' were planned with academic women at universities in New Zealand, using a questionnaire format which paralleled the 'open-ended' questionnaires used in the UK. The choice of these research methods is considered below. In addition to the qualitative research methods and data, quantitative data in the form of statistics, collected by the Universities Statistical Record from universities in the UK, using a number of variables, was assessed and analysed. A more limited statistical profile of universities in New Zealand was undertaken using data from the New Zealand Ministry of Education.

A number of issues emerge in the context of understanding the process of research and analysis. It is important to emphasize at the outset that the *two sets of data* drawn from universities in the UK and New Zealand are *not directly comparable* and that no claim is made to this effect. The data were collected using different methods of data collection within different academic and cultural contexts. Thus, there are clearly recognized difficulties in terms of comparability, in relation to the nature of the findings and the claims that can be made regarding the data. As a result, considerable caution has been exercised in making claims from the findings based on direct comparability. However, where appropriate, parallels have been drawn in patterns of differentiation, discrimination and disadvantage for academic women in the academies of the UK and New Zealand.

Secondly, empirical data were also collected, using different methods, from academic women at universities in the UK and New Zealand based on their experience of the academy. It is important to establish the way 'experience' is framed in this research. Academic women's experience in the context of UK and New Zealand data is understood as both differentiated and contradictory. That is, traditional notions of a universal women's experience are challenged in this research. To this end analysis of the data is framed with an analytical focus which raises questions about concepts such as 'subjectivity', 'identity', 'difference' and 'location' for different groups of academic women and assessed in terms of how academic women experience, and are differentially positioned within, the academy in the UK and New Zealand.

Thirdly, empirical data in the form of statistics on the position of academic women at universities in the UK and New Zealand is drawn on to define and articulate more clearly how academic women are positioned within the academy around a number of issues including: grade of appointment; grade and method of employment; and distribution across subject departments. Statistical data drawn on in the UK is more extensive and was framed in terms of the specific requirements of this research. The data drawn on from New Zealand are more limited and have been adapted from government statistics for the purpose of this research. The methods of data collection in the two academic and cultural contexts are outlined below.

Quantitative data

Quantitative data in the form of statistics on the position of academic women at universities in the UK provide a statistical profile of the academy. Statistical data drawn from the Universities Statistical Record (USR) from universities in England and Wales provide the basis for an analysis of the position of academic women for the period 1970–90 around a number of specified variables including:

- The number of academic staff by gender in the following grade of post and the equivalent research grade: professor; reader/senior lecturer; lecturer at universities (England and Wales) as at 31 December 1991.
- Academic staff (teaching/research and research) by grade, sex and method of employment at universities (England and Wales) for the years 1980–91 as at 31 December in each year stated.
- Academic staff by grade, sex and specific cost centres* for the years 1972–91 at universities in England and Wales as at 31 December in each year stated.

  * specific cost centres covered:
  1 Clinical medicine   21 Civil engineering
  7 Nursing   31 Other social studies
  9 Biochemistry   34 Language based studies
  10 Psychology   37 Education
  15 Physics
  17 Mathematics

Due to changed patterns of collection and presentation of data by the USR, statistics for the period 1972–83 on cost centres appear in a different form and are categorized as main subject departments. Further, cost centre 31 'Other social studies' is not recorded as a separate category before 1983.

Analysis covers aggregates of universities in England and Wales. Specific information on individual institutions proved impossible to present, or to get, because of the requirement of confidentiality made by a number of universities. A number of universities were unhappy with the idea of presenting 'league tables' of statistics on the appointment and promotion of women academics. Aggregates of universities include, University of London, University of Oxford and Cambridge and universities in England and Wales. Comparable statistics from new universities and polytechnics in England and Wales proved more elusive. A period of communication between June–September 1992 failed to persuade the Department For Education (DFE) to assist in the production of equivalent statistical material to the USR for new universities and polytechnics.

Statistical data on the position of academic staff in universities in New Zealand proved difficult to obtain. Direct contact made with universities in New Zealand proved unsuccessful. Statistical data for the period 1970–92 taken from the Ministry of Education publication 'Education Statistics of New Zealand' was provided by the Association of University Staff of New Zealand (AUSNZ). As a result a more limited statistical profile of the New Zealand academy for that period is presented.

Qualitative data – UK

Twenty 'old' and 'new' universities in the UK were selected from a wider sample of 50 universities and polytechnics, consisting of 15 universities and five (new) universities and polytechnics. An initial selection of 50 old and new universities and polytechnics in England and Wales was made consisting of 37 traditional universities and 13 'new' universities and polytechnics. The selection of traditional and new universities attempted to combine traditional 'redbrick' and 'campus' universities. Universities and polytechnics were combined which had a 'traditional' reputation and ethos specializing in the classical arts or sciences, compared with universities and polytechnics with a strong reputation in the field of innovation and 'radicalism'. Letters were sent to registrars/admissions officers requesting information on equal opportunities policy, committees, and so on, as well as information on any policy/strategies used to encourage promotion opportunities for women academics.

Sample of Universities/Polytechnics (UK)

1. University of Bristol
2. University of Cambridge
3. University of Wales, Cardiff
4. University of East Anglia
5. University of Essex
6. University of Exeter
7. University of Kent
8. University of Leicester
9. University of London – Goldsmiths College
10. London School of Economics and Political Science
11. University College London
12. Oxford University
13. University of Sussex
14. University of Warwick
15. University of York
16. University of Central England (previously Birmingham Polytechnic)
17. University of Brighton (previously Brighton Polytechnic)
18. University of Westminster (previously Central London Polytechnic)

19. Oxford Brookes (previously Oxford Polytechnic)
20. South Bank University (previously South Bank Polytechnic)

The 20 universities/polytechnics were sent 10 copies each of questionnaires entitled 'Researching the Experience of Women Academics in Higher Education' (see Appendix 2). The questionnaires were forwarded to university registries. A memo was included requesting that the registries distribute the questionnaires to a 'range of women academics in different faculties and in different grade of post. Women academics by definition could include lecturers and research workers'. A large number of universities/polytechnics asked about distribution strategies. There was some concern/resistance from registries regarding confidentiality over the identity of the academics contacted and in regard to distribution. Clarification on this was given by phone and/or letter. The overwhelming response, on the part of the registries, was to deal with the matter in a helpful and conscientious way and despite a degree of clustering in the distribution most universities/polytechnics made a selection from across the disciplines (departments) and across the grades. Only two universities initially refused to distribute the questionnaires. The University of Wales at Cardiff returned the questionnaires on the grounds of lack of time. However, a covering letter and the return of the questionnaires to Cardiff resolved the issue. The University of Oxford proved more problematic. In the case of Oxford and Cambridge, the issue of distribution was potentially problematic because of the 'college' structure. A single college had been selected at both Oxford and Cambridge and the college contacted directly. In the case of the University of Cambridge, this proved unproblematic. In the case of Oxford University, the response was less successful. Questionnaires were initially returned from the college contacted and advice was given to forward them to the Central Admissions Office. The machinery of the Oxford Colleges clearly proved too unwieldy for the distribution of the questionnaires and a letter was finally received from another Oxford College on 15 January 1993, over 6 months after the questionnaires had been forwarded, advising that the questionnaires had been sent to 10 women academics in Oxford. Only one response was received from the University of Oxford.

Guidance on distribution, restating the guidelines already set out in the 'Memorandum to Registries' was given, and further clarification provided if required. Some clustering became evident where some universities had selected women in senior posts. But in the main most universities/polytechnics chose a range of women academics from across the grades and the disciplines. Of the 200 questionnaires distributed by registries, 108 (54 per cent) were returned. A further nine questionnaires were received in New Zealand, between June and July 1993 from a series of redirections in the UK. However, they proved too late to be included. Thus, the total number of returned questionnaires was 117. The breakdown of returns from different universities was as follows:

		Returns
1.	University of Bristol	5
2.	University of Cambridge	5
3.	University of Wales Cardiff	7
4.	University of East Anglia	7
5.	University of Essex	7
6.	University of Exeter	6
7.	University of Kent	6
8.	University of Leicester	6

9. Goldsmiths College London	6
10. London School of Economics and Political Science	5
11. University College London	3
12. University of Oxford	1
13. University of Sussex	6
14. University of Warwick	7
15. University of York	7
16. University of Central England (Birmingham Polytechnic)	7
17. University of Brighton (Brighton Polytechnic)	nil returns
18. University of Westminister (Central London Polytechnic)	nil returns
19. Oxford Brookes (Oxford Polytechnic)	7
20. South Bank University (South Bank Polytechnic)	7
+ unidentified institutions	3
+ 1 (wrongly sent) male academic	1
Total	108

Qualitative data – New Zealand

While I was undertaking the empirical research in the UK, I applied for and was offered the post of lecturer in sociology at a university in New Zealand. This move had quite profound implications for the research. The appointment to a lectureship in sociology at Massey University in New Zealand, made the original time-frame of undertaking 30 'in-depth' interviews with academic women in universities in the UK problematic. A decision was made in London in August 1992 to shift that dimension of the research to New Zealand. It was decided to contact at least two universities in New Zealand with a view to organizing 30 'in-depth interviews' with academic women at universities in New Zealand.

The rationale behind this decision had both pragmatic and positive research elements and implications. First, there was a real necessity for a decision to be made that would maintain coherence in the collection of data and crucially avoid loss of momentum. The data collection process in the UK had proved fascinating in its responses, efficient in its operation and implementation, and had aroused considerable interest and support from both institutions and individuals within the institutions. Secondly, there was a need for a practical and workable solution to a major logistical problem. Thirdly, there was also a need for a practical solution to maintain the continuity of focus, that is the focus on the experience of academic women in the academy. Fourthly, the research to be undertaken in New Zealand could be seen to provide some parallels with UK academics' experience of the academy, as far as this was feasible. It was recognized from the outset that no direct comparisons could be made between the data collected in the UK and New Zealand. Finally, the 'in-depth' interviews with academic women in New Zealand would highlight issues of role modelling and mentorship, as experienced by academic women, in a context where mechanisms, such as mentorship, have a higher profile in research terms and in practice.

In planning the 'in-depth' interview schedule the experience gained from an analysis of the questionnaire returns from women academics in the UK was used to sharpen the focus and define the issues more clearly. Planning for the 'in-depth' interviews involved a number of considerations. Emphasis was put on a greater degree of openness in terms of the structure of the questions with a large number of supplementary questions to encourage the widest consideration of issues. In addition, the phrasing of the questions was refined to avoid the use of terms which might confuse or lead to ambiguity. Emphasis was given to continuity of research objectives and issues. The in-depth interviews enhanced the qualitative focus of the research. The choice of universities for selection of women academics in New Zealand, was made partly to parallel the same process of selection that had been made in the UK.

Selection of universities in New Zealand consisted of traditional, established universities with fairly 'conservative' programmes of study, and the campus universities with a greater emphasis on a range of innovative programmes of study. The choice of universities in New Zealand had also been informed by a more specific reference point, that of my experience of applying for university positions in New Zealand. I had made applications to Waikato and Auckland Universities in New Zealand before being offered a post at Massey University; a lectureship in women's studies at Waikato, and a lectureship in education at Auckland. I had been shortlisted at Waikato, but not by Auckland. The process of communication with the different universities had given me an insight into 'the institutional climate' of universities in New Zealand.

The appointment to the post at Massey University in August 1992, and the commencement of the post in January 1993, led to a fairly early decision that, apart from a 'piloting' role, Massey University would not be used directly in the research. However, the pilot interviews at Massey University are drawn on to some extent in later chapters, as a number of reports had emerged from Massey University regarding the status of academic women (Cox and Poole, 1989; Massey University, 1989; Worth, 1992), and this was clearly a major area of concern and debate.

The two universities initially selected were the University of Auckland and the University of Waikato (Hamilton). The University of Auckland is a large established university which is strong in traditional subject areas, such as Anthropology, Psychology and Education. The University of Waikato is a smaller, newer university, with a number of innovative programmes and a large women's studies programme, and a very strong commitment to equal opportunities issues in both policy and practice. Contact by letter was made with these universities in September 1992 to gain permission and request information on women academics at the two universities. Permission was granted by the universities who provided information on all women academics with designation (grade) and subject area.

Selection of academic women – New Zealand

Whereas the selection of the 200 women academics in the UK had been made by university registries, in New Zealand the task of selection was undertaken by the researcher and author of this text. A number of reasons gave rise to this situation. First, there was a need for a clear distribution of academic women from different subject areas and different grades. The selection of academic women in UK institutions, as made by registries, had resulted in a degree of clustering of academic women in senior positions. This could have been purely coincidental, but there was a feeling that this process of selection on the part of registries could possibly have produced a more favourable response to promotion issues and equal opportunities issues more generally. Further, the nature of 'in-depth' interviews requires the establishment of a rapport with the interviewees in advance of the interview itself.

A more personal approach by letter establishes the nature and credentials of the research as being undertaken 'on behalf of' academic women and not as the basis of research 'on academic women' by the academy. The selection of academic women did not attempt to be representative of academic women in New Zealand universities as a whole, but to provide some insight into the experiences of academic women within the academy in New Zealand.

Interviews with academic women in New Zealand

In making the selection, a number of criteria were involved. Thirty women academics were selected from the Universities of Auckland and Waikato, and Massey University. A great deal of support and interest had been generated in the research as a whole at Massey University. In addition, and independently of any decision to include Massey University in the research, the University had provided through the Massey University Research Fund (MURF) monies to cover travel, interviewing and transcription costs for the in-depth interviews in New Zealand, which greatly facilitated the research work in New Zealand. Further, the Human Ethics Committee at Massey University had 'vetted' the work and supported the 'ethical' dimension of it. In this context, a Human Ethics Information sheet and Consent form was sent to all participants in the research to allow the transcribed material included in the interviews, to be recorded and published.

Selection was made on the same basis as selection had been made in the UK: 'distribution of a range of women academics across different faculties and in different grade of post'. Women academics by definition could include lecturer and research worker. Some of the women academics were well known in terms of scholarship in the area of feminism/women's studies. No deliberate attempt was made to include these women. If anything an attempt was made to limit those women academics who were involved in women's studies so that the research would not be skewed in a particular direction. An additional variable included in the selection of women academics in NZ was the date of appointment/duration/length of service. This information had been provided by the universities and selection was made from both longstanding and more recent appointments. Issues of tenure are clearly important here, that is the relationship between length of service and tenure was an area that needed to be explored in the interviews. There had been some movement of women academics either between the universities or beyond, and some alterations had to be made. However, the final selection remained as close as possible to the original selection. The category also included administrative posts, specifically equal employment opportunities officers (EEOO). Although these posts are designated administrative, rather than strictly academic posts, in terms of conditions of appointment, they have been included in the research because EEOOs in New Zealand are categorized as academic women and in addition they provided invaluable background on equal employment opportunities policy and equal opportunities issues in the New Zealand academy.

Thirty academic women at three universities in New Zealand were approached and asked to participate in the 'in-depth' interviews. Of the 30 academic women initially approached, 23 interviews were eventually undertaken. There was one refusal, one withdrawal because the interviewee was hospitalized, one was unable to reschedule the interview and did not return the questionnaire, and four did not reply (despite repeated attempts to make contact). The 23 interviews included: one professor; one associate professor; four senior lecturers (one half-time); 12 lecturers; one senior tutor; one assistant lecturer; three academic women (administration). Interviewees were drawn from the following subject areas and departments: law; women's studies; physics; sociology; maths and statistics; business studies; psychology; English; education; economics; Maori studies; social anthropology. An analysis of academic women's experience in the academy in New Zealand is outlined in Chapter 4.

Appendix 2: Questionnaire – Researching the Experience of Women Academics in Higher Education

All answers to questions will be treated in confidence.

Name (Optional)   Title

Position held   Institution

Section 1 – Present post
Q1 How many years have you held your current post?
Q2 Is this your first appointment with the university/polytechnic?
Q3 If *yes* what and where was your previous post?
     If *no* what post did you previously hold with the university/polytechnic?

Section 2 – Promotion opportunities
Q4 Please indicate which of the following posts you hold:
     a) Professor/head of department
     b) Reader/senior lecturer
     c) Lecturer
     d) Research worker
Q5 What type of tenure does the post carry?
     a) until retirement
     b) no specific term of contract
     c) fixed-term contract
     d) probationary
     e) other
Q6 Would you regard your present post as being a promotion on your last post?
Q7 If *yes* would you see the promotion in terms of
     i) academic status
     ii) job satisfaction
     iii) financial reward
     iv) a combination of the above
     v) other
Q8 If *no* can you give reasons

Q9 Does your post carry a recognized career structure?
Q10 Do you feel you have been made aware of promotion opportunities in your present institution?
Q11 Have you ever had a 'professional review'?
Q12 If *yes* could you outline any positive results?
If *no* could you benefit from a professional review? Outline ways in which you might benefit.
Q13 Have you ever been encouraged to apply for a more senior post in your present institution?

Section 3 – Areas of responsibility
Q14 Can you identify areas of academic responsibility in addition to those of lecturing/researching for which you have responsibility, e.g. pastoral function.
Q15 Do you serve on any departmental/faculty committees?
If *yes* please specify
Q16 Do you currently serve on any university/polytechnic committees/decision-making bodies?
Q17 How is membership of university/polytechnic committees decided?
Q18 *Either (for lecturing staff)*
Have you been given the opportunity to be involved in the establishment of new courses?
or (for research workers)
Have you been given the opportunity to make an input to the development of research programmes?

Section 4 – Equal opportunities policy
Q19 How important is an equal opportunities policy to the ethos of HE institutions?
Q20 Do you think the existence of an equal opportunities policy and practice has an impact on academic relationships?
If *no*, why?
If *yes*, please explain in what way?
Q21 What do you regard as the most important equal opportunities issues?
Q22 How significant is an equal opportunities policy, in the recruitment of students current under-represented in HE, e.g. black students, women returners, students with disabilities?
Q23 Has the university/polytechnic adopted an equal opportunities statement?
Q24 Does the university/polytechnic have an equal opportunities committee?
Q25 Are the aims of the equal opportunities committee available to all academic staff and students?
If *yes*, in what form?
Q26 How often does the equal opportunities committee meet?
Q27 Are you aware of the types of issues addressed by your equal opportunities committee?
Q28 How is membership of the equal opportunities committee decided?

Section 5 – Discrimination
Q29 What would you regard as issues of discrimination in a higher education context?
Q30 Does the university/polytechnic provide information in relation to the existence of procedures (e.g., grievance procedures) for dealing with issues of discrimination?

Q31 Are you aware of grievance procedures in the handling of issues of discrimination?

Q32 Have you experienced discrimination in your present post?
If *yes* could you briefly explain.

Q33 Are you aware of any issue of sexual harassment arising in your present institution?

Section 6 – Role modelling/mentorship

Role modelling – operates when a person is used as a reference for imitation using the model to create a feeling of self identification. Role modelling can be used as a strategy for breaking down stereotypes.

Mentorship – is the active process of positive sponsorship by more experienced persons towards less experienced persons, e.g. academic/student roles.

Q34 What areas of academic life do you think role modelling/mentorship most lend themselves to?

Q35 Do you think the idea of role modelling/mentorship is a useful strategy in breaking down gender stereotyping in academic relationships?

Q36 Have you any experience of mentorships as a strategy for breaking down gender stereotyping in academic relationships?

Q37 Do you think that the idea of mentorship is a useful one to extend to tutor/student relationships?

Q38 Would you say that role modelling is a useful strategy for adoption in the supervision/postgraduate researcher relationship?

Q39 Would you prefer to be given a choice in the matter of the gender of a supervisor?

Q40 Would the idea of role modelling/mentorship be a strategy you would support if adopted as an aspect of a university/polytechnic equal opportunities policy?

Thank you very much for contributing to this survey.
Please return using the attached envelope.

Appendix 3: Massey University – Academic Salaries in 1993**

	Step	Salary rate from 1.7.90
Assistant lecturer	1	31,200
	2	32,760
	3	34,320
	4	35,880 bar *
Lecturer	1	37,440
	2	38,584
	3	39,728
	4	40,872
	5	42,016
	6	43,160
	7	44,304
	8	45,448 bar §
	9	46,800
	10	47,944
	11	49,088 bar §
Senior lecturer	1	52,000
	2	54,184
	3	56,368
	4	58,656
Normal career point	5	60,944 bar §
	6	63,232 bar §
	7	65,156 bar §
	8	67,080 bar §
Associate professors		69,680 to 75,920
Professors		80,080 to 99,840

Note: An increment to the next higher step is automatic annually until a bar is reached.
* Assistant lecturers are employed for a maximum of three years. There is no promotion over the bar. Applications for lectureships are to be made in response to advertisements.
§ Promotion to a higher grade is on application or recommendation. To be eligible for promotion the appointee must have their appointment confirmed. This is usually considered in the third year of appointment.

8 October 1990
** The salary scale was revised on 1 January 1995. The new salary scale at Massey University is outlined on pages 150–1.

Notes

Introduction

1. 'Discourse' is a key concept in this research. Discourse is often used to refer to words or texts, but it can be understood as more than that. Michèle Barrett, in *The Politics of Truth: From Marx to Foucault* (1991), distinguishes between 'discourse theory' in terms of understanding a broader based notion of discourse in relation to social processes and power relations and 'discourse' in terms of an analysis of text or textuality. Discourse, as used here is discourse as used in the former sense and refers to ways of constituting meaning which is specific to particular groups, cultures and historic periods. It is drawn from the work of Michel Foucault, who used it to highlight the multifaceted nature of power. The concept of discourse is centrally important for feminism. To develop strategies which challenge masculinist hegemonic assumptions and social practices, feminism must investigate the discursive 'sites' of male power as they are articulated and legitimized in institutional structures of power and forms of knowledge. The academy is a typical example of this. Feminist poststructuralist Chris Weedon in her important text *Feminist Practice and Poststructuralist Theory*, explains 'discourse' as 'competing ways of giving meaning to the world and of organising social institutions and processes' (Weedon, 1987: 36). The meanings used to understand and form our experiences and shape institutional structures are an expression of a set of complex and multiple power relations. Thus, the term discourse facilitates an analysis of the organization and operation of power in academic institutions.
2. For Foucault 'discourse' is a set of 'practices' rather than structures. The term 'discourse' gives rise to a number of related concepts, since discourses exist in 'discursive fields' giving rise to 'discursive formations' or groups of regulated practices. Foucault (1984: 102) maintains that the point is, not where discourses come from, nor what interests they represent, but what 'effects of power and knowledge they ensure' and what makes their use necessary. There is no all-powerful subject which manipulates discourse; rather 'discoursing subjects' (that is, people who produce and deploy discourses) form part of the 'discursive field' (Foucault, 1991: 58).
3. Empirical investigation involves any factually based enquiry carried out in any

given area of sociological study. The emphasis of this type of investigation is concerned with issues of fact rather than theoretical or moral issues.
4. Aotearoa is the Maori name for New Zealand and means 'The land of the long white cloud'.

1   Jobs for the Boys: Academic Women in the UK, 1900–1990

1. It has been shown elsewhere (see Walby, 1990) that there was a shift in the form and degree of patriachy from a private to a public form. The significance of the debate was considered for locating education within the structures of public patriarchy in my doctoral thesis 'Gender, power and the academy' (1995). It was argued that whereas in private patriarchy, the primary strategy is exclusionary, within public patriarchy it is segregationist and subordinating. The academy as a public patriarchal structure was investigated and an attempt made to chart and assess the level of 'closure' that existed and continues to exist for academic women within the academy. To what extent such closure was enforced at a decentralized level was also investigated.

2. First wave feminism is sometimes known as 'old wave', 'the term usually refers to the mobilization of the suffrage movement in America and England between 1890 and 1920, although an organized "feminist" movement for women's suffrage had existed for 40 years earlier. Contemporary feminism dates from the early 1970s with the strength of "second wave" or "new wave" feminism and its search for the political bases on which contemporary feminism rests. But both movements share similar characteristics, for example a use of militant tactics. First wave feminism represents organized feminism with an emphasis on reforms in family law and economic opportunities, and international associations symbolized, in America, by the 1848 Geneva Falls Convention of Women. . . . The term "first wave" of course is only relevant for feminist movements in the Western world' (Humm, 1989: 78).

3. Earlier studies which cover the same general topic are less systematic in the breadth of their analysis. These studies include Rita McWilliams Tulberg (1975) *Women at Cambridge*, London, Victor Gollancz; Jessie Bernard (1974) *Academic Women*, New York, Meridian Books. A more recent article is John McAuley's (1987) 'Women Academics – a case study in inequality', A. Spencer and D. Podmore (eds) *In a Man's World: Essays on Women in Male Dominated Professions*, London, Tavistock.

4. The tables are drawn from Rendel's analysis of women academics at universities in the UK in the first half of this century. As Rendel indicates there is some difficulty in making comparisons between the figures for 1966 and 1975, as shown in Table 1.6. As she points out, the figures for 1912–1930/1 were drawn from the *Commonwealth Universities Yearbook*, whereas the figures for 1966 and 1975 were drawn from the returns to the University Grants Committee (UGC). This makes direct comparison between these years difficult because the UGC figures did not include statistics on part-time staff, whereas the *Yearbook* did include these figures.

5. The category 'Other' as used by the Universities Statistical Record refers to other related staff, e.g., research assistants, laboratory assistants, language support assistants.

6. The classification schemes were as used by the Universities Statistical Record for grade of employment, method of employment, and subject department/cost centre codes.

7. Rendel (1984) shows that the relationship between vertical and horizontal segregation is more complicated than might first appear. She observes that the representation of women in different subject areas showed greater variation in the 1970s than previously. Rendel shows that the distribution and representation of women academics in subject departments or cost centres is quite complex and the presence of academic women in professional posts has more than a numerical significance. As Rendel (1984) notes, even quite a small number of women professors can influence the shape of a subject, and the visibility of women in it, in terms of research, publications and appointments.

2   Women's Experience of the UK Academy

1. The distribution of women academics by grade of post in the categories of teaching/research and research resulting from the distribution made by registries/admissions officers did show clustering around some senior grades, particularly in the teaching/research area. The number of respondents in the categories of professor/HOD and senior lecturer was disproportionately high compared to their numbers nationally. The number of respondents who were lecturers was lower than their numbers nationally. The difference in gradings between polytechnics and universities produced four respondents in the category of principal lecturer from the grading system in the polytechnics. There is no equivalent in the university grading system. In addition, despite the clear instructions for distribution as indicated in the covering letter to registries defining women academics in terms of lecturing and researching staff, three questionnaires were sent to staff in administrative categories. One senior administrative officer and two administrative officers returned questionnaires and their views proved a valuable additional source of information. Within the teaching/researching category the respondents included: one senior research fellow, three research fellows and one teaching fellow. The distribution of women academics by grade of post in the category of Research tended to parallel the national distribution.
2. It is recognized in the UK that the concept of 'tenure' does not apply *de jure* since the Education Reform Act (1988).
3. Several respondents had difficulty with this section of the questionnaire and the difficulties varied from problems of definition of terms and problems of semantics to issues to do with the concepts of role modelling and mentorship. The unfamiliarity of British academics with the concept of mentoring is a key issue here, and this is apparent in the response of academic women at universities in the UK. Similar questions did not raise the same problems when used in the context of 'in-depth interview format' in New Zealand where the concepts are more familiar.
4. The *Report of the Hansard Society Commission on Women at the Top* (1990) notes, 'positive action' is a little used provision of the Sex Discrimination Act which allows 'positive action', in the sense of a degree of affirmative action, to be taken without breaching the principle of non-discrimination. 'The Sex Discrimination Act does not permit discrimination in favour of women in making appointments to public offices and posts, nor in recruitment' (Hansard Society, 1990: 95). However, the Act permits organizations to give 'women only access' to facilities for training that would assist them to obtain work in areas in which they are significantly under-represented. 'Positive action' strategies as defined by the Sex Discrimination Act 1975 and the Race Relations Act 1976 are identified by a number of universities.

5. Recent figures show that black students in the UK are *not* under-represented in terms of *access*, although their *experience* of university is a discriminary one (see Bird, 1996).

3   Academic Women in Aotearoa/New Zealand, 1970–1990

1. Aotearoa is the Maori name for New Zealand and is politically important in its post-colonial identity. As indicated earlier Aotearoa means 'Land of the long white cloud'.
2. Responses from universities in New Zealand to a request for information on this issue met with negative responses from all but one university.
3. The term 'Pakeha' is a contested one in New Zealand society. It is used to apply to those of white European descent who were born in New Zealand. It is also used to apply more generally to the white European-born immigrant who has 'settled' in New Zealand, but whose cultural reference points are European. It is sometimes used by Maori in more general political terms to refer to white non-Maori.
4. An 'indigenous feminist methodology' is one which acknowledges the specific cultural and historical dimensions of 'the local' in undertaking research. Typical of such an approach is Sue Middleton's development of 'life history' as oral history which she maintains is a more authentic feminist methodology for Aotearoa.
5. Margaret Wilson was until 1996 Dean of the Law School at Waikato University, New Zealand.
6. Figures for the ethnic distribution of the population in New Zealand based on figures for the 1991 Census are as follows:

	%
European	78.8
New Zealand Maori	9.6
Pacific Island, Polynesian	3.9
Chinese	1.1
Indian	0.8
Other	5.0
Not specified	0.8

7. The term 'continuance' has replaced 'tenure' in universities in New Zealand. However 'continuance', certainly for a wide range of posts probably up to professorial level, does not mean permanent or until retirement regardless of structural or organizational changes. There are a variety of different types of appointment being made in New Zealand universities, many on a short-term contractual basis. All posts, particularly non-contractual posts (i.e. those not on a fixed term), carry a probationary period of between 1–3 years. After that point 'continuance' may be granted. Tenure is used here in a conceptual sense to indicate permanence or a career position as opposed to a contractual position.

4   Academic Women's Experience of the Academy in Aotearoa/New Zealand

1. Selection was made on the same basis as in the UK, i.e. distribution of a range of women academics across different university faculties and in different grades

of post. An exact equivalent of the role of research worker in the UK appeared not to exist in the same form in New Zealand. As a result, the category lecturer (all grades) was mainly defined in terms of teaching/research. Two other factors played a part in the selection of women academics. The role of the equal employment opportunities officer (EEOO) is a relatively new one in New Zealand universities, as it is in universities in the UK. Although these posts are counted as administrative, as opposed to strictly academic posts in terms of conditions of appointment, they have been included in this research and are seen by many academic women as academic posts. An additional variable included in the selection of women academics in New Zealand was the date of appointment/duration/length of service. This information had been provided by the universities and selection was made from both longstanding and more recent appointments. Some of the women academics listed were well known in terms of scholarship, particularly those writing in the area of feminism/women's studies. An attempt was made to limit the inclusion of academic women in these areas so that the research would not be skewed in a particular direction.

2. The selection of women academics did not attempt to be representative of academic women in New Zealand universities. The findings of this research do not attempt to update the findings of reports such as the *Report on the Status of Academic Women at Massey University* (1989). However, the number of interviews undertaken compare well with the interviews undertaken by earlier research/reports. Wilson in the *Report on the Status of Academic Women in New Zealand* (1986) undertook 25 in-depth interviews, and the *Report on the Status of Academic Women at Massey University* (1989) included 18 in-depth interviews.

3. Inevitably, therefore, there will be a loss of data in terms of subject specific comments due to the need to avoid any linking of grade of post with subject area.

4. While there is some variation in the categories used, an attempt has been made to provide comparability with the reports cited earlier and documented elsewhere (Chapter 3). The categories used in relation to the reports on the status of academic women in New Zealand and which also frame the In-depth Interview Schedule are as follows:

   (i) Academic status (position on lecturer scale)
   (ii) Academic status at first appointment
   (iii) Tenure
   (iv) Level of teaching/workload
   (v) Promotion/career development
   (vi) Discrimination
   (vii) Committee membership
 (viii) Mentorship
   (ix) Equal opportunities issues

5. Vasil (1993) draws on self-efficacy theory as developed in the work of Bandura (1986) *Social Foundations of Thought and Action: Social Cognitive Theory.* 'According to Bandura, self-efficacy beliefs or individuals' perceptions of confidence in their ability to perform a given task, influence whether the task will be attempted, the amount of effort that will be expended and persistence in the face of obstacles. Self-efficacy beliefs are acquired and shaped by four main sources of information from the environment: performance accomplishments (successful performances of the given behaviour), vicarious learning or modelling, emotional arousal, and

verbal support and encouragement from others. Thus self-efficacy theory provides a cognitively based explanation of how socialization translates into behaviour' (Vasil, 1993: 144).

6. In New Zealand there are two dimensions associated with equal opportunities policy. The first, equal employment opportunities policy (EEOP), is the most common in terms of policy implementation and legislation. The second, equal educational opportunities policy (EDOP), is more concerned with general issues of equity in education and applies more to students, whereas EEOP really refers to academic and general staff appointments. Most universities in New Zealand, indeed the three universities used in the research, have adopted EEOP but not EDOP.

5   Gender, Power and the Academy: Patterns of Discrimination and Disadvantage for Academic Women in the UK and Aotearoa/New Zealand

1. ───

As of 1 January 1995 the lecturer scale has been amended and the revised scale is as follows:

Assistant lecturer	Step 1	31,500	*Research officer*	1	31,500
	Step 2	33,000		2	33,000
	Step 3	34,500		3	34,500
	Step 4	*36,000* bar		4	*36,000* bar

Lecturer	Step 1	39,500		5	39,500
	Step 2	41,000		6	41,000
	Step 3	42,500		7	42,500
	Step 4	44,000		8	44,000
	Step 5	*45,500* bar		9	*45,500* bar
	Step 6	47,000		10	47,000
	Step 7	48,500		11	48,500
	Step 8	*50,000* bar		12	*50,000* bar

Senior lecturer/senior research officer

	Grand-parented Scale	*Range 1*
	(To 1 January 1995)	(From 1 January 1995)
	Step 1 52,000	52,000
	Step 2 54,184	to
	Step 3 56,368	62,000 bar
	Step 4 58,656	
	Step 5 *60,944* bar	*Range 2*
	Progression to maximum step	62,001
	of new Range 1, i.e. $62,000, is	to
	available from 1 October 1995.	72,000 bar

Associate professor	*Range*
	69,000
	to
	77,000 bar

Professor		*Range* 80,000 to 102,000 bar
Tutor	Step 1	31,500
	Step 2	33,000
	Step 3	34,500
	Step 4	*36,000* bar
	Step 5	37,500
	Step 6	*39,500* bar
Senior tutor	Step 1	41,000
	Step 2	42,500
	Step 3	*44,000* bar
	Step 4	45,500
	Step 5	*47,000* bar
Graduate assistants		17,438

Bibliography

Acker, S. (1980) Women, the other academics, *British Journal of the Sociology of Education*, 1, 1, 81–91.

Acker, S. (ed.) (1984) *Women and Education: World Yearbook of Education*. London, Kogan Page.

Acker, S. (1987) Feminist theory and the study of gender and education, *International Review of Education*, 33, 419–35.

Acker, S. (1988) Teachers, gender and resistance, *British Journal of Sociology of Education*, 9, 3, 307–22.

Acker, S. (1989a) The problem with patriarchy, *Sociology*, 23, 2, 235–40.

Acker, S. (1989b) Making gender visible. In R. Wallace (ed.) *Feminism and Sociology*. London, Sage.

Acker, S. (ed.) (1989c) *Teachers, Gender and Careers*. Lewes, Falmer Press.

Acker, S. (1994) *Gendered Education*. Buckingham, Open University Press.

Acker, S. and Warren Piper, D. (eds) (1984) *Is Higher Education Fair To Women?* Guilford, Nelson.

Adkins, L. (1992) Sexual work and the employment of women in the service industries. In M. Savage and A. Witz (eds) *Gender and Bureaucracy*. Oxford, Blackwell Publishers/Sociological Review.

Aisenberg, N. and Harrington, M. (1988) *Women of Academe: Outsiders in the Sacred Grove*. Amberst, MA, University of Massachusetts Press.

Allen, F. (1990) *Academic Women in Australian Universities*, Monograph No. 4, Affirmative Action Agency. Canberra, Australian Government Publishing Service.

Arnot, M. (1981) Culture and political economy: dual perspectives in the sociology of women's education, *Educational Analysis*, 3, 1, 97–116.

Arnot, M. (1992a) Feminism, education and the new right. In M. Arnot and L. Barton (eds) *Voicing Concerns – Sociological Perspectives on Contemporary Education Reforms*. Oxford, Triangle Books.

Arnot, M. (1992b) Feminist perspectives on education for citizenship, paper presented at the *International Sociology of Education Conference, Citizenship, Democracy and the Role of the Teacher*. Birmingham, Westhill College.

Arnot, M. (1993a) Introduction. In M. Arnot and K. Weiler (eds) *Feminism and Social Justice*. London, Falmer Press.

Arnot, M. (1993b) A crisis in patriarchy? British feminist educational politics and state regulation of gender. In M. Arnot and K. Weiler (eds) *Feminism and Social Justice*. London, Falmer Press.

Arnot, M. and Weiler, K. (eds) (1993) *Feminism and Social Justice*. London, Falmer Press.

Association of University Teachers (1989) *AUT Woman*, No. 17. London, AUT.

Bacchi, C. (1993) The brick wall: why so few women become senior academics, *Australian Universities Review*, 86, 1, 36–41.

Bandura, A. (1986) *Social Foundations of Thought and Action: Social Cognitive Theory*. Englewood Cliff, NJ, Prentice-Hall.

Barrett, M. (1980) *Women's Oppression Today: Problems in Marxist Feminist Analysis*. London, Verso.

Barrett, M. (1987) The concept of 'difference', *Feminist Review*, 26, Summer, 29–42.

Barrett, M. (1990) Feminism's turn to culture, *Woman: A Cultural Review*, 1: 22–4.

Barrett, M. (1991) *The Politics of Truth. From Marx to Foucault*. Stanford, Stanford University Press.

Barrett, M. (1992) Words and things: materialism and method in contemporary feminist analysis. In M. Barrett and A. Phillips (eds) *Destabilizing Theory. Contemporary Feminist Debates*. Cambridge, Polity Press.

Barrett, M. and McIntosh, M. (1985) Ethnocentrism and socialist feminist theory, *Feminist Review*, 20, 23–47.

Barrett, M. and Phillips, A. (eds) (1992) *Destabilizing Theory: Contemporary Feminist Debates*. Cambridge, Polity Press.

Bartky, S.L. (1988) Foucault, femininity and the modernization of patriarchal power. In I. Diamond and L. Quinby (eds) *Feminism and Foucault: Reflections on Resistance*. Boston, Northeastern University Press.

Bell, C. and Roberts, H. (eds) (1984) *Social Researching, Politics, Problems and Practice*. London, Routledge.

Benhabib, S. and Cornell, D. (eds) (1987) *Feminism as Critique*. Cambridge, Polity Press.

Bernard, J. (1974) *Academic Women*. New York, Meridian Books.

Best, S. and Kellner, D. (1991) *Postmodern Theory: Critical Interrogations*. London, Macmillan.

Bird, J. (1996) *Black Students and Higher Education: Rhetorics and Realities*. Buckingham, Open University Press.

Blackburn, R.M. and Jarman, J. (1993) Changing inequalities in access to British universities, *Oxford Review of Education*, 19, 2, 197–215.

Blackmore, J. and Kenway, J. (eds) (1988) *Gender Issues in the Theory and Practice of Educational Administration and Policy*. Waurn Ponds, Deakin University.

Bognanno, M.F. (1987) Women in professions: academic women. In K. Koziara, M. Moskow and L. Tanner (eds) *Working Women: Past, Present, Future*. Washington, DC, Bureau of National Affairs.

Bordo, S. (1990) Feminism, postmodernism and gender scepticism. In L. Nicholson (ed.) *Feminism/Postfeminism*. London/New York, Routledge.

Bowles, G. and Duelli-Klein, R. (eds) (1983) *Theories of Women's Studies*. London, Routledge.

Braidotti, R. (1991) *Patterns of Dissonance: A Study of Women in Contemporary Philosophy*. Cambridge, Polity Press.

Bristol Polytechnic (1990) *Equal Opportunities Policy Statement*. Bristol Polytechnic, Bristol.

British Sociological Association (1975) *Report of the Working Party on the Status of Women in the Profession*. London, BSA.

British Sociological Association (1977) *Sociology Without Sexism: A Source Book*. London, BSA.

Brittan, A.(1989) *Masculinity and Power*. Oxford, Basil Blackwell.

Brittan, A. and Maynard, M. (1984) *Sexism, Racism and Oppression*. Oxford, Basil Blackwell.

Brown, C. (1981) Mothers, fathers and children: from private to public patriarchy. In L. Sargent (ed.) *Women and Revolution: A Discussion of the Unhappy Marriage of Marxism and Feminism*. Boston, South End Press.

Brown, H. (1992) *Women Organising*. London; New York, Routledge.

Burgess, R.G. (1985) *Issues in Educational Research: Qualitative Methods*. Lewes, Falmer Press.

Burgess, R.G. (1988) Conversations with a purpose: The ethnographic interview in educational research. In R.G. Burgess (ed.) *Conducting Qualitative Research*. New York, JAI Press.

Butler, J. (1990) *Gender Trouble: Feminism and the Subversion of Identity*. London, Routledge.

Byrne, E.M. (1987) *Role Modelling and Mentorship and Policy Mechanisms: The Need for New Directions*. Brisbane, University of Queensland.

Cain, M. and Finch, J. (1981) Towards a rehabilitation of data. In P. Abrams, R. Deem, J. Finch and P. Rock (eds) *Practice and Progress: British Sociology 1950– 1980*. London, Allen and Unwin.

Cain, M. (1993) Foucault, feminism and feeling. What Foucault can and cannot contribute to feminist epistemology. In C. Ramazanoglu (ed.) *Up Against Foucault. Explorations of Some Tensions between Foucault and Feminism*. London, Routledge.

Campbell, K. (ed.) (1992) *Critical Feminism: Arguments in the Disciplines*. Milton Keynes, Open University Press.

Cannan, J. and Griffin, C. (1990) The new men's studies: part of the problem or part of the solution. In J. Hearn and D. Morgan (eds) *Men, Masculinities and Social Theory*. London, Unwin Hyman.

Carby, H. (1982) White woman listen! Black feminism and the boundaries of sisterhood. In *The Empire Strikes Back: Race and Racism in '70s Britain*. Centre for Contemporary Cultural Studies, University of Birmingham. London, Hutchinson.

Chisholm, L. (1984) Comments and reflections on action research in education, *Girls and Occupational Choice Working Paper 2*. University of London, Institute of Education.

Chisholm, L. and Holland, J. (1984) Sinking or swimming: the experience of developing affirmative action collaborative research in schools, *Girls and Occupational Choice Working Paper 3*, University of London, Institute of Education.

Chisholm, L. and Woodward, D. (1979) The progress and experiences of women graduates in the labour market. In R. Deem (ed.) *Women and Education: A Reader*. London, Routledge.

Clegg, S. (1985) Feminist methodology – fact or fiction?, *Quality and Quantity*, 19, 83–97.

Cockburn, C. (1983) *Brothers: Male Domination and Technological Change*. London, Pluto Press.

Cockburn, C. (1985) *Machinery of Male Dominance: Men, Women and Technological Change*. London, Pluto Press.

Cockburn, C. (1986a) The material of male power. In Feminist Review Collective (ed.) *Waged Work: A Reader*. London, Virago.

Cockburn, C. (1986b) The relations of technology: what implications for theories of sex and class? In R. Crompton and M. Mann (eds) *Gender and Stratification*. Cambridge, Polity Press.

Cockburn, C. (1988) The gendering of jobs: workplace relations and the reproduction of sex segregation. In S. Walby (ed.) *Gender Segregation at Work*. Milton Keynes, Open University Press.

Cockburn, C. (1990) Men's power in organisations: 'Equal Opportunities' intervenes. In J. Hearn and D. Morgan (eds) *Men, Masculinities and Social Theory*. London, Unwin Hyman.

Cockburn, C. (1991) *In the Way of Women. Men's Resistance to Sex Equality in Organisations*. London, Macmillan.

Codd, J.A., Harker, R.K. and Nash, R. (eds) (1990) *Political Issues in New Zealand Education*, 2nd edn. Palmerston North, Dunmore Press.

Collinson, D.L. and Collinson, M. (1989) Sexuality in the workplace: the domination of men's sexuality. In J. Hearn, D. Sheppard, P. Tancred-Sheriff and G. Burrell (eds) *The Sexuality of Organisation*. London, Sage.

Committee of Vice-Chancellors and Principals of the Universities of the United Kingdom (1991) *Guidance on Equal Opportunities in Employment in Universities*. London, CVCP.

Connell, R.C. (1987) *Gender and Power: Society, the Person and Sexual Politics*. Cambridge, Polity Press.

Connell, R.W. (1990) The state, gender and sexual politics, *Theory and Society*, 19, 507–44.

Cook, J. and Fonow, M. (1986) Knowledge and women's interests: issues of epistemology and methodology, in feminist sociological research, *Sociological Inquiry*, 56, 2–29.

Coser, R.L. (1981) Where have all the women gone? Like the sediment of a good wine they have sunk to the bottom. In C. Epstein, C. Fuchs and R.L. Coser (eds) *Access to Power: Cross National Studies of Women and Elites*. London, Allen and Unwin.

Coward, R. (1992) *Our Treacherous Hearts: Why Women Let Men Get Their Way*. London, Faber and Faber.

Cox, S. and Poole, R. (1989) *Women and Promotion*. Unpublished Position Paper. Palmerston North, Massey University.

Crompton, R. (1987) Gender, status and professionalism, *Sociology*, 21, 413–28.

Crompton, R. and Jones, G. (1984) *White Collar Proletariat? De-Skilling and Gender in Clerical Work*. London, Macmillan.

Crompton, R. and Sanderson, K. (1989) *Gendered Jobs and Social Change*. London, Unwin Hyman.

David, M. (1989) Prima donna inter pares? Women in academic management. In S. Acker (ed.) *Teachers, Gender and Careers*. Lewes, Falmer Press.

David, M.E. (1994) Engendering education – feminism and the sociology of education. In S. Acker (ed.) *Gendered Education*. Milton Keynes, Open University Press.

Davis, D. and Astin, H. (1990) Life cycle, career patterns and gender stratification in academe: Breaking myths and exposing truths. In S. Lie and V. O'Leary (eds) *Storming the Tower: Women in the Academic World*. London, Kogan Page.

Deem, R. (ed.) (1980) *Schooling for Women's Work*. London, Routledge.

Deem, R. (1981) State policy and ideology in the education of women, 1944–1980, *British Journal of the Sociology of Education*, 2, 2, 131–43.

DEET (Department of Education, Employment and Training) (1993) *Higher Education Series, Female Academics*, Report No. 18, August.

Delphy, C. (1984) *Close to Home*. London, Hutchinson.

Derrida, J. (1976) *Of Grammatology*. Baltimore, Johns Hopkins University Press.

Derrida, J. (1978) *Writing and Difference*. London, Routledge and Kegan Paul.

Diamond, I. and Quinby, L. (eds) (1988) *Feminism and Foucault: Reflections on Resistance*. Boston, Northeastern University Press.

Di Nitto, D., Yancey, P., Harrison M. (1982) Sexual discrimination in higher education, *Higher Education Review*, 14, 2, 33–54.

Di Stefano, C. (1990) Dilemmas of difference: Feminism, modernity and postmodernism. In L. Nicholson (ed.) *Feminism/Postfeminism*. London/New York, Routledge.

Drakich, J., Smith, D.E., Stewart, P., Fox, B. and Griffith, A. (1991) *Status of Women in Ontario Universities: Final Report, Vol. 1: Overview*. Toronto, Ministry of Colleges and Universities, Government of Ontario.

Du Bois, B. (1983) Passionate scholarship: notes on values, knowing and method in feminist social science. In G. Bowles and R. Duelli-Klein (eds) *Theories of Women's Studies*. London, Routledge.

Duelli-Klein, R. (1983) How to do what we want to do: thoughts about feminist methodology. In G. Bowles and R. Duelli-Klein (eds) *Theories Of Women's Studies*. London, Routledge.

Duelli-Klein, R. (1984) The intellectual necessity for women's studies. In S. Acker and D. Warren-Piper (eds) *Is Higher Education Fair to Women?* Guilford, Nelson.

Eichler, M. (1986) The relationship between sexist, non-sexist, woman centred and feminist research. In T. McCormack (ed.) *Studies in Communication*, 3. Toronto, JAI Press.

Eichler, M. (1988) *Non-Sexist Research*. London, Allen and Unwin.

Eisenstein, H. (1990) Femocrats, official feminism and the uses of power. In S. Watson (ed.) *Playing the State: Australian Feminist Interventions*. London, Verso Press.

Eisenstein, H. (1991) *Gender Shock: Practising Feminism on Two Continents*. Boston, Beacon Press.

Eisenstein, Z.R. (ed.) (1979) *Capitalist Patriarchy*. New York, Monthly Review Press.

Eisenstein, Z.R. (1981) *The Radical Future of Liberal Feminism*. New York, Longman.

Eisenstein, Z.R. (1984) *Feminism and Sexual Equality*. New York, Monthly Review Press.

Evans, M. (1993) A faculty for prejudice, *The Times Higher Education Supplement*, 12 November.

Exum, W.H. (1983) Climbing the crystal stair: values, affirmative action and minority faculty, *Social Problems*, 30, 4, 383–9.

Faludi, S. (1992) *Backlash: The Undeclared War Against Women*. London, Chatto and Windus.

Ferguson, K.E. (1984) *The Feminist Case Against Bureaucracy*. Philadelphia, Temple University Press.

Finch, J. (1984) It's great to have someone to talk to: the ethics and politics of interviewing women. In C. Bell and H. Roberts (eds) *Social Researching: Politics, Problems and Practice*. London, Routledge.

Finch, J. (1986) *Research and Policy: The Use of Qualitative Methods in Social and Educational Research*. Lewes, Falmer Press.

Finkelstein, M.J. (1984) *The American Academic Professor*. Colombus, Ohio State University Press.

Flax, J. (1990) Postmodernism and gender relations in feminist theory. In L. Nicholson (ed.) *Feminism/Postmodernism*. London/New York, Routledge.

Fonow, M. and Cook, J. (eds) (1991) *Beyond Methodology: Feminist Scholarship as Lived Research*. Bloomington, Indiana University Press.

Foucault, M. (1972) *The Archaeology of Knowledge*. London, Tavistock.

Foucault, M. (1973a) *The Order of Things: An Archaeology of the Human Sciences*. New York, Vintage Books.

Foucault, M. (1973b) *The Birth of the Clinic*. London, Tavistock.

Foucault, M. (1977) *Discipline and Punish: The Birth of the Prison*. Harmondsworth, Penguin.

Foucault, M. (1980a) Truth and power. In C. Gordon (ed.) *Power/Knowledge – Selected Interviews and other Writings 1972–77 By Michel Foucault*. Brighton, Harvester Press.

Foucault, M. (1980b) Two lectures. In C. Gordon (ed.) *Power/Knowledge – Selected Interviews and other Writings 1972–77 by Michel Foucault*. Brighton, Harvester Press.

Foucault, M. (1980c) *Power/Knowledge: Selected Interviews and other Writings 1972–1977*. C. Gordon (ed.) and C. Gordon, L. Marshall, J. Mepham, K. Soper (trans). New York, Pantheon Books.

Foucault, M. (1982) The subject and power, L. Sawyer (trans.). In H.L. Dreyfus and P. Rabinow (eds) *Michel Foucault: Beyond Structuralism and Hermeneutics*. Chicago, University of Chicago Press.

Foucault, M. (1984) *The History of Sexuality, Vol.1*. London, Allen Lane.

Foucault, M. (1988) On power. In L. Kritzman (ed.) *Michel Foucault: Politics, Philosophy, Culture: Interviews and other Writings 1977–1984*. London, Routledge.

Foucault, M. (1991) Politics and the study of discourse. In G. Burchell, C. Gordon and P. Miller (eds) *The Foucault Effect: Studies in Governmentality*. London, Harvester.

Franzway, S., Court D. and Connell, R.W. (eds) (1989) *Staking a Claim: Feminism, Bureaucracy and the State*. Sydney, Allen and Unwin.

Fraser, N. (1989) *Unruly Practices. Power, Discourse and Gender in Contemporary Social Theory*. Cambridge, Polity Press.

Fraser, N. and Nicholson, L. (1990) Social criticism without philosophy. In L. Nicholson (ed.) *Feminism and Postmodernism*. London/New York, Routledge.

Freeman, B.C. (1977) Faculty women in the American university. In P. Altback (ed.) *Comparative Perspectives on the Academic Profession*. New York, Praeger.

Fulton, O. (1993) Women catch up, *The Times Higher Education Supplement*, 16 July, ii–iii.

Gatens, M. (1991) *Feminism and Philosophy*. Cambridge, Polity Press.

Gatens, M. (1994) The dangers of a woman-centred philosophy. In *The Polity Reader in Gender Studies*. Cambridge, Polity Press.

Gavey, N. (1989) Feminist poststructuralism and discourse analysis: contributions to feminist psychology, *Psychology of Women Quarterly*, 13, 459–75.

Gelb, J. (1989) *Feminism and Politics*. Berkeley, University of California Press.

Giddens, A., Held, D., Hillman, D., Hubert, D., Seymour, D., Stanworth, M. and Thompson, J. (eds) (1994) *The Polity Reader in Gender Studies*. Cambridge, Polity Press.

Graham, H. (1983) Do her answers fit his questions: women and the survey method. In E. Gamarnikow, D. Morgan, J. Purvis and D. Taylorson (eds) *The Public and the Private*. London, Heinemann.

Grant, J. (1987) I feel therefore I am: a critique of female experience as the basis for a feminist epistemology, *Women and Politics*, 17, Fall, 99–114.

Griffiths, M. (1980) Women in higher education: a case study of the Open University. In R. Deem (ed.) *Schooling for Women's Work*. London, Routledge.

Grimshaw, J. (1993) Practices of freedom. In C. Ramazanoglu (ed.) *Up Against Foucault. Explorations of Some Tensions between Foucault and Feminism*. London, Routledge.

Grosz, E. (1986) What is feminist theory? In C. Pateman and E. Grosz (eds) *Feminist Challenges: Social and Political Theory*. Sydney, Allen and Unwin.

Grosz, E. (1990a) Contemporary theories of power and subjectivity. In S. Gunew (ed.) *Feminist Knowledge: Critique and Construct*. London, Routledge.

Grosz, E. (1990b) A note on essentialism and difference. In S. Gunew (ed.) *Feminist Knowledge: Critique and Construct*. London, Routledge.

Gunew, S. (1990) Feminist knowledge: critique and construct. In S. Gunew (ed.) *Feminist Knowledge: Critique and Construct*. London, Routledge.

Halberg, M. (1992) Feminist epistemology: an impossible project, (extracted). In S. Hall, D. Held and T. McGrew (eds) *Modernity and Its Futures*. Cambridge, Polity Press.

Halford, S. (1992) Feminist change in a patriarchal organisation: the experience of women's initiatives in local government and implications for feminist perspectives on state institutions. In M. Savage and A. Witz (eds) *Gender and Bureaucracy*. Oxford, Blackwell Publishers/The Sociological Review.

Halsey, A.H. (1990) The long open road to equality, *Times Higher Education Supplement*, 20 February.

Halsey, A.H. (1992) *Decline of Donnish Dominion: The British Academic Professions in the Twentieth Century*. Oxford, Clarendon.

Halsey, A.H. (1992a) *Opening Wide the Doors of Higher Education*. Briefings for the Paul Hamlyn Foundation, National Commission on Education 1–4 August. Oxford.

Halsey, A.H. and Trow, M. (1971) *The British Academics*. London, Faber and Faber.

Hammersley, M. (1992) On feminist methodology, *Sociology*, 26, 2, 187–206.

Hanmer, J. (1990) Men, power and the exploitation of women. In J. Hearn and D. Morgan (eds) *Men, Masculinities and Social Theory*. London, Unwin Hyman.

Hansard Society for Parliamentary Government (1990) *Report of the Hansard Society Commission on Women at the Top*. London, The Hansard Society.

Haraway, D. (1988) Situated knowledges: the science question in feminism and the privilege of partial perspective, *Feminist Studies*, 14, 3.

Harding, J. (ed.) (1986) *Perspectives on Gender and Science*. Lewes, Falmer Press.

Harding, S. (1986) *The Science Question in Feminism*. Milton Keynes, Open University Press.

Harding, S. (ed.) (1987a) *Feminism and Methodology*. Milton Keynes, Open University Press.

Harding, S. (1987b) Conclusions: epistemological questions. In S. Harding (ed.) *Feminism and Methodology*. Milton Keynes, Open University Press.

Harding, S. (1990) Feminism, science and the anti-enlightenment critique. In L. Nicholson (ed.) *Feminism/Postmodernism*. London, Routledge.

Harding, S. (1991) *Whose Science? Whose Knowledge?: Thinking From Women's Lives*. Milton Keynes, Open University Press.

Harding, S. (1993) Re-inventing ourselves as other: more new agents of history and knowledge. In L. Kauffman (ed.) *American Feminist Thought at Century's End*. Oxford, Basil Blackwell.

Hartmann, H. (1979) Capitalism, patriarchy and job segregation by sex. In Z.R. Eisenstein (ed.) *Capitalism, Patriarchy and the Case for Socialist Feminism*. New York, Monthly Review Press.

Hartsock, N. (1987) The feminist standpoint: Developing the ground for a specifically feminist historical materialism. In S. Harding (ed.) *Feminism and Methodology.* Milton Keynes, Open University Press.

Hartsock, N. (1990) Foucault on power: a theory for women? In L. Nicholson (ed.) *Feminism/Postmodernism.* London; New York, Routledge.

Hearn, J. (1982) Notes on patriarchy, professionalization and the semi-professions, *Sociology,* 16, 2, 184–202.

Hearn, J. (1992) *Men in the Public Eye – The Construction and Deconstruction of Public Men and Public Patriarchies.* London, Routledge.

Hearn, J. and Morgan, D. (eds) (1990) *Men, Masculinities and Social Theory.* London, Unwin Hyman.

Hearn, J. and Parkin, P.W. (1987) *'Sex' at 'Work': The Power and Paradox of Organisation Sexuality.* Brighton, Wheatsheaf.

Hearn, J. and Parkin, P.W. (1992) Women, men, management and leadership, in N. Adler and D. Izraeli (eds) *Women in Management Worldwide,* 2nd edn. New York, M.E. Sharpe.

Hearn, J., Sheppard, D.L., Tancred-Sheriff, P. and Burrell, G. (1989) *The Sexuality of Organisation.* London, Sage.

Hekman, S. (1990) *Gender and Knowledge: Elements of a Postmodern Feminism.* Cambridge, Polity Press.

Helmreich, R.L., Spence, J.T., Beane, W.E., Lucker, G.W. and Matthews, K.A. (1980) Making it in academic psychology: demographic and personality correlates of attainment, *Journal of Personality and Social Psychology,* 39, 896–908.

Heward, C. and Taylor, P. (1992) Women at the top in higher education: Equal opportunities policies in action? *Policy And Politics,* 20, 1.

Hinds, H., Phoenix, A. and Stacey, J. (eds) (1992) *Working Out: New Directions in Women's Studies.* London, Falmer Press.

Hirsch, M. and Keller, E.F. (eds) (1990) *Conflicts of Feminism.* New York, Routledge.

hooks, b. (1984) *Feminist Theory: From Margin to Centre.* London, South End Press.

Hughes, B. (1980) Women in the professions in New Zealand. In P. Bunkle (ed.) *Women in New Zealand Society.* Wellington, Allen and Unwin.

Humm, M. (1989) *The Dictionary of Feminist Theory.* Hemel Hempstead, Harvester Wheatsheaf.

Irwin, K. (1988) Maori, feminist academic, *Sites,* 17, 30–8.

Irwin, K. (1992) Towards theories of Māori feminism. In R. Du Plessis (ed.) *Feminist Voices.* Auckland, Oxford University Press.

Jackson, D. (1980) Women working in higher education: a review of the position of women in higher education and policy developments, *Higher Education Quarterly,* 44, 4, Autumn, 297–324.

Jayaratne, T.E. (1983) The value of quantitative methodology for feminist research. In G. Bowles and R. Duelli-Klein (eds) *Theories of Women's Studies.* London, Routledge.

Jones, J.M. and Lovejoy, F.H. (1980) Discrimination against women academics in Australian universities, *Signs,* 5, 3, Spring, 518–26.

Kanter, R.M. (1975) Women in the structure of organisations. In M. Millman and R.M. Kanter (eds) *Another Voice.* New York, Anchor Books.

Kauffman, L. (ed.) (1993) *American Feminist Thought at Century's End – A Reader.* Oxford, Basil Blackwell.

Kelly, A. (1978) Feminism and research, *Women's Studies International Quarterly,* 225–32.

Kelly, J. (1979) The doubled vision of feminist theory: a postscript to the 'women and power' conference, *Feminist Studies,* 5, 1, Spring, 216–27.

Kenway, J. (1988) *Practice of Educational Administration and Policy*. Waurn Ponds, Deakin University.

Kenway, J. (1990) *Gender and Education Policy: A Call for New Directions*. Waurn Ponds, Deakin University.

Kenway, J. (1993) Gender matters in educational administration and policy: a feminist introduction. In J. Blackmore and J. Kenway (eds) *Gender Issues in the Theory and Practice of Educational Administration and Policy*. Waurn Ponds, Deakin University.

Kenway, J. (1994) *Economising Education: The Post-Fordist Directions*. Waurn Ponds, Deakin University.

Kenway, J. (ed.) (1995) *Marketing Education: Some Critical Issues*. Waurn Ponds, Deakin University.

King, C. (ed.) (1993) *Through the Glass Ceiling: Effective Senior Management Development for Women*. Wirral, Tudor.

Lather, P. (1989) Postmodernism and the discourses of emancipation: precedents, parallels and interruptions, *Women's Studies Association (NZ) Conference Papers 1989*. Lincoln, WSA.

Lather, P. (1991) *Getting Smart. Feminist Research and Pedagogy within the Postmodern*. London, Routledge.

Lees, S. (1991) Feminist politics and women's studies: struggle, not incorporation. In J. Aaron and S. Walby (eds) *Out of the Margins: Women's Studies in the Nineties*. London, Falmer.

Lodge, J. (1975) New Zealand women academics: some observations on their status, aspirations and professional achievement, unpublished paper. Political Studies Department, University of Auckland.

Lown, J. (1990) *Women and Industrialization*. Cambridge, Polity Press.

MacKinnon, C. (1979) *The Sexual Harassment Of Working Women: A Case of Sex Discrimination*. New Haven, Yale University Press.

MacLeod, M. and Saraga, E. (1988) Challenging the orthodoxy: towards a feminist theory and practice, *Feminist Review*, 28, 16–55.

Manchester Polytechnic (1991) *Equal Opportunities Policy*. Manchester Polytechnic, Manchester.

Martin, B. (1988) Feminism, criticism and Foucault. In I. Diamond and L. Quinby (eds) *Feminism and Foucault*. Boston, Northeastern University Press.

Massey University (1989) *Report on the Status of Academic Women at Massey University*. Palmerston North, Massey University.

Maynard, M. (1989) Theory and theorising. In R. Burgess (ed.) *Investigating Society*. York, Longman.

McAuley, J. (1987) Women academics – a case study in inequality. In A. Spencer and D. Podmore (eds) *In a Man's World: Essays on Women in Male Dominated Professions*. London, Tavistock.

McNay, L. (1992) *Foucault and Feminism*. Cambridge, Polity Press.

McNeil, M. (1993) Dancing with Foucault. Feminism and power-knowledge. In C. Ramazanoglu (ed.) *Up Against Foucault. Explorations of Some Tensions between Foucault and Feminism*. London, Routledge.

McRobbie, A. (1982) The politics of feminist research: between talks, text and action, *Feminist Review*, 12, 46–58.

McWilliams-Tullberg, R. (1975) *Women at Cambridge*. London, Gollancz.

Middleton, S. (1983) On being a feminist educationalist doing research on being a feminist educationalist . . . Reflections on life history analysis as feminist research methodology. Conference paper. Australian Association for Research in Education. Canberra, AARE.

Middleton, S. (1983) Sexism, racism, consciousness raising and praxis: some reflections and dilemmas of a university teacher, *New Zealand Cultural Studies Working Group Journal*, 6, 23–36.

Middleton, S. (1984) The sociology of women's education as a field of academic study, *Discourse*, 5, 1, October, 42–62.

Middleton, S. (1987) Schooling and radicalisation: Life histories of New Zealand feminist teachers, *British Journal of Sociology of Education*, 8, 2, 169–89.

Middleton, S. (1988) Researching feminist educational life histories. In S. Middleton (ed.) *Women and Education in Aotearoa*. Wellington, Allen and Unwin.

Middleton, S. (ed.) (1988) *Women and Education in Aotearoa*. Wellington, Allen and Unwin.

Middleton, S. (1989) Educating feminists: a life history study. In S. Acker (ed.) *Teachers, Gender and Careers*. Lewes, Falmer Press.

Middleton, S. (1993) *Educating Feminists: Life Histories and Pedagogy*. New York, Teachers College Press, Columbia University.

Middleton, S. (1993) A post-modern pedagogy for the sociology of women's education. In M. Arnot and K. Weiler (eds) *Feminism and Social Justice*, London, Falmer Press.

Middleton, S., Codd, J. and Jones, A. (eds) (1990) *New Zealand Education Policy Today: Critical Perspectives*. Wellington, Allen and Unwin.

Mies, M. (1983) Towards a methodology for feminist research. In G. Bowles and R. Duelli-Klein (eds) *Theories of Women Studies*. London, Routledge.

MoEdNZ (Ministry of Education New Zealand) (1990, 1991, 1992, 1993) *Education Statistics of New Zealand*. Wellington, Ministry of Education.

Moi, T. (1985) Power, sex and subjectivity: feminist reflections on Foucault, *Paragraph*, 5, 95–102.

Moi, T. (1989) Men against patriarchy. In L. Kauffman (ed.) *Gender and Theory: Dialogues on Feminist Criticism*. Oxford, Basil Blackwell.

Morgan D.H.J. (1981) Men, masculinity and the process of sociological enquiry. In H. Roberts (ed.) *Doing Feminist Research*. London, Routledge and Kegan Paul.

Morgan, K.P. (1987) The perils and paradoxes of feminist pedagogy, *Resources for Feminist Research*, 16, 3, 48–52.

Morgan, K.P. (1987) Bibliography of feminist philosophy and theory, *Resources for Feminist Research*, 16, 3, 89–103.

Morris-Matthews, K. (1993) 'For and about women: Women's Studies in New Zealand universities 1973–1990'. Unpublished DPhil thesis. University of Waikato.

NTEU (National Tertiary Education Union) (1995) *Limited Access: Women's Disadvantage in Higher Education Employment*. Melbourne, NTEU.

Nicholson, L. (ed.) (1990) *Feminism/Postmodernism*, London; New York, Routledge.

O'Neill, A.M. (1992) The equal opportunity myth: women in New Zealand educational institutions. In Su Olssen (ed.) *The Gender Factor*. Palmerston North, Dunmore Press.

Oakley, A. (1981) Interviewing women: a contradiction in terms. In H. Roberts (ed.) *Doing Feminist Research*. London, Routledge.

Over, R. (1982) Research productivity and the impact of male and female psychologists, *American Psychologist*, 37, 24–31.

Ozga, J. (ed.) (1993) *Women in Educational Management*. Buckingham, Open University Press.

Page, D. (1986) The first lady graduates: women with degrees from Otago University, 1885–1900. In B. Brooks, C. Macdonald and M. Tennant (eds), *Women in History: Essays on European Women in New Zealand*. Wellington, Allen and Unwin.

Park, A.M. (1991) Women working in higher education. Unpublished MPhil Thesis. University of Oxford.

Park, A.M. (1992) Women, men, and the academic hierarchy: exploring the relationship between rank and sex, *Oxford Review of Education*, 18, 3, 227–39.

Pateman, C. (1980) Women and consent, *Political Theory*, 8, 2, 149–68.

Pateman, C. (1988) *The Sexual Contract*. Cambridge, Polity Press.

Pateman, C. and Grosz, E. (eds) (1986) *Feminist Challenges: Social and Political Theory*. Sydney, Allen and Unwin.

Pere, R. (1983) *Ako: Concepts and Learning in Maori Traditions*, Monograph. Hamilton, University of Waikato.

Pettmann, J. (1988) All the women are white. All the blacks are men . . . racism, sexism and sociology. Paper presented at the Australian Sociological Association Conference. Canberra, Australia National University.

Phillips, Anne (1987) *Feminism and Equality*. Oxford, Basil Blackwell.

Phillips, A. (1991) *Engendering Democracy*. Cambridge, Polity Press.

Phillips, A. (1992) Universal pretentions in political thought. In M. Barrett and A. Phillips (eds) *Destabilizing Theory*. Cambridge, Polity Press.

Phizacklia, Annie (1988) Entrepreneurship, ethnicity and gender. In S. Westwood and P. Bhachu (eds) *Enterprising Women: Ethnicity, Economy and Gender Relations*. London, Routledge.

Pohatu, G.H. (1988) The Watts report: implications for the Maori presence in southern universities: an opinion, *New Zealand Journal of Educational Studies*, 23, 1, 75–85.

Pringle, R. (1989) *Secretaries Talk: Sexuality, Power and Work*. London, Verso.

Pringle, R. and Watson, S. (1990) Fathers, brothers, mates: the fraternal state in Australia. In S. Watson (ed.) *Playing the State*. London, Verso.

Pringle, R. and Watson, S. (1992) 'Women's interests' and the post-structuralist state. In M. Barrett and A. Phillips (eds) *Destablizing Theory*. Cambridge, Polity Press.

Rabinow, P. (ed.) (1984) *The Foucault Reader*. London, Penguin.

Ramazanoglu, C. (1986) Ethnocentricism and socialist feminist theory: a response to Barrett and McIntosh, *Feminist Review*, 22, 83–6.

Ramazanoglu, C. (1987) Sex and violence in academic life or you can keep a good woman down. In J. Hanmer and M. Maynard (eds) *Women, Violence and Social Control*. London, Macmillan.

Ramazanoglu, C. (1989) *Feminism and the Contradiction of Oppression*. London, Routledge.

Ramazanoglu, C. (1992) Feminist methodology: male reason versus female empowerment, *Sociology*, 26, 2, May, 207–12.

Ramazanoglu, C. (ed.) (1993) *Up Against Foucault. Explorations of Some Tensions between Foucault and Feminism*. London, Routledge.

Ramazanoglu, C. and Holland, J. (1993) Women's sexuality and men's appropriation of desire. In C. Ramazanoglu (ed.) *Up Against Foucault. Explorations of Some Tensions between Foucault and Feminism*. London, Routledge.

Ransom, J. (1993) Feminism, difference and discourse: the limits of discursive analysis for feminism. In C. Ramazanoglu (ed.) *Up Against Foucault. Explorations of Some Tensions between Foucault and Feminism*. London, Routledge.

Reekie, G. (1994) Feminist history after Foucault. Paper presented at *Foucault: The Legacy Conference*. Surfers Paradise, Australia, July 1994.

Rees, T. (1989) Contract research: a new career structure? *AUT Woman*, 16, 1, 4.

Reinharz, S. (1983) Experiential analysis: A contribution to feminist research methodology. In G. Bowles and R. Duelli-Klein (eds) *Theories in Women's Studies*. London, Routledge.

Reinharz, S. (1992) *Feminist Methods in Social Research*. Oxford, Oxford University Press.

Rendel, M. (1980) How many women academics 1912–76? In R. Deem (ed.) *Schooling for Women's Work*. London, Routledge.

Rendel, M. (1984) Women academics in the seventies. In S. Acker and D. Warren-Piper (eds) *Is Higher Education Fair to Women?* Guildford, Nelson.

Roberts, H. (1981) Some of the boys won't play any more: the impact of feminism on sociology. In D. Spender (ed.) *Men's Studies Modified – The Impact of Feminism on the Academic Disciplines*. Oxford, Pergamon Press.

Riujs, A. (1993) *Women Managers in Education: A Worldwide Progress Report*. Coombe Lodge Report, Vol. 23, Nos 7–8. Bristol, The Staff College.

Roberts, H. (ed.) (1981) *Doing Feminist Research*. London, Routledge.

Roberts, H. (1984) A feminist perspective on affirmative action. In S. Acker and D. Warren-Piper (eds) *Is Higher Education Fair to Women?* Guilford, Nelson.

Sanderson, K. (1990) Meanings of class and social mobility: the public and private lives of women civil servants. In H. Corr and L. Jamieson (eds) *The Politics of Everyday Life*. London, Macmillan.

Savage, M. and Witz, A. (eds) (1992) *Gender and Bureaucracy*. Oxford, Blackwell Publishers/The Sociological Review.

Sawicki, J. (1991) *Disciplining Foucault: Feminism, Power and the Body*. London, Routledge.

Schoen, L.G. and Wincour, S. (1988) An investigation of the self-efficacy of male and female academics, *Journal of Vocational Behaviour*, 32, 307–20.

Simeone, A. (1987) *Academic Women*. South Hadley MA, Bergin and Garvey.

Smart, B. (1986) The politics of truth and the problem of hegemony. In D.C. Hoy (ed.) *Foucault: A Critical Reader*. Oxford, Basil Blackwell.

Smith, A. (1991) Women in university teaching, Conference of the New Zealand Association for Educational Research. Knox College.

Smith, D. (1979) A peculiar eclipsing: Women's exclusion from men's culture, *Women's Studies International Quarterly*, 1, 4, 281–96.

Soper, K. (1993) Productive contradictions. In C. Ramazanoglu (ed.) *Up Against Foucault: Explorations of Some Tensions between Foucault and Feminism*. London, Routledge.

Spencer, A. and Podmore, D. (eds) (1987) *In a Man's World: Essays on Women in Male Dominated Professions*. London, Tavistock Publications.

Spender, D. (1981) Education: the patriarchal paradigm and the response to feminism. In D. Spender (ed.) *Men's Studies Modified – the Impact of Feminism on the Academic Disciplines*. Oxford, Pergamon Press.

Spender, D. (ed.) (1981) *Men's Studies Modified – the Impact of Feminism on the Academic Disciplines*. Oxford, Pergamon Press.

Spender, D. (ed.) (1982) *Invisible Women: The Schooling Scandal*. London, Writers and Readers Publishing Co-op.

Spender, D. (1983) *Women of Ideas and What Men Have Done to Them*. London, Ark.

Sperling, G. (1991) Can the barriers be breached? Mature women's access to higher education, *Gender and Education*, 3, 2, 199–213.

Spivak, Gayatri Chakravorty (1983) Displacement and the discourse of woman. In M. Mrupnick (ed.) *Displacement: Derrida And After*. Bloomington, Indiana University Press.

Stanko, E. (1985) *Intimate Intrusions: Women's Experience of Male Violence*. London, Routledge.

Stanko, E. (1988) Keeping women in and out of line: sexual harassment and occupational segregation. In S. Walby (ed.) *Gender Segregation at Work*. Milton Keynes, Open University Press.

Stanley, L. (1984) How the social science research process discriminates against women. In S. Acker and D. Warren Piper (eds) *Is Higher Education Fair to Women?* Guilford, Nelson.

Stanley, L. (ed.) (1990) *Feminist Praxis*. London, Routledge.

Stanley, L. and Wise, S. (1979) Feminist research, feminist consciousness and experiences of sexism, *Women's Studies Quarterly*, 2, 3, 359–74.

Stanley, L. and Wise, S. (1983a) *Breaking Out: Feminist Consciousness and Feminist Research*. London, Routledge.

Stanley, L. and Wise, S. (1983b) Back into the personal or our attempt to construct feminist research. In G. Bowles and R. Duelli-Klein (eds) *Theories of Women's Studies*. London, Routledge.

Stanley, L. and Wise, S. (1990) Method, methodology and epistemology in feminist research processes. In L. Stanley (ed.) *Feminist Praxis*. London, Routledge.

Statistics Canada (1992) *Teachers in Universities 1988/89*. Ottawa, Ministry of Industry, Science and Technology.

Survey Committee of the Cambridge University Women's Action Group (CUWAG) (1988) *Report on the Numbers and Status of Academic Women in the University of Cambridge*. Cambridge, CUWAG.

Sutherland, M. (1985) *Women Who Teach in Universities*. London, Trentham Books.

Universities Statistical Record (1984) *University Standard Classification of Academic Subjects*. Cheltenham, USR.

Taylor, J. (1995) Research in UK Departments of Sociology: an analysis based upon the 1992 Research Assessment Exercise Database, *Sociology*, 29, 3, August, 513–29.

Universities Statistical Record (1992) *Staff Analysis Nos S28203, S28332, S28388, S28638, S28639, S28640*. Cheltenham, USR.

University College London (1991) *Report of the Senior Promotions Procedures Working Group*. London, University College.

University College London (1992) *Academic Staff Handbook*. London, University College.

University College London, Goldsmith's College (1991) *Equal Opportunities Code of Practice*. London, University of London Goldsmith's College.

University of Auckland (1988) *Report of the Committee Established to Review the Position of Academic Women on the Staff of the University of Auckland*. Auckland, University of Auckland.

University of Cambridge (1987) Report of the Council of the Senate on Equal Opportunities in Employment, *Cambridge University Reporter*, 28 May 1987. Cambridge, Cambridge University.

University of East London (1992) *Equal Opportunities Policy Statement*. London, University of East London.

University of Essex (1991) *Policy Statement on Equal Opportunities*. Colchester, University of Essex.

University of Keele (1991) *Equal Opportunities at Keele.* Staffordshire, University of Keele.

University of Kent (1991) *Equal Opportunities Policy Statement: Sexual and Racial Harassment.* Canterbury, University of Kent.

University of Kent (1991) *Equal Opportunities Policy Statement and Guidelines.* Canterbury, University of Kent.

University of Leicester (1992) *Equal Opportunities Policy Statement.* Leicester, University of Leicester.

University of Liverpool (1992) *Statistical Profile 1992 Workforce Audit.* Liverpool, University of Liverpool.

University of Liverpool (1984) *Equal Opportunities Code of Practice.* Liverpool, University of Liverpool.

University of London Queen Mary and Westfield College (1992) *Equal Opportunities in Employment Policy Statement.* London, University of London Queen Mary and Westfield College.

University of Manchester (1991–2) *Equal Opportunities in Employment: Code of Practice.* Manchester, University of Manchester,

University of Nottingham (1992) *Equal Opportunities Policy.* Nottingham, University of Nottingham.

University of Southampton (1991) *Equal Opportunities Policy.* Southampton, University of Southampton.

University of Sussex (1992) *Equal Opportunities Policy Statement.* Brighton, University of Sussex.

University of Wales Cardiff (1991) *Equal Opportunities Policy Constitution of the Equal Opportunities Committee.* Cardiff, University of Wales.

University of Wales Cardiff (1992) *Code of Practice on Harassment.* Cardiff, University of Wales.

University of Warwick (1986) *Equal Opportunities in Employment Policy.* Warwick, University of Warwick.

University of York (1988) *Equal Opportunities Policy* (revised 1992). York, University of York.

University of York (1988) *Statement on Sexual Harassment.* York, University of York.

Vasil, L. (1992) Self-efficacy, expectations and causal attribution for achievement among male and female university faculty, *Journal of Vocational Behaviour,* 41, 259–69.

Vasil, L. (1993) Gender differences in the academic career in New Zealand universities, *New Zealand Journal of Educational Studies,* 28, 2, 143–63.

Walby, S. (1985) Spacial and historical variations in women's employment. In L. Murgatroyd, D. Shapiro, J. Urry, S. Walby, A. Warde with J. Mark-Lawson (eds) *Localities, Class and Gender.* London, Pion.

Walby, S. (1986) *Patriarchy at Work.* Cambridge, Polity Press.

Walby, S. (ed.) (1988) *Gender Segregation at Work.* Milton Keynes, Open University Press.

Walby, S. (1989) Theorizing patriarchy, *Sociology,* 23, 2, 213–34.

Walby, S. (1990) *Theorizing Patriarchy.* Oxford, Basil Blackwell.

Walters, P. (1987) Servants of the Crown. In A. Spencer and D. Podmore (eds) *In a Man's World: Essays on Women in Male Dominated Professions.* London, Tavistock Publications.

Watson, S. (ed.) (1990) *Playing the State: Australian Feminist Interventions.* London, Verso Press.

Watson, S. (1992) Femocratic feminisms. In M. Savage and A. Witz (eds) *Gender and Bureaucracy*. Oxford, Blackwell Publishers/The Sociological Review.

Watson, S. (1995) Reclaiming social policy. In B. Caine and R. Pringle (eds) *Transitions – New Australian Feminisms*. St Leonards NSW, Allen and Unwin.

Weedon, C. (1987) *Feminist Practice and Poststructuralist Theory*. Oxford, Basil Blackwell.

Weiler, K. (1988) *Women Teaching for Change: Gender, Class and Power*. New York, Bergin and Garvey.

Weiler, K. (1993) Feminism and the struggle for a democratic education: a view from the United States. In M. Arnot and K. Weiler (eds) *Feminism and Social Justice*. London, Falmer Press.

Weiner, G. (1986) Feminist education and equal opportunities: unity or discord? *British Journal of Sociology of Education*.

Weiner, G. (1989) Feminism, equal opportunities and vocationalism: the changing context. In H. Burchell and V. Millman (eds) *Changing Perspectives on Gender*. Milton Keynes, Open University Press.

Weiner, G. and Arnot, M. (eds) (1987) *Gender Under Scrutiny*. Oxford, Pergamon.

West, C. (1990) The new cultural politics of difference. In R. Ferguson, M. Gever, T. Minh-ha and C. West (eds) *Out There: Marginalization and Contemporary Cultures*. Cambridge, MIT Press.

Westwood, S. (1984) *All Day, Every Day: Factory and Family in the Making of Women's Lives*. London, Pluto Press.

Westwood, S. (1990) Racism, black masculinity and the politics of space. In J. Hearn and D. Morgan (eds) *Men, Masculinities and Social Theory*. London, Unwin Hyman.

Westwood, S. and Bhachu, P. (eds) (1988) *Enterprising Women: Ethnicity, Economy and Gender Relations*. London, Routledge.

Wilson, M. (1986) *Report on the Status of Academic Women in New Zealand*. Wellington, Association of University Staff of New Zealand.

Witz, A. (1990) Professions and patriarchy: gender and the politics of occupational closure, *Sociology*, 24, 4.

Witz, A. (1992) *Professions and Patriarchy*. London, Routledge.

Witz, A. and Savage, M. (1992) The gender of organisations. In M. Savage and A. Witz (eds) *Gender and Bureaucracy*. Oxford, Blackwell Publishers/The Sociological Review.

Worth, H. (1992) *Report on Issues Affecting Academic Staff at Massey University*. Auckland Uniservices, University of Auckland.

Yates, L. (1990) *Theory/Practice Dilemmas: Gender Knowledge and Education*. Waurn Ponds, Deakin University.

Yates, L. (1993) Feminism and Australian state policy: Some questions for the 1990s. In M. Arnot and K. Weiler (eds) *Feminisms and Social Justice*. London, Falmer Press.

Yeatman, A. (1988) Contemporary issues for feminism and the politics of the state. In J. Blackmore and J. Kenway (eds) *Gender Issues in the Theory and Practice of Educational Administration and Policy*. Waurn Ponds, Deakin University.

Yeatman, A. (1990) *Bureaucrats, Technocrats, Femocrats: Essays on the Contemporary Australian State*. Sydney, Allen and Unwin.

Zimmeck, M. (1986) Jobs for the girls: the expansion of clerical work for women. In A. John (ed.) *Unequal Opportunities: Women's Employment in England, 1800–1918*. Oxford, Blackwell.

Zimmeck, M. (1988) The new women and the machinery of government: a spanner in the works. In R. McLeod (ed.) *Government and Expertise: Specialists, Administrators and Professionals, 1860–1919*. Cambridge, Cambridge University Press.

Index

academic institutions, as male-
    dominated hierarchies, 1
academic status, at first appointment,
    New Zealand universities, 76–8,
    86, 88–90, 121
Acker, S., 4, 7, 20, 22, 23, 24, 27, 128,
    129
affirmative action, xi, 118, 126, 131
age at first appointment, New Zealand
    academic women, 84, 90
age discrimination, and UK women
    academics, 48, 49, 60
Aisenberg, N., 1
Allen, F., 1, 24
Annual Abstract of Statistics, 9, 19
Aotearoa, see New Zealand
appraisal
    New Zealand universities, 99–101,
    124
    UK universities, 40, 41–3, 123–4
Arnot, M., 2–4, 128, 129, 130, 131,
    132
assistant lecturers
    New Zealand universities, 86, 87
    numbers of, 68
    UK universities, numbers of women,
    10, 12
associate professors
    New Zealand, and promotion, 97
    UK women, and appraisal, 41
Association of University Teachers, xi
Auckland University (academic
    women at), 64, 72

admissions and enrolment
    coordinator, 106–7
appraisal process, 100
    and equal opportunities, 115–16,
    117, 118
    experiences of discrimination,
    111–12
    and mentorship, 113, 114–15
    promotion opportunities, 93–4, 95,
    97, 98–9
    responsibilities and workload, 105,
    106–7, 109
    tenured staff, 79, 91, 92–3
AUSNZ (Association of University
    Staff of New Zealand), 72, 91
Australia, 24, 72
    academic women in New Zealand
    from, 73
    'femocrats', 7
AUT (Association of University
    Teachers), 50
authority, see leadership positions

Bacchi, C., 24
Barrett, M., 32–4
'Beyond the Glass Ceiling', 129
Blackburn, R.M., 9, 16, 17
Blackmore, J., 1, 129
Bognanno, M.F., 1
botany, in UK universities, women
    academics in senior posts, 15
Bryson, C., xi
Byrne, E.M., 1

Cambridge University (academic
    women at)
  experiences of, 50
  in leadership positions, 38
  numbers of, 10, 12, 13
Canadian universities, 7, 24
career structure
  New Zealand universities, 97–9,
    122
  UK universities, 40, 43, 60
  see also appraisal; promotion
caregiving
  discriminatory practices around,
    125
    in UK universities, 48–9, 60
  failure to recognize status, 121
  New Zealand women academics
    caregiver status, 74, 98
    and discrimination, 110
    and promotion, 98–9
    and workload, 109
class, and discriminatory behaviour,
    UK academic women, 48
committee membership/
    administration
  New Zealand academic women, 83
    and productivity, 105, 108–9
  UK academic women, 45–7, 60
committees, equal opportunities,
    58–9
Commonwealth Universities Yearbook, 11
confidentiality, and women academics
    in New Zealand, 85–8
Connell, R.W., 130
contract researchers, women in UK
    universities, x, 36, 42, 60
contractually-based posts
  New Zealand universities, 122, 123
  UK universities, 39–40, 41
Council of British Archaeology, 39
counselling, and New Zealand women
    academics, 104, 105
Coward, R., 129
critical feminism, 5

David, M., 11, 16
David, M.E., 129
Deem, R., 11, 16
DEET (Department of Employment,
    Education and Training), 1, 24

departmental/faculty committee
    membership, UK women
    academics, 46–7
Derrida, Jacques, 34
Dex, S., xi
difference, 33–5
  in academic women's experiences,
    35–8
  as experiential diversity, 33–4
  and feminist poststructuralism,
    119–20
  feminist theory on, 4
    and New Zealand research, 65–6
  from equality to, 130, 131
  as positional meaning, 34
differentiation, patterns of, 120
discourse, and feminist
    poststructuralism, 5, 119, 120
discrimination, 125–6
  and equal opportunities policies, 56
  and feminist politics, 111–12, 125
  Hansard Society Commission
    Report on, 38, 47–8
  in New Zealand universities, 72,
    81–2, 84, 109–12
    and promotion, 95, 112, 121,
    122–3
  patterns of, 120
  UK academic women's experiences
    of, 36, 47–50, 60
  Wilson report on, 81–2, 127
doctoral status
  and male academics, 121
  in New Zealand universities
    and productivity, 101–2, 124
    and promotion, 121
Drakich, J., 7, 24

education policies, *see* higher
    education policies
EEOP (equal employment
    opportunities policy), New
    Zealand universities, 84, 115–18,
    126
egalitarianism, ideology of, in New
    Zealand, 62
Eisenstein, H., 4, 129, 130
Eisenstein, Z.R., 7
equal opportunities
  committees, 58–9

and Conservative education policies
(UK), 128–9
effectiveness of legislation, xi
and gender and educational policy
analysis, 130
and liberal democratic societies, 131
and mentoring, 51, 53
principle of, 2–3
UK academic women's experience
of, 36
equal opportunities policies (EOPs),
117–18
New Zealand universities (EEOP),
84, 115–18, 126
and practice, 121
in UK universities, 54–9, 60–1, 126
and academic relationships, 55,
56
and practice, 55–7, 58–9, 61
ethnicity
and discriminatory behaviour, UK
academic women, 48, 60
in New Zealand, 63

Faludi, S., 129
family commitments
in New Zealand universities
and promotion, 97–9
and workload, 107–8
feminism
and educational policy, 2–7
first wave, 8–9
and UK academic women's
experiences, 35–6, 49
Feminism and Social Justice (Arnot and
Weiler), 3
feminist epistemology, in New
Zealand research, 63, 64
feminist management strategies, 129
feminist methodology, in New
Zealand, 63, 64, 65–6
feminist politics, and discrimination,
111–12, 125
feminist poststructuralism, 4–5,
119–20, 130
and New Zealand feminist research,
65–6
and women's experience, 32–5
feminist research, in New Zealand,
63–4

feminist standpoint epistemology, 34
feminist theories, 128–32
'femocrats', 7
Finkelstein, M.J., 68
first wave feminism, 8–9
fixed-term contracts, women in UK
universities, 39, 40, 41
Foucault, Michel, 34
Franzway, S., 7, 129
Freeman, B.C., 1
Fulton, O., 19–20

Gelb, J., 4, 7
gender politics, and the role of the
state, 129–30
gender stereotyping, and role
modelling/mentorship, 52

Halsey, A.H., 17, 19, 29
Hansard Society Commission Report,
1–2
on discrimination, 38, 47–8
on equal opportunities policies,
54
on promotion of women academics,
39
harassment
physical, 49–50
sexual, 48, 50–1, 60, 112
verbal, 49–50
Haraway, Donna, 37
Harding, S., 34, 37, 38
Harrington, M., 1
heads of department (HOD)
in New Zealand universities, 83,
100–1, 124
and discrimination, 110
Helmreich, R.L., 101
hierarchical organization systems, in
academic institutions, 1
higher education policies
Conservative (UK), 128–9
and feminism, 2–7
and state ideology, 11, 16
Hirsch, M., 4
HOD, *see* heads of department
(HOD)
Hughes, B., 64

Irwin, K., 64

Jarman, J., 9, 16, 17
Jones, Alison, 64

Keller, E.F., 4
Kenway, J., 1, 129–30
King, C., 129

Lacan, Jacques, 34
leadership positions
  gendered nature of power in, 120
  New Zealand universities, 82, 87–8
  UK universities, 38–43
lecturers
  New Zealand universities, 86
    and academic status, 89–90
    numbers of, 68, 71
    and promotion, 121
  UK universities
    academic status, 76, 78
    and appraisal, 42
    by gender, 26–7
    numbers of women, 10, 12, 19,
      21, 22, 23, 24, 29
  see also senior lecturers
Lincoln University (New Zealand),
  tenured staff, 79
Lodge, J., 84
London University, number of women
  academics, 10, 12, 13, 23

McWilliams-Tulberg, R., 11
male academics, 124
  in New Zealand universities, 69–72
    and the delegation of
      responsibilities, 104
    and discrimination, 110
    heads of department, 100–1, 124
    and productivity, 102
  in positions of power, 120
  in UK universities
    discriminatory behaviour, 47–50
    numbers of, 25–7
    and sexual harassment, 51
    in subject groups, 18, 28
male students, 19, 20
Maori society, role of women in, 65
Maori women, 63, 64, 82, 127
  students, 104
marital status, academic women in
  New Zealand, 73–4

Massey University (academic women
    at), 72
  academic status, 76, 88–9, 90
  and the appraisal process, 100
  and discrimination, 110, 112
  and equal opportunities, 116–17
  marital status, 73
  and mentorship, 113–14
  papers presented by, 81
  and positions of authority, 82
  and promotion, 94–5, 95–6
  and tenured posts, 92
  tenured staff, 79
  *see also Report on the Status of
    Academic Women at Massey
    University*
maternity leave
  in New Zealand universities, 111
  in UK universities, 48, 50, 56, 61
men, *see* male academics
mentorship
  in New Zealand universities,
    112–15, 126
  in UK universities, 51–4, 60, 126
Middle Ages, women at European
    universities, 8
Middleton, Sue, 64, 65–6, 85
Morris-Matthews, K., 24, 64, 66, 67,
    68, 84, 86
multi-culturalism, in New Zealand, 63

national identity issues, in New
    Zealand, 63
New Zealand, xi, 6–7
  'academic community' in, 63
  academic staff, by gender and
    method of employment, 69–72
  academic women, 62–84
    age at first appointment, 84
    and appraisal, 99–101, 124
    committee membership/
      administration, 83, 105
    confidentiality and anonymity,
      85–8
    and discrimination, 81–2, 84, 95,
      109–12, 121, 122–3
    Maori, 64, 73, 127
    marital status, 73–4
    and mentorship, 112–15, 126
    numbers of, 68–72, 73

'older', 121–2
papers at conferences, 79–80
productivity, 79–81, 84, 101–9,
124
promotion, 80–1, 93–9, 122–3
publications, 79, 80, 81, 93–4
and sexual harassment, 112
status at first appointment, 76–8,
86, 88–90, 121
status of, 72–8, 86–7, 88–90
tenured posts, 78, 90–3, 122
EEOP (equal employment
opportunities policy), 115–18,
126
feminist research in, 63–4
heads of department (HOD), 83,
100–1, 124
indigenous feminist methology in,
65–6
Maori women, 63, 64
students, 104
students
numbers of women, 66–8
Pacific Island and Maori, 104
subjects taken by, 66, 67
*see also under names of individual
universities*
NTEU (National Tertiary Education
Unit), 1, 24

occupational segregration, vertical and
horizontal, 17
'old civic' universities, number of
women academics, 10, 12, 13
'older' academic women, New
Zealand, 121–2
O'Neill, A.M., 62, 63, 66
Open University, 17
Otago University (New Zealand), 64,
72
tenured staff, 79
Over, R., 101
Oxford University, number of women
academics, 10, 12, 13
Ozga, J., 129

Pacific Island students, 104
Pacific Island women, 127
Page, Dorothy, 64
parenting

discriminatory practices around, 125
in UK universities, 48–9, 60
New Zealand academic women,
107–8
and discrimination, 110
part-time positions
New Zealand universities
and discrimination, 111
by gender, 69, 70, 71
UK universities
academic women in, 24, 25, 26,
27, 31
by gender, 27
part-time students, UK universities, 17,
19–20
Pateman, C., 130
patriarchy
in academic institutions, 1, 126
and power, 130
patronage, and UK women academics,
48, 51
Pere, Rose, 65
physical harassment, UK women
academics' experiences of, 49–50
physics, in UK universities, posts held
by academic women, 30–1
positive action, 117, 118, 126
post-colonialism, and feminism, 131
postgraduate supervision
and mentoring, 53
and UK women academics, 43, 44
postmodernism, and feminism, 130,
131
poststructuralism, *see* feminist
poststructuralism
power
and feminist poststructuralism, 5,
120
gender and leadership positions, in
UK universities, 38–43
and liberal democratic societies, 131
male academics in positions of, 120
and patriarchy, 130
relationships, and the appraisal
process, 100–1
Pringle, R., 129, 130
productivity of academic women, 121,
124–5
New Zealand, 79–81, 84, 101–9, 124
UK, 43, 60

professional development, and
    appraisal, 43
professional experience, and academic
    status, women at New Zealand
    universities, 89
professional qualifications, New
    Zealand universities, 77, 78, 90
professors
    New Zealand universities
        and academic leadership, 87–8
        academic status, 76, 78
        and committee work, 109
        numbers of women, 68, 69–70,
            71, 75
        and promotion, 97, 123
    UK universities
        and appraisal, 41
        by gender, 25–6, 27
        by subject group, 15, 28
        experiences of women, 50
        numbers of women, x, 10, 12, 17,
            19, 21, 22, 23, 24, 25–6, 29
    see also associate professors
promotion
    as a equal opportunity issue, 57, 60
    New Zealand academic women,
        80–1, 93–9
        and discrimination, 95, 112, 121,
            122–3
        and heads of departments
            (HOD), 83
        and publications, 79
    UK women academics, 39–43, 50,
        60, 123
    Wilson report on, 80–1, 93
psychology, in UK universities, posts
    held by academic women, 29, 30
publications of academic women
    in New Zealand, 79, 80, 81, 93–4
    in the UK, 43

racism, and equal opportunities
    policy, 117
radical feminism, and New Zealand
    feminist research, 65
Ramazanoglu, C., 1, 5–6, 11, 32, 49
readers
    New Zealand universities
        academic status, 76, 78
        numbers of, 68, 70, 71

UK universities
    and appraisal, 41
    by gender, 25, 26, 29
    by subject group, 15
    numbers of women, 10, 12, 19,
        21–2, 23, 25, 29
Reagan, Ronald, 129
Rendel, M., 8, 10, 11–15, 16–17, 23,
    27, 29
*Report on the Status of Academic Women
    at Massey University*, 73, 78–9, 81,
    82, 121
    and committees, 83
    and discrimination, 109–10
    and promotion, 93
*Report on the Status of Academic Women
    in New Zealand, see* Wilson,
    Margaret
research productivity, 102
research programmes, 'client-led', 45
research workers
    New Zealand universities, academic
        status, 76, 78
    UK universities
        and appraisal, 42
        numbers of women, 19
responsibilities, *see* workloads
Riujs, A., 129
role modelling
    in New Zealand universities, 114
    and UK women academics, 51–4, 60

Schoen, L.G., 101
self-efficacy, 102
senior lecturers
    New Zealand universities, 86
        numbers of, 68, 70, 71
        promotion to, 121
    UK universities
        academic status, 76, 78
        and appraisal, 41
        by gender, 25, 26
        numbers of women, 10, 12, 21–2,
            23, 25, 29
        by subject area, 15
Sewell, R., xi
sexism
    and equal opportunities policy, 117
    New Zealand academic women's
        experiences of, 82, 84

sexual harassment
  and New Zealand universities, 112
  and UK women academics, 48,
    50–1, 60
short-term contracts, women in UK
  universities, x, 40
Simeone, A., 1, 68, 101, 103
Smith, A., 1, 68
Smith, Linda, 64
social justice theories, and feminism,
  131
social sciences, in UK universities,
  number of women academics, 14,
  15, 16
Sperling, G., 129
Spivak, Gayatri Chakravorty, 34
Stanko, E., 51
state, role of the, and gender politics,
  129–30
Statistics Canada, 24
Stockman, N., xi
students
  in New Zealand universities
    numbers of women, 66–8
    Pacific and Maori, 104
  and role modelling/mentoring, 51,
    52
    academic women's relationships
      with, 104–5
  in UK universities, 19–20
    numbers of women, 9, 16, 17, 19,
      20
    part-time, 17, 19–20
subject areas
  in New Zealand universities
    and research productivity, 102
    women academics, 86
    and women students, 66, 68
  in UK universities, 29–31
    gender of academic staff, 18, 28
    numbers of academic women,
      14–16, 19
subjectivity, and feminist
  poststructuralism, 119
Sutherland, M., 9

'target groups', 117, 118, 126
teaching workload, 121
  and New Zealand women
    academics, 102–3, 104–5

tenure (continuance) of posts
  in New Zealand universities, 78,
    90–3, 122
    and discrimination, 112
  in UK universities, 39–40, 41
'tokenism', at Auckland University,
  115–16
Tulle-Winton, E., xi

undergraduates, *see* students
United Kingdom, xi
  academic staff by gender, 21–9
  academic women
    and appraisal, 40, 41–3, 123–4
    exclusion for, 11–15
    numbers of, x, 10, 11–14
    promotion, 39–43, 50, 60, 123
    by subject areas, 14–16
  Conservative education policy,
    128–9
  students, 19–20
    numbers of women, 9, 17, 19, 20
    part-time, 17, 19–20
  tenure of academic posts, 39–40,
    41
  *see also under names of individual
    universities*
United States, 72
  academic women in New Zealand
    from, 73
  mentorship experiences, 52–3
  Moral Right crusade, 129
Universities Funding Council, 20
Universities Statistical Record (USR),
  17, 21
University of Canterbury (New
  Zealand), tenured staff, 79
University Grants Committee, 11
university/polytechnic committee
  membership, UK academic
  women, 46–7

Vasil, L., 24, 68, 74, 77, 87, 98, 101–3,
  107–8, 115, 121, 124–5
verbal harassment, UK women
  academics' experiences of, 49–50
Victoria University, tenured staff, 79
violence
  in academic life, 5–6
  UK universities, 49–50

Waikato University (academic women
    at), 64
  appraisal process, 99–101
  and committee work, 108–9
  and discrimination, 110–11
  and equal opportunities, 115
  position of 'chair', 87–8
  promotion opportunities, 96, 97, 123
  tenured staff, 79, 91
  workload, 103, 105, 105–6
Walby, S., 130
Watson, S., 129, 130
Weiler, K., 1, 3, 131, 132
Weiner, G., 128
West, C., 131
Wilson, Margaret
  *Report on the Status of Academic
    Women in New Zealand*, 72, 73, 74,
    77, 79, 84, 86, 121, 126–7
  and academic status at first
    appointment, 88

and discrimination, 81–2
and heads of department, 83
and promotion, 80–1, 93
and tenure, 90–3, 122
and women in positions of
    authority, 82
and workload, 103
Winocur, S., 101
Witz, A., 130
women's colleges, senior posts for
    academic women, 13
workloads of academic women, 124–5
  New Zealand, 79, 102–9, 124
  United Kingdom, 43–7, 61, 124
Worth, H., 102

Yates, L., 1, 7, 129, 130–1
Yeatman, A., 7, 129, 130
'young civic' universities, number
    of women academics, 10, 12,
    13

The Society for Research into Higher Education

The Society for Research into Higher Education exists to stimulate and coordinate research into all aspects of higher education. It aims to improve the quality of higher education through the encouragement of debate and publication on issues of policy, on the organization and management of higher education institutions, and on the curriculum and teaching methods.

The Society's income is derived from subscriptions, sales of its books and journals, conference fees and grants. It receives no subsidies, and is wholly independent. Its individual members include teachers, researchers, managers and students. Its corporate members are institutions of higher education, research institutes, professional, industrial and governmental bodies. Members are not only from the UK, but from elsewhere in Europe, from America, Canada and Australasia, and it regards its international work as among its most important activities.

Under the imprint *SRHE & Open University Press*, the Society is a specialist publisher of research, having some 60 titles in print. The Editorial Board of the Society's Imprint seeks authoritative research or study in the above fields. It offers competitive royalties, a highly recognizable format in both hardback and paperback and the worldwide reputation of the Open University Press.

The Society also publishes *Studies in Higher Education* (three times a year), which is mainly concerned with academic issues, *Higher Education Quarterly* (formerly *Universities Quarterly*), mainly concerned with policy issues, *Research into Higher Education Abstracts* (three times a year), and *SRHE News* (four times a year).

The Society holds a major annual conference in December, jointly with an institution of higher education. In 1994 the topic was 'The Student Experience' at the University of York. In 1995 it was 'The Changing University' at Heriot-Watt University in Edinburgh and in 1996, 'Working in Higher Education' at Cardiff Institute of Higher Education. Conferences in 1997 include 'Beyond the First Degree' at the University of Warwick.

The Society's committees, study groups and branches are run by the members. The groups at present include:

Teacher Education Study Group
Continuing Education Group
Staff Development Group
Excellence in Teaching and Learning

Benefits to members

Individual

Individual members receive:

- *SRHE News*, the Society's publications list, conference details and other material included in mailings.
- Greatly reduced rates for *Studies in Higher Education* and *Higher Education Quarterly.*
- A 35 per cent discount on all SRHE & Open University Press publications.
- Free copies of the Proceedings – commissioned papers on the theme of the Annual Conference.
- Free copies of *Research into Higher Education Abstracts.*
- Reduced rates for conferences.
- Extensive contacts and scope for facilitating initiatives.
- Reduced reciprocal memberships.
- Free copies of the *Register of Members' Research Interests.*

Corporate

Corporate members receive:

- All benefits of individual members, plus.
- Free copies of *Studies in Higher Education.*
- Unlimited copies of the Society's publications at reduced rates.
- Special rates for its members e.g. to the Annual Conference.
- The right to submit application for the Society's research grants.

Membership details: SRHE, 3 Devonshire Street, London
WIN 2BA, UK. Tel: 0171 637 2766. Fax: 0171 637 2781.
email: srhe@clus1.ulcc.ac.uk
Catalogue: SRHE & Open University Press, Celtic Court,
22 Ballmoor, Buckingham MK18 1XW. Tel: 01280 823388.
Fax: 01280 823233. email: enquiries@openup.co.uk

EQUAL OPPORTUNITIES IN COLLEGES AND UNIVERSITIES
TOWARDS BETTER PRACTICES

Maureen Farish, Joanna McPake, Janet Powney and Gaby Weiner

This book is the *first* attempt to consider the effectiveness of equal opportunities policies for staff (in colleges and universities) after the policies have been passed and implemented. It suggests future strategies for policy-makers and equal opportunities 'activists' in the light of the findings which concerns structure, policy coherence and policy contradiction.

It provides an account, through the detailed case-studies of three educational institutions (one further education college, one 'new' and one 'old' university) of how equal opportunities policy-making has developed over the last decade and what gains have been made. It also examines the complexity of trying to judge the effectiveness of such policies by viewing policy from a number of standpoints including those of managers and policy-makers, those charged with implementing the policies (for instance, equal opportunities or women's officers), and those at the receiving end. In trying to unravel the complexity, what emerges is the importance of institutional history and context as well as policy structure and content.

Contents
Setting the context of equal opportunities in educational organizations – Borough college incorporated: case study – Town university: case study – Metropolitan university: case study – Critical moments and illuminative insights – Codifying policy and practice – Contrasting contexts – Shared themes – Munro bagging: towards better practices – Appendix: research methodology – Bibliography – Index.

224pp   0 335 19416 8 (Paperback)   0 335 19417 6 (Hardback)

LEADING ACADEMICS

Robin Middlehurst

At a time of major change in higher education, the quality of university leadership is an issue of key importance. Whether heading a research team, planning curriculum innovations, managing a department of running an institution, effective leadership is required. Yet how well is the idea of leadership understood? How is leadership practised in the academic world? What special characteristics are needed to lead autonomous professionals?

This book, based on research in universities, is the first comprehensive examination of leadership in British higher education. Robin Middlehurst critiques contemporary ideas of leadership and examines their relevance to academe. She explores the relationship between models of leadership and practice at different levels of the institution. She argues for a better balance between leadership and management in universities in order to increase the responsiveness and creativity of higher education.

Contents
Part 1: Thinking about leadership – What is leadership? – The new leadership – Organizational images – Leadership and academe: traditions and change – Part 2: Practising leadership – Institutional leaders – Collective leadership – Leading departments – Individuals and leadership – Part 3: Developing leadership – Leadership learning – Endings and beginnings – Bibliography – Index.

c.192pp   0 335 09988 2 (Paperback)   0 335 09989 0 (Hardback)

STRESS IN ACADEMIC LIFE

Shirley Fisher

Academic life is becoming increasingly stressful. Academics are suffering from increased government control and monitoring; from financial cuts and work overload; from the difficult balancing act between their teaching, research and administration roles. They experience the everyday stresses of doing a creative job within an increasingly uncreative environment; of both developing relationships with students and assessing their performance; of seeking promotion or settling for non-promotion as opportunities for advancement have become more limited; of maintaining self-esteem as their status in the community appears to decline. At the same time they are aware of the increasing stress suffered by their students: their fear of failure, financial pressures, homesickness, impending examinations, uncertain prospects, and their balancing of academic and social lives.

Shirley Fisher provides an overview of the effects of stress on performance, daily efficiency and health, and reports the results of research into stress in academic environments (for both staff and students). She explores the origins and nature of academic stress, personal vulnerabilities and coping mechanisms and proposes ways in which individuals can be helped, emphasizing how working conditions and practices must be changed in order to reduce stress in academic life.

Contents
What is stress? – Stress and efficiency in daily behaviour – Life, stress and health – Stress and control in health and well-being – Stress in students – Examination stress – Creativity and context – Stress in academic staff – Overload and division of labour – Coping with stress in academics – Bibliography – Index.

100pp   0 335 15720 3 (Paperback)